D0066468

Practical Newspaper Reporting

Practical Newspaper Reporting

4th edition

David Spark and Geoffrey Harris

Los Angeles | London | New Delhi
Singapore | Washington DC

© David Spark and Geoffrey Harris 2011
First published 2011

Apart from any fair dealing for the purposes of research
or private study, or criticism or review, as permitted
under the Copyright, Designs and Patents Act, 1988, this
publication may be reproduced, stored or transmitted in
any form, or by any means, only with the prior permission
in writing of the publishers, or in the case of reprographic
reproduction, in accordance with the terms of licences issued
by the Copyright Licensing Agency. Enquiries concerning
reproduction outside those terms should be sent to the
publishers.

SAGE Publications Ltd
1 Oliver's Yard
55 City Road
London EC1Y 1SP

SAGE Publications Inc.
2455 Teller Road
Thousand Oaks, California 91320

SAGE Publications India Pvt Ltd
B 1/I 1 Mohan Cooperative Industrial Area
Mathura Road
New Delhi 110 044

SAGE Publications Asia-Pacific Pte Ltd
33 Pekin Street #02-01
Far East Square
Singapore 048763

Library of Congress Control Number: 2009943205

British Library Cataloguing in Publication data

A catalogue record for this book is available from
the British Library

ISBN 978-1-84787-896-0
ISBN 978-1-84787-897-7 (pbk)

Typeset by C&M Digitals (P) Ltd, Chennai, India
Printed by MPG Books Group, Bodmin, Cornwall
Printed on paper from sustainable resources

Mixed Sources
Product group from well-managed
forests and other controlled sources
www.fsc.org Cert no. SA-COC-1565
© 1996 Forest Stewardship Council
FSC

Contents

Abbreviations used in this book

BJR	*British Journalism Review*
BT	*Belfast Telegraph*
Digging Deeper	*Digging Deeper, A Canadian Reporter's Research Guide*, Robert Cribb, Dean Jobb, David McKie and Fred Vallance-Jones, Oxford, 2006.
FT	*Financial Times*
McNae	*McNae's Essential Law for Journalists*, Tom Welsh, Walter Greenwood and David Banks, Oxford, 2007.
Mail	*Daily Mail*
MEN	*Manchester Evening News*
NE	*The Northern Echo*
PCC	Press Complaints Commission
YP	*Yorkshire Post*

Foreword

Practical Newspaper Reporting, first published in 1966, was the second book commissioned by the National Council for the Training of Journalists. The first was a collection of essays and reminiscences by prominent writers. This completely rewritten fourth edition has a new chapter on how the internet is changing journalism, and extended chapters on investigative reporting and on religion and diversity. It looks in greater detail at controversies over ethics. It reviews the ferment of ideas that the internet's impact has inspired.

It has a new publisher, Sage Publications. I am very grateful to Mila Steele of Sage for taking it on after the original publishers, Heinemann/Focal Press, withdrew from publishing books about newspapers. I am very grateful also to my wife, Audrey, who has put up not just with 18 months' writing but an eight-month rewrite reflecting the growing importance of the internet.

I would also like to express gratitude for the kind comments on the book jacket from Sir Harold Evans and Sir Simon Jenkins, and for the encouragement I received from my fellow author, Geoffrey Harris; from the book's previous editor, Freddie Hodgson, and from Barry Lowe of Thames Valley University and David Kelly, former managing director of North of England Newspapers.

Sadly, Geoff, well known for his training of journalists for Mirror Group and United Newspapers, died in September 2009, before this came out.

I am very grateful to those who have helped, especially Karl Schneider, editorial development director at Reed business magazines, who gave me a new insight into reporting on the web. Other helpers I would like to thank include Peter Barron (editor), Lauren Pyrah and other members of the staff of *The Northern Echo*; Syed Belal Ahmed, Mohammed Azam, Guy Black (the *Daily Telegraph*), Karen Burke (Methodist media office), Charlie Campbell (*Wanstead Guardian*), Dayo Duyile (Nigeria), Matthew Engel (*Financial Times*), Dave Evans (*Ilford Recorder*), Eddie Gibb (Redbridge Borough Council), Tom Ilube (Garlik Consultancy), Swarn Singh Kandola, Steve Kingham (the *Sun*), Mike Morrissey (my contemporary at *The Northern Echo*), Martin Mulligan (*Financial Times*), Rita Payne (former Asia editor at BBC World TV), N. Ravi (*The Hindu*, for his contribution to Chapter 15), Amitabh Soni, my son Ian Spark (for his advice on pictures), Phil Vinter (video editor, *Birmingham Mail*), Nick White (MTP plc, who wrote the comments on Tesco's accounts) and my Westminster Press contemporaries Hugh Lawrence (who wrote the section about reporting Westminster) and Milly Lewy.

George Viner of the National Union of Journalists criticized the original *Practical Newspaper Reporting* for not covering the national press. There are many quotations from the nationals this time. Young journalists are bound to look to the nationals as both models and future employers and so I have discussed national as well as regional practice, warts and all. I have avoided attributing the warts to named writers.

In 1966, reporters still wrote on typewriters. Now they write on computers and are expected to take pictures, compose videos, write blogs. They may even compose TV programmes. Their words are distributed not just in print but online. ITN provides a service for iPhones.

In 'The Future of Journalism' (at www.bbc.co.uk/blogs/theeditors/Future_of_journalism.pdf), published by the BBC College of Journalism in 2009, Kevin Marsh, the college's editor, proclaims the death of the story, hitherto the heart of a writing journalist's work. He argues that the story tells a partial truth – what the journalist has seen and learned before an arbitrary deadline – about something classed as news. At its best, the story has reduced the asymmetry between people and power, by spannering the truth out of the powerful. But, in Marsh's view, national newspapers have undermined the credibility of the story by publishing slanted and untrue copy. The internet offers a far wider pool of information. If journalists are to gainsay Marsh, they must convince the public they are trustworthy.

For there is a job to do, a need for trustworthy helpers in the ocean of information. Les Hinton, chief executive of the *Wall Street Journal's* publishers, says the internet has unleashed an epidemic of amplified ignorance (*BJR*, September 2009). In the same *British Journalism Review*, *Guardian* editor Alan Rusbridger stresses the continuing value of reliable professional journalists: *We can reach an extremely large audience – in the* Guardian's *case some 30 million unique users around the world. At our best, we can report quickly, knowledgeably, accurately, readably, comprehensibly and trustworthily.*

Members of the public have come forward as citizen journalists, sending in words and pictures electronically from every corner of the world and every scene of mayhem. Tina Brown of the web-based Daily Beast told Andrew Marr (BBC1, 7 06 09) that many Beast stories are researched and sent in by obsessives. The Beast lacks control over their obsessions and it can't call on them when they're doing their day job. To provide a comprehensive news or information service, you still need paid and dedicated staff. But who will pay them?

In the regional press, staff numbers have fallen steadily. During the profitable years before the credit crunch, many managements failed to strengthen their journalism *see Local papers: an obituary*, Matthew Engel, *BJR*, June 2009).

According to Claire Enders of Enders Analysis, advertising in the local and regional press was down a third in the first quarter of 2009 (*FT*, 18 06 09). She expected half the local and regional papers to be gone in five years. This is serious for democracy. American researchers have shown that fewer candidates ran for municipal office and fewer voters voted after the *Cincinnati Post* died in 2007 (*FT*, 23 05 09).

The audience and the advertisers are migrating from newspapers and television to the web, especially its social sites. Google earned more than ITV in 2008 (*FT*, 30 07 09). The *Financial Times* also reported (28 08 09): *Volkswagen launched the latest version of its Golf GTI without using television or print advertising, relying almost entirely on free 'buzz' online.*

Many newspapers have been attracted by the web's offer of near-free distribution. But they have lost car advertisements to the Autotrader site, houses to Rightmove ('We have a million homes for sale or rent', says its TV advertisement). The BBC, warm and dry in the good ship Licence Fee, makes for the shore. Meanwhile, ITV and the press flounder in deep water, losing buoyancy from advertising and sales all the while.

Andrew Currah of Oxford University (*What's Happening to Our News*, Reuters Institute, 2009) found that newspaper managements launched websites not knowing how they would make enough money. He found it unlikely that the digital marketplace would ever provide a robust enough economic foundation for news services fulfilling the civic functions which newspapers now fulfil. He was hopeful that editors could nevertheless build online audiences for distinctive journalism, and not simply follow the whims of the mouse-clicking public. But such services would need subsidy or cross-subsidy, he believed.

The digital audience has proved, in the main, financially disappointing for the news media. The *Guardian*'s international online success has come at a price. Guardian News and Media lost £90 million over a year (*FT*, 5 08 09).

According to McKinsey, quoted by Curragh, web readers spend under 3 per cent of their online time on news sites. Mostly, they go there via Google rather than directly. Or they may be attracted by a recommendation on Facebook. Having arrived, they stay only a few minutes. People spend eight times as long reading a newspaper. So there may be life and money in newspapers yet, despite the rising cost of producing them.

Les Hinton, of the *Wall Street Journal*, wrote in the September *BJR*: *I don't know why paper gets such a bad rap. If it were invented today, it would be the wonder of the age. Light. Totally portable. Drop it and it doesn't break. No batteries. No reboots.* And the *Wall Street Journal* is selling more printed copies.

Rupert Murdoch announced (*FT*, 6 08 09) that he was going to charge users of all News Corporation's websites. News sites with something special to offer already charge, from the *Wall Street Journal* (a million subscribers) to Malaysia's independent *Malaysiakini* (minimum fee £3.50 a month). But, for sites in competitive fields, charging is dodgier. They could lose clicks and, with them, advertising. The most popular British news site, the BBC's, will still be free. One way or another, journalists and the media, not just the BBC, must bring in enough money to pay their way. No one is yet sure how they will do it.

Derek Smail, chairman of African Media Investments, speaking at a Commonwealth Journalists Association meeting in London (27 01 10), pinned his hopes for a commercially successful relaunch of the banned *Daily News*, Zimbabwe, on a link with mobile phones. Dominic Young, director of strategy and product development at Rupert Murdoch's News International, expressed confidence that, 'as long as journalists provide what people want, they will survive in the new age'.

David Spark

1 News and how to find it

News is what someone decides to publish as news

'His fingers sped like an express train on his portable typewriter, clattering away the news in paragraphs.' Thus, in *Reporting Politics in Nigeria* (2008), Dayo Duyile describes Alhaji Lateef Teniola, his one-time news editor at the *Nigerian Tribune*. What was this 'news' that Teniola was clattering away? News might be defined as what someone somewhere – in a newspaper, on the air, on the internet – decides to publish as news. But is it still a useful concept? Kevin Marsh, editor of the BBC College of Journalism, has proclaimed the death of the news story (*see* 'The Future of Journalism', BBC College, 2009). The killer is the internet which has erased the distinction between news and information.

However, people who publish information on current issues and events still need to decide what to publish and what not to. News remains a handy word for what they publish. And 'story' remains a handy word for that piece of news which a journalist is covering.

News is not necessarily new

News is not necessarily new, in the just-happened sense. As Marsh points out, almost any information, however old, is new to someone. (A new task for journalists is to connect people to information on the internet that they would want to know but might have missed.) At a press day in Cambridge, Professor Robert Mair explained how, two or three years before, he had arranged injections of grout into the ground below the Big Ben tower to keep it upright while the vast Westminster underground station was excavated beside it. A page editor at the *Financial Times* rejected the story as old. But the *Evening Standard* published a double page about it. The story was new to *Standard* readers.

Editors or other publishers can publish just about any information they wish. However, they want to engage their public and to identify its wants and needs. They can easily see which stories online are looked at the most. Sport occupies more space because it engages so many people. *25 pages of sport*, the *Western Mail* announced proudly (16 03 09).

Celebrity news also scores: while the digg and reddit websites, where readers select and vote for the stories, suggest an appetite, too, for weird pictures and weak jokes, with the occasional flash of idealism – a reddit posting urged twitterers to tweet as from Tehran (17 06 09), thereby taking the heat off local twitterers demonstrating against President Ahmadinejad's re-election.

Editors face a choice between being guided by the ever-changing currents of the clickstream and seeking to establish a news policy which builds up a loyal audience. The *Daily Mail* and the *Guardian*, with their distinctive editorial attitudes, have built up large audiences online in the United States.

Web readers like attitude. BBC man James Painter writes in *Counter-Hegemonic News* (Reuters Institute, 2008): 'There is a growing view that opinionated news is becoming more popular than fair, balanced and neutral news, especially among the young.' But, as Painter also points out, news with an agenda, particularly a government's agenda, can be unfair.

News must interest readers, fit the paper's news framework

No editor, not even a website publisher, can publish everything. Editors must therefore create a framework for their publications' news judgments. News which comes within this framework will be published. News outside it won't. So a magazine about carpets will concentrate on carpets. A local paper will concentrate on local people. News publications' frameworks of news judgment are usually divided into compartments. Some sections are for sport, others for news from a particular area, or for national news, foreign news, the arts or lifestyle. 'Lifestyle' – homes, hobbies and fashions – attracts people even if they have little interest in the community they live in.

How do gatekeepers decide what to publish?

Editors are gatekeepers, deciding what will and what will not be published. They usually have other gatekeepers to help them. Their decisions are influenced by professional and social assumptions. They need to be in tune with their readers. In the early years of the *Daily Nation*, Nairobi, in the 1960s, gatekeepers from Britain were not well suited to the African audience they wanted to attract (*Birth of a Nation*, by Gerard Loughran, Tauris, 2010). Here are some points that gatekeepers may consider:

Is it an event?

The media primarily report what has happened, is happening or will happen. Michael Schudson, an American professor of journalism, wrote in *Why Democracies Need an Unlovable Press* (Polity Press, 2009):

6 That is what serves democracy: the irresistible drive of journalists to focus on events, including those that powerful forces cannot anticipate and often cannot manage.   9

But non-events can also be news. Thelondonpaper (11 11 08) reported that the Stephen Lawrence Centre in south-east London had not reopened, nine months after vandals smashed its windows.

Does it concern a conflict?

One of the earliest known news stories describes in pictures an Egyptian victory and the fate of defeated Hittites. Conflict, whether armed, political, social, religious, local or on the sportsfield, is news. Conflict and controversy excite people. Schudson (2009) sees as part of the press's necessary unlovability its love of conflict and dissent.

When did it happen?

Reports to hand when work on an edition begins are likelier to be used than those sent in late, though editors will strive to include big last-minute news. (Online, however, news unfolds continuously.)

Is it unexpected, unusual?

Dog bites man is not news, we are told. Man bites dog *is* news.

Is it big?

A bomb that kills 80 people in Iraq is news. A bomb that kills one person may be ignored. The more bombs go off, the bigger the bomb needed to create a bang in the media. (Conversely, a small bomb in Israel will make headlines if it is the first for a year.)

Mike Amos, a *Northern Echo* columnist, got a tip that Sheila Clarke, in the Teesdale village of Gainford, had been the oldest Englishwoman to go abroad on Voluntary Service Overseas. She was then 65. Mike found two other elderly Gainford women with much to tell. One had become a Buddhist and an expert in interpreting handwriting. The stories of three made a better column than a story of just one.

Is it about people?

Western media and readers see news in personal terms. They see political debate as a battle of personalities rather than ideas. Health news almost always concentrates on particular patients. Many news stories are about celebrities – people whom other people want to know about. The pressure of the clickstream favours news about people and celebrities.

Who's involved?

Dog bites man is not news. But, in a local paper, *Dog bites mayor* is news. So was *Former French President Chirac hospitalized after mauling by his clinically depressed poodle* (*Mail* online, 21 01 09). News depends on who's involved.

When gunmen ambushed the Sri Lankan cricket team in Lahore in March 2009, British media praised the British match referee, Chris Broad, who shielded a wounded colleague. They scarcely noticed the coach driver who stayed in his seat and drove the Sri Lankans to safety.

Relatives, associates, even animals of well-known people can make news. So can the sufferings and successes of children and the elderly. Former TV newscaster Anna Ford complained (*BJR*, September 2007):

> So often the concentration was on a paedophile, a dead girl or two, some sort of traumatic, overdeveloped event about a child … I think the crunch came when Bruce Forsyth's wife's dog was missing at a time when a lot of other things were going on. And I said: 'Is this really one of the 12 most important things happening today?'

Does it stir feelings?

Anna Ford did not think Mrs Forsyth losing her dog was news. But animal stories rouse emotions. Many women would sympathize with Mrs Forsyth. Stories about children rouse emotions similarly.

Discussions on television usually generate heat rather than light. But the speakers' anger attracts viewers. Radio listeners around the world love phoners-in who say outrageous things. Tony Blair remarked in a Reuters Institute speech (12 06 07): 'Something that is interesting is less powerful than something that makes you angry or shocked.'

Is it entertaining?

Celebrities, children and animals are also news because their exploits and mishaps are entertaining.

Swiss newspapers savour humorous news. A political festival, with free food and the Steppin' Stompers, clashes with a major football match (*Baseler Allgemeine Zeitung*, 31 05 08). A sense of humour can make news more readable.

Is someone coming or going?

New appointments to important jobs are news. So are the departures – and deaths – of prominent or intriguing people. News has been defined as learning someone died who you never knew was alive.

Was it hidden?

After years in which the details of the Al-Yamamah aircraft deal between Britain and Saudi Arabia were kept secret, it was news when *Guardian* journalists discovered these details could include big payments to a prince.

The *Daily Mail* discovered a forgotten jungle in Cornwall (27 11 08). Newsnight (BBC2, 25 11 08) exposed overcrowded Iraqi jails like Black Holes of Calcutta.

Is it important?

Elections are news because they are important. They can change the government or control of the local council. Importance does not necessarily get news into the media or command the attention of the clickstream. Really important news demotes or drives out smaller news. In *Reporting Politics in Nigeria* (2008), journalism educator Dayo Duyile tells how he wrote a lead story for the *Nigerian Tribune* about a village murder. This was displaced by another story he wrote, on a national pay rise. Then the president of Nigeria's near-neighbour, Togo, was murdered. The village killing and the pay rise were both relegated to the back page.

Is it dangerous?

We read and listen to news to learn about the dangers that might affect us: terrorism, teenagers, taxes, tempests.

Are there any pictures?

Pictures are central to newspaper layout and vital to TV. Coverage of the final days and aftermath of the Sri Lankan civil war in 2009 was restricted by the army's success in keeping reporters and photographers away.

Where is it?

Geography is important, even for publications that cover the world. All the world news is on the BBC website but only some of it appears on TV news. British journalists assess overseas countries ruthlessly. The United States comes top for foreign news value – American stories are often presented as if they were British. The *Daily Mail* front page (28 08 09) reported: *This girl of 11 was snatched off the street 18 years ago. Yesterday she reappeared.* You had to turn to page 5 to discover it happened in California. Europe scores because of the UK's membership of the European Union – but Europe is considered a bit dull. The Middle East and Pakistan score because they pose terrorist threats and British troops are in Afghanistan. Suffering in once-British-ruled Palestine fosters guilt.

Being in the news has given Darfur, Congo and Zimbabwe a start on other parts of Africa. China and India are gaining news value, because of their trading and working links with Britain and their importance in the world economy. Other areas of the world get little notice in the British media unless they suffer a major disaster or hide some scandal. African journalists complain that British media see Africa in terms of Aids, famine and war.

Media geography is different abroad. *El Pais* (Spain) features the Middle East and Latin America. Al Jazeera TV's English service tries to see the news from the perspective of poorer people in poorer countries. It publishes less American and European news than CNN and BBC World (*see* James Painter, *Counter-Hegemonic News*, Reuters Institute, 2008).

Is it easy to grasp?

News media – written and read or heard in a hurry – prefer the simple to the complicated. They want cures to be cures and they want them available from the health service straight away. They like clear contrasts between good and evil, heroes and terrorists. 'Modern journalism doesn't do complicated,' wrote Andrew Gilligan of the *Evening Standard* (Press Gazette, 18 01 08).

In truth, the world and its rights and wrongs are not as simple as journalists can make them appear. It is a great skill to explore the complexities of the real world and make them easy for busy people to grasp.

Does it relate to the news agenda?

A wide range of media commonly have the same news agenda, concentrating on a limited group of major stories. Having decided to invest in covering such a story – the disappearance of three-year-old Madeleine McCann in Portugal in 2007, for instance – the media do not easily let it go.

The agenda depends on or relates principally to:

- major events – fighting, disasters, sports, demonstrations, parades, epidemics
- celebrity – national and local
- news flagged up by newsmakers – politicians, councils, bloggers, sports clubs, TV presenters
- media tradition – crime has long been a media standby
- history, both recent (terrorism, global warming, the 2007–9 recession) and more distant (anniversaries). World-war anniversaries get a special flogging because of the wars' importance to British self-image
- jobs
- services – health, schools, transport, fuel, food supply
- expert reports
- local relevance, for local media
- above all, television and its cousin, the internet

TV has a triple effect. What happens on TV can be news, even for a local paper since local people will have seen it. Second, TV pictures can make events bigger news. Third, TV creates and nurtures celebrities. Jade Goody, whose early death from cancer in 2009 received saturation coverage in the media, owed her celebrity to two TV reality shows.

Good news and bad news

The media are accused of concentrating on bad news. This is inevitable if people look to the media for information about dangerous events. Dangerous events are bad news. However, good news is published, too: new jobs as well as disappearing jobs; medical discoveries and sporting victories; stories of people who have done wonderful things at home and abroad. Readers are hungry for what is modern and optimistic.

A journalist who writes or broadcasts a good-news story takes a risk that everything is as it seems. In practice, the medical breakthrough may not be. The imaginative scheme may fail. Even truly good news can have a short life. William Graham, a talented Jamaican sculptor who made mannequins for shop windows, could not be found in his workshop in a London railway arch six months after the *Financial Times* published a profile of him. Burglars had put him back on the dole.

Hard news and soft news

Journalists have been taught that there should be a reason why news is published now, not tomorrow or next week. The media receive hard news, of important events which just took place, for example, Usain Bolt wins the 2008 Olympic 100 metres. They also receive soft news, for example, Usain Bolt prepares for the 2012 Olympics, a story which could be published any day up to 2012.

Hard news drives out soft, in print and on air, but not necessarily online where both can be published together. The clickstream likes soft news, about celebrities, animals, children. Soft news tells people what life is about and how people live it. It gets used because it is entertaining or a touch bizarre – *Cloudy days help the memory* (*Telegraph* and *Mail*, 18 04 09); *Health officials provide chip shops with salt-saving shakers* (*MEN*, 19 03 09). The *Daily Mirror* and the *Sun* entertain readers with minor news that is hard to credit, for instance: *A TV mogul who set up a station to show Muslims as peaceful has been charged with beheading his wife* (*Daily Mirror*, 17 02 09); '*A mayor raked in £18,000 as a benefits cheat* (*Sun*, 6 02 09).

Media accept a responsibility to keep their audiences in touch with important situations even though they are neither hard news nor entertaining. Channel 4's 'Unreported World' scours the planet for such situations.

Finding news: news services

You can find news worldwide on the websites of the BBC, CNN and Google News and of national newspapers. You can receive news alerts direct to your computer from the BBC and other agencies. Google provides an RSS reader, gathering the latest from websites of your choice.

Former BBC political correspondent Nicholas Jones showed in his blog – www. nicholasjones.org.uk – how newspapers used their websites to be first with the news in May/June 2009. Daily at 9pm, before the TV news, the *Daily Telegraph* website published a taster of its next disclosures about MPs' expenses. The *Guardian* website disclosed at 12 noon on June 3, the eve of local and European elections, the Hotmail plot to rally MPs to oust Gordon Brown. Ex-minister Hazel Blears, who left the government on the eve of polling, apologized for this in a video interview on the website of the *Manchester Evening News*.

Again, you can get news from the websites of news agencies – the Press Association (for UK news), Reuter and the Associated Press – if your paper subscribes to them and gives you an access code. On a split screen, you can use your mouse to drag highlighted passages from the agencies into your work. News websites rely heavily on agency news.

Other news on the internet

John Darwin reappeared in 2007, five years after disappearing in a canoe off Seaton Carew, Hartlepool. Nearly everyone had thought him dead, including – it seemed – his wife Anne who was in Panama. Then a reader of the *Daily Mirror* typed John, Anne and Panama into Google Images. Up came a picture of John and Anne in Panama the year before. So Anne had known all along that John was alive. The Darwin affair shows how the internet can help find a story, or a new twist to an old one.

A blogger, Guido Fawkes, disclosed on the internet the smears about Conservative leaders and MPs supplied by Downing Street aide Damian McBride for a Labour blog (12 04 09). Stories can crop up anywhere on the net. Court documents about Électricité de France spying on Greenpeace were unearthed by an investigative website Mediapart (*FT*, 21 04 09). An *Evening Standard* placard in London in April 2009 read *Queen's G20 gibe a hit on YouTube* – the YouTube site often runs replays of significant news incidents. The same month, an awkwardly smiling Prime Minister Gordon Brown used YouTube to announce a plan to reform MPs' expenses.

There is news on the social networks – Facebook, MySpace, Bebo. A police officer resigned after posting on Facebook a sardonic comment on the death of Ian Tomlinson at a London protest (BBC, 30 04 09).

The easiest networking site to search is that of the microblogging service, Twitter. Go to http://search.twitter.com and you will see links to 'trending topics', the most popular current stories. Or you can type into Twitter's search panel a subject or celebrity of your choice. Relevant tweets will appear on the screen. Most may be banal. But you may find usable comments. If you are pursuing a moving story, Twitter could be first with the next piece of news. Tweets are limited to 140 characters, so people write them quickly, providing what could be the first tip of an incident. Twitter made headlines when gunmen attacked Mumbai hotels in November 2008. People trapped in rooms sent out tweets. Twitter can provide leads on local as well as international stories. When Darlington Football Club went into administration in March 2009, http://twitter.com/saveDFC told you what was going on.

The BBC has received striking pictures from the public – of the South-East Asian tsunami tidal wave in 2005, of the Buncefield oil depot fire in 2005, of Sheffield floods in 2007. It has desks checking and handling user-generated news. Pictures, in particular, need checks on where and when they were taken. An appeal for pictures of floods can bring in pictures from previous years.

Comments and recommendations drive web activity. On a slack news day, you could google the name of a local hotel and select – from Google's list of recommended pages – one on www.tripadvisor.co.uk. Tripadvisor collects reviews from hotel visitors, ranging from very good to terrible. It also publishes what the reviewers say. Ask the hotel for a response. Has it dealt with any complaints in the reviews?

www.reviewcentre.com publishes restaurant reviews by county, and even by town. On the basis of the reviews, it gives restaurants a thumbs up or a thumbs down. You could try a meal at a thumbs-downed restaurant and see what you think.

Calls and contacts

Journalists find news by calling regularly on informants and contacts – the police, fire stations, football and sports clubs, members of parliament, councils, companies, ministers of religion, friends in pubs and clubs. Every paper or broadcasting station needs to identify people on whom it can call regularly to check what has happened or is about to happen.

The diary

The office diary, listing courts, council meetings and other forthcoming news events, is central to news gathering. The diary can help to ensure that stories which recur or run on for several days continue to be covered. However, competing media have similar diaries with similar entries. Off-diary news is valuable because competitors may not have it.

News from public relations

Tourism Queensland's contest to fill the best job in the world – caretaker of an attractive island – generated media coverage worth $100 million from an outlay of $1.2 million (*FT*, 28 08 09).

Public relations has established itself as a major channel for news. It serves not only commerce and government. Charities, too, turn to PR people to put their case. According to Liz Lewis Jones, director of the Chartered Institute of Public Relations, over 30,000 PR people deal with the media. That's not counting press officers for government and other organizations. A third of them are in the CIPR, which has a strict code of ethics. They organize events and initiatives. They send handouts and e-mails. Like Tourism Queensland, they play the internet. They make the work of their clients plain for reporters and the public. Their task is to help their clients sell their wares and pills and points of view, not necessarily to provide objective, dispassionate reporting. They recruit the celebrated and the sick to say what the client wants said. Former Reuterman Daniel Simpson writes: *Reporters lack the time they need to find stories, so they rely on pre-packaged content from the PR industry* (*BJR*, September 2009).

Don't put handouts straight in the paper or online. Ask a few questions.

News from the mail

Many letters and publications arrive in media offices. They make announcements. They draw attention to forthcoming events. Newsletters contain news which may be of interest to a wider circle than their readership. Letters to an editor raise issues and comment on situations. Letters in the *Ilford Recorder* (23 03 06) protested at the threat to Ilford's oldest building from rubbish and the new flats being built next door. Council minutes are a mine of information. In the 1960s and 1970s they recorded the shady construction deals which were to become the scandal of the day.

Don't assume that every news story submitted by a member of the public needs to be rewritten. If it reads well as it stands, leave it alone. Making changes risks introducing errors.

Your own newspaper or service

You need to know what your colleagues are reporting. Your paper may contain leads for new stories. Scan the advertisements, including the small advertisements. *Belfast Telegraph* columnist Lindy McDowell spotted a page advertising 60 bankruptcies, a sign of the local cost of the credit crunch (6 05 09).

In October 2008, lawyers advertised in eight newspapers for people who might have skin problems because of gas emitted by a drying agent in Chinese-made leather sofas.

Other publications

Look at national and local newspapers and magazines; listen to broadcasts. They, too, can give you leads.

Someone watching BBC 1's University Challenge 2009 was sharp enough to realize that Gail Trimble of Corpus Christi College, Oxford, was the outstanding competitor. This led to several news stories about her, and a controversy over whether she was too clever by half. Controversy also followed broadcaster Ray Gosling's account of smothering his gravely ill partner (BBC1, 15.02.10).

National media often publish stories of local interest or import. BBC4 (24 11 08) featured Peters, a Huddersfield department store. A church minister on Songs of Praise had been ill-treated as an illegitimate child in a Spanish orphanage and then brought to Britain by a man from North Shields. Persimmon, Britain's biggest housebuilder, suspended new projects (the *Independent*, 25 04 08). Was it building in your local area?

The *Big Issue* (21 01 08) published an advertisement seeking a man last seen two years earlier selling his paintings in Churchill Square, Brighton. He was being sought by a woman who gave two phone numbers, one of them in Belgium. Here was an intriguing story for a Brighton newspaper. Readers will recall seeing the artist and his pictures. What did they show? How long had he been around? What was the Belgian connection? The idea for an *FT Magazine* feature about Morocco's leading TV host seems to have come from a book (9 02 10).

Brief reports on television leave obvious questions unanswered. At the end of 2007, the Russian government threatened not to send an art exhibition to Britain, because of possible legal claims. Who might have a claim? (It turned out that the collections of two merchants were nationalized soon after the Russian Revolution. Heirs had tried to get them back.)

Many stories are framed by assumptions worth questioning. We must cut carbon emissions by 80 per cent by 2050. Who said so? What is the expected result? Why not 75 per cent or 85 per cent? At what cost to a householder in comfort and/or cash?

The news behind the news

Many routine news engagements give clues to other stories, anything from a chatty paragraph for a gossip column to a major scoop. Major announcements may be made during media visits to industrial plants. Sports reporting thrives on what goes on off the pitch or the track.

In 1986 the BBC gave the media a preview of a TV series entitled 'The Monocled Mutineer' about a mutiny by British soldiers at Étaples, France, during the First World War. The historical adviser for the series thought it presented fiction misleadingly as fact. He did not believe that the monocled mutineer shown leading the mutiny was actually at Étaples at the time.

Follow up what you see and hear

If you walked down Wanstead High Street, north-east London, at the end of August 2009, you would have seen that a travel agent's shop had suddenly been cleared out. A note on the door protested that holidaymakers had been stranded. Then, at the beginning of September, the shop reopened. What was going on? It made a lead story for the *Wanstead Guardian*.

What and who you notice in your daily life can be news. Potatoes have jumped in price. The windows of a bar are blanked out with newspaper. A prominent modern church has disappeared. Monica, a Romanian gypsy, sells the *Big Issue* outside the Somerfield store in all weathers. Who is she? Why is she here? Does she make any money? Couldn't she do something more rewarding? (In 2008, Romanians had a right to live in Britain but not take jobs outside a limited range.) A leaflet is handed out at Whipps Cross Hospital, North-East London in September 2009, saying that consultants are contactable and the hospital can be e-mailed about appointments. Both these facts are important to patients. A blood testing centre at Wanstead Hospital sports a notice saying that only 50 people will be bled that day. Others, beyond the 50, come and leave. But some stay put. They insist on their blood samples being taken – after all, the session is scheduled to continue a further 90 minutes, and they have taken time off work. If this happens other days, what has gone wrong with local blood testing? Philip Stephens of the *Financial Times* was incensed by the hassle he endured at Heathrow Airport. He wrote about it. Many other people were incensed as well, forcing the government and the British Airports Authority to react.

Casual conversation can offer a clue to an unusual story. A friend remarked that Germans dominated solar-power sales overseas. It turned out that a new, low-wage industry making solar panels had sprouted in a dying industrial area south of Berlin.

Mike Morrissey, a freelance who has been sending a dozen stories a week to the *Darlington and Stockton Times* from the seaside town of Saltburn, recalls four local scoops. They drew attention to news important for local people that could have gone unnoticed:

1. In December 2007 he found buried in a lengthy council document the news that houses might be built on hitherto undeveloped coastal land between Saltburn and the neighbouring settlement, Marske. When the *D&S Times* reported this, 60 Saltburn people crammed into the parish council meeting room to protest.

2. A local activist told him in summer 2008 that a community bobby was being transferred out of Saltburn. After this was reported, 1000 people signed petitions and the chief constable rescinded the transfer.

3. He followed up a claim by a speaker at a public meeting that a ward at Brotton Hospital (near Saltburn) had been closed.

4. He heard that, without public announcement, a Brotton golf club in financial trouble had been bought by a local landowner. The purchase saved 50 jobs.

Questions

1. How does your publication define news?

2. What does it particularly concentrate on?

3. What stories would it not publish?

4. What themes or campaigns is it pursuing?

5. What does it not cover which you would like it to cover?

6. In what ways do you agree or disagree with your publication's choice of news?

7. Answer these questions for a TV news service.

2 Pursuing news: what do I need to know?

It shocked me that so many journalists had allowed the story to be written for them. The West Midlands Police and CPS allegations were taken at face value.

Kevin Sutcliffe (BJR, March 2008)

Having selected or been assigned to a news story, a reporter needs to ask 'What do I need to know?' Essentially, I need to know what the story is, with enough detail and explanation for readers to understand it and see it in its context.

In the quote above, Kevin Sutcliffe, deputy head of news and current affairs at Channel 4, was complaining that journalists had too readily accepted imprecise allegations from police and the Crown Prosecution Service against Undercover Mosque, an investigation into inflammatory preaching. (Channel 4 showed that police transcripts of what was said were flawed.)

Stories are not necessarily as reporters expect or news editors envisage or publicists present them. In the 1980s, the Save the Children Fund held a press conference about its efforts to feed starving Ethiopians in a camp in Tigray, Northern Ethiopia. Inquiries at Oxfam showed that people were starving because the government was bombing insurgent-held areas.

Find the real story: it may not be how it looks

Stories can change with every informant you talk to. So talk to as many as you can. Columnist Matthew Engel wrote in the *FT Magazine* (19 05 07) about a report in the *New York Times*, prompted by a police tip-off: *For more than half an hour thirty-eight respectable citizens in Queens watched a killer stalk and stab a woman on three separate occasions. Not one person telephoned the police during the assault.* This got the commentators commenting. How terrible that 38 people should stand by while a woman was stabbed. However, a lawyer showed that not all the 38 were eyewitnesses. None could have watched for half an hour because the woman and her assailant would have been visible only a few moments. Probably no more than three people saw the woman stabbed. So the 38 were not such uncaring citizens after all.

The year 2009 saw publication of the English translation of *People Like Us*, by Joris Luyendijk who spent five years reporting in Egypt, Lebanon and Palestine for Dutch newspapers and TV (Soft Skull Press). The real story in Egypt was life in a dictator-ruled poorhouse run by corrupt thugs. He could not tell it before because, in a dictatorship, it is hard to get anyone to describe what their life is like. Dictators don't like grasses.

He also believes that the events of the Israeli–Palestinian conflict are largely staged for TV. He compares the news to a wrapped loaf of bread. Correspondents pretend they've baked the loaf 'while, in fact, all we've done is put it in its wrapping'. The challenge of reporting is to find the real story, not simply wrap the story that someone else has concocted.

Have a questioning mind

You need the sort of mind that asks questions when a news story breaks. Why did it happen? How did it happen? What were the circumstances?

Shildon, a small railway town off the beaten track in South-West Durham, is a centre of credit-card fraud, reported the *News of the World* (6 09 09). Why Shildon? Are the fraudsters local or simply using Shildon addresses? Again, if so, why? What goods are they acquiring? Who is being defrauded?

A £12 billion scheme to computerize health records has ground to a halt (FT, 28 10 08). Why? What were the difficulties? *15000 mostly elderly investors have lost over £34 million in the biggest international boiler-room share scam so far uncovered (FT, 14 03 08)*. What is a boiler-room scam? How did this one work? Were people in your area among the losers? (A boiler-room is a call centre selling dud shares.)

During an attack in 2008/9, when Israel kept reporters out of Gaza, pictures emerged of a Gazan father kissing his dead son. Jeremy Bowen, the BBC's Middle East editor, was asked afterwards how he would have followed these up if he had been able to get into Gaza. He replied: 'I would have found out who he was, gone to his house, found his personal story, what his life was going to be like now and who he thought the culprits were' (C4, 22 01 09).

Suppose you pursued the story about the hospital blood tests session from which people were turned away (*see* Chapter 1, p. 11). You would first want to know whether this story was worth pursuing. Was it an isolated occurrence or did it happen every day? Was it happening elsewhere in the area? If so, why? You would need the hospital trust's side of the story – why was it not coping better with the demand for blood tests? Why were more people being sent for tests than, it seems, could easily be tested? You could go to the test centre the next day and find out what happened. (At this particular Wanstead centre you could talk to people outside in the street. Under the

Press Complaints Commission Code, speaking to people inside a hospital requires an executive's permission.) You would find people had taken time off work or taken children out of school. The session was supposed to run from 9.00 am to 12.15. So, even though only one woman was taking blood samples, she could have taken them from 90 people. Why limit the number to 50, which meant ending the session at 10.45? You still need to be asking 'Why?' when you are collecting information, so that you can explain what you are told.

The *Financial Times* reported (10 11 09) *Each unit of social housing now requires a much larger government grant than before the credit crunch.* Why should this be? The crunch can hardly have made homes more expensive to build. So is an affordable rent, post-crunch, lower than before? Or is there less subsidy from full-price house sales?

Ways of finding out

There are three main ways of finding things out: by reading written material, going to events, and talking to people.

Written material

The internet Internet information comes with a health warning. It may be inaccurate or it may be less than the full story. Some sites – for example, the *Guardian* – attach a history to their articles but many do not make it clear who wrote their articles or when. Check with a real, live person if you can. At the least, this should make the facts more certain and it could bring the story to life.

The websites of reputable governments and universities are reliable usually. If a site belongs to an organization you have never heard of, search for the organization itself to see what it is about. Another check is to google 'link': followed by the website's address, for example link:www.dodgywebsite.co.uk. This shows you other sites to which the site is linked.

When all this has been said, however, the internet comes in very handy. If you need the minutes of your local council, you can find them on its website. If you cover football, you will know the website of the football club.

For a reporter sitting at a computer, the quickest access to written facts is usually through Google. Type a few well-chosen, correctly spelled words into Google's search panel, and you quickly find out where Urlay Nook is, who wrote A Colour Symphony, who holds a given job in the government and how to spell his/her name. You can find or check, too, the details of past events, if they are back in the news.

A search engine may turn up information in a large website more quickly than you can search the site yourself. Google turned up the Sally Murrer case in the Press Gazette website (*see* Chapter 12, pp. 159–60).

Google, in its reply to your search, lists first a few 'sponsored links', which are advertisements. Then it lists web pages in the order it judges will be most useful to you. A million or more pages may be in some way relevant to your query. Google puts first the pages it expects most likely to assist you. It represents each page with a headline and a sentence or two of text. Often, you will quickly see what you seek in these sentences. If not, click on a headline to open the page you think likeliest to give you an answer. If the page is a long document, or a book, it may not open at the information you require. Type Control and F to find a word or words deep in a document. If it's a book, there is probably a page-turning system.

High up in a Google list of web pages will probably be a Wikipedia site. On a vast range of subjects, Wikipedia provides search engines and their users with comprehensive, simply written information. In 2007, melamine came into the news because Chinese manufacturers were adding it to food and feed. But what was it? A Wikipedia article gave the answer. Answers.com provides a broader range of responses, from several encyclopedias and dictionaries. The *Encyclopedia Britannica* (www.britannica.co.uk) is another alternative but has to be paid for.

Among Google's responses to your query you may find background information you were not specifically looking for. A search for Laos and drugs in May 2009 – when a Briton, Samantha Orobator, faced a drugs charge in Laos – turned up a travel site (Matadorpulse.com) with a link to an article on how to avoid drugs charges in South-East Asia. It also told the stories of foreigners accused of drug trafficking.

Web searching requires patience. Not all searches are immediately successful. Google failed to turn up a single English eighteenth century sculptor. At the other extreme, if you google the name of someone not very well known, Google may provide thousands of listings, most of them relating to other people, probably Americans, with the same name. (A new search engine, Wolfram Alpha, has abandoned web searches. It searches its own database instead.)

You can extend your search of the web or make it more precise.

1. Try Dogpile, www.dogpile.com. Dogpile is a meta-crawler. It trawls through the results of Google and other search engines and gives you the top slice. It turned up the final result of Shiv Malik's court battle with the police (*see* Chapter 14, pp. 188–9).

2. Put in double quotes a title, name or phrase you seek, for example "Seven Years War". This will give you results for Seven Years War only, and reject pages that simply contain the words seven, years and war.

3. Add a search word, putting it immediately after a plus sign, for instance "John Jones" +solicitor. "Hold the front page" + "family courts" brought up, on the Holdthefrontpage website, a list of media-law articles including two or three on family courts.

4. "John * Jones" will give you John Joneses who use a middle name. You can also use an asterisk if you are seeking a title or quotation and cannot remember a word in it.

5. Use less common search words that are specific to your search.

6. Put in OR if you want results for either of two names or items. Mumbai OR Bombay will give you results for both the old and new names of the city. Cricket +Mumbai OR Bombay will give you pages relating to both Mumbai and Bombay cricket.

7. Put an asterisk after the root of the word you want. Agricult* will give you results for agriculture, agricultural, agriculturist.

8. You can confine your search to a particular site – "Fiona Bruce" site:www.bbc.co.uk will give you pages about Fiona Bruce from the BBC's site only.

9. Try advanced search. This refines your search in several ways at once. Clicking on Google's advanced search, for example, produces a questionnaire on which you can specify which words must be in the replies, what phrase must appear in a particular form, which alternative names or items you are interested in, and which words you want to rule out as no good to you. (For instance, if you were seeking David Spark, author of this book, you would rule out Media Solutions, San Francisco, run by another David Spark.) Google's advanced search also offers Google Book Search (which looks in books), Google News Archive Research (for history) and Google Scholar (which finds articles written by particular people or on particular subjects). If your computer gives you a customized version of Google, you may need to open the main Google search engine www.google.co.uk to get an advanced search.

10. Search Lexis-Nexis, if you or your employer subscribe to it. Lexis-Nexis is a database containing billions of documents. It is strong in court records and newspaper files.

11. Try a specialized directory or search engine. www.findlaw.com covers the law, http://medlineplus.gov is the American National Library of Medicine's Medline service. For the UK, there is NHS Direct at www.nhsdirect.nhs.uk.

Martin Huckerby has written *The Net for Journalists,* a detailed beginners' guide to internet research, mainly intended for journalists in developing countries. It contains many links to useful sites. It was published online in 2006 by Unesco, the Thomson Foundation and the Commonwealth Broadcasting Association. You can find it on http://portal.unesco.org/ci/en/files/21010/11387936529net_for_journalists.pdf/net_for journalists.pdf. You can also try www.pressclub.ch/doc/the_net_for_journalists.pdf.

Wikipedia   A web encyclopedia written and amended by web users. Its vast scope and enlightening explanations show what can be achieved by non-professionals on the web.

Part of the theory underlying it was that contributors' errors would be corrected by other contributors. However, it turned out that some wrote or made amendments for less worthy reasons. Some have changed facts to support political arguments. Some have introduced disparaging remarks. In March 2009, a student planted a fake quote from French composer Maurice Jarre. It appeared in media obituaries (*Mail*, 26 08 09). In any event, there is no guarantee that the more knowledgeable contributors will prevail over the less.

In 2009, Wikipedia announced it was appointing thousands of editors, to check changes in articles about living people. Wikipedia illustrates how much users can do for the internet. But such public participation can be wrecked by people with questionable motives or one-track minds.

Twitter   People who sign up with Twitter are asked to become followers of other twitterers. Alan Rusbridger, editor of the *Guardian*, has explained (*BJR*, September 2009) how *Guardian* reporter Paul Lewis garnered material from scores of Twitter followers who attended the G20 anti-bankers protest near the Bank of England in April 2009. It included a video from a New York fund manager who realized that he had captured the moment when news-seller Ian Tomlinson was pushed over by a police officer, shortly before he died from a heart attack.

You can use your own site as well as Twitter to seek stories and opinions from readers and viewers. The BBC asked viewers 'Is it OK to hug the Queen?' after she was hugged by Barack Obama's wife, Michelle. To find blogs on a subject you want to pursue, simply type into Google the subject plus blogs – for example 'MPs expenses blogs'. There is a directory, blogcatalog.com.

Other written material   There is still a lot of printed paper around – hand-outs, reports, publications, newspapers, old newspaper files. Local information is probably not on the web, apart from newspaper, council and company websites.

Don't put complete trust in what other journalists have previously written. It is common for one journalist's error to be copied by many more. Ask yourself whether what you have read is likely to be right. In *Public Affairs for Journalists* (Oxford, 2009), James Morrison asserts that more than half of people aged over 65 have a disabling condition requiring long-term care. A second glance shows that this depends on the definition of a disabling condition and long-term care. If it includes people taking pills long-term for rheumatism and hypertension, Morrison's statement becomes more convincing. But you would want to check with an expert how to read it.

Going to events

Attending events is another way to pursue news. They could be accidents, fires, meetings, marches, courts, conferences, press conferences, concerts, sports matches. (Always stay to the end. Something important can happen or be said at the last moment.) Going to an event, you will get a better grasp of what happened, and your description of the place will help the readers picture it. You may also find eyewitnesses.

Speaking to people

These three approaches – reading, going, interviewing – are interdependent. You will be better able to ask questions, cover an event or write up a handout if you know what has already been written. And, if you are writing up a handout, you need a live quote. At a meeting, you may need to check that you have accurately heard what was said. You may need to tease out, from behind the fine words, what the story actually is, how the new industrial process works.

Who to ask   At a meeting, the best person to speak to is probably there and available. In other situations you have to find someone, and you may be passed from one to another. When you have located good informants, keep their contact details. You will probably need them again. Be courageous. Try to interview the decision-makers, not second-rankers or PR representatives. Top people may brush you off, but you may get valuable copy.

If the story is about an incident or situation, you first need the people who know what it is about and have authority to talk to you: managers, police superintendents, fire officers, head teachers, trade union officials. The police and other organizations have press officers who will give the general picture.

You also need the people who were there when it happened, or arrived soon after: eyewitnesses, the first police officer on the scene. *'It was very, very windy, and suddenly the ship lurched away from the quayside. Two passengers and one of the staff were in the water and it took ten to 15 minutes to get them out,'* said Douglas Campbell, 68, a retired Scotland Yard detective (the *Daily Telegraph*, 29 10 08).

If the story concerns something possibly amiss, you may need help from unauthorized people – the teacher complaining against dismissal, the employee who is not receiving the minimum wage, the ex-official who knows about the council's cosy relationship with a local contractor. Ex-members and ex-employees can be useful if you want to know what really goes on inside an organization. A Channel 4 film-maker who went to the Philippines to see a jail's enthusiastically dancing prisoners found out from a former inmate that the dancing was not entirely voluntary.

Many people you speak to will expect you to have read the relevant documents on the web. Before an interview with a Redbridge official for the local government chapter of this book, it was necessary to look through the Local Government Act 2000 and the Redbridge Borough Council's constitution.

Many stories require an understanding of the science or the technology or the theology or the law or a foreign country. If you need someone to explain to you, university staff will usually help. A university's press office will point you in the right direction. The university may also list its experts online. The website https://profnet.prnewswire.com suggests experts, mainly American: www.experts.com finds expert witnesses.

The British Medical Association press office (020 7387 4499) can usually suggest a doctor who will explain a disease or a treatment. Just about every disease and condition also has its national charity, traceable through Google. The charity may have local branches. There may be local charities also.

Don't be too awed by experts and managers. Give ordinary people a hearing.

Finding those you need to find   You may not be able to find immediately the people you need. Here are some suggestions:

Your contacts book – Always write down contact details for people you speak to. Keep a note of any indication where well-known people live. You may need them.

Who's Who – Lists the great and the good, often with contact details.

Phonebook – Worth trying, even if many people are ex-directory. You can ring people of the same name, if it is important enough to justify the intrusion. They could be related to the person you need. The website www.infobel.com/teldir will look people up for you in phonebooks all over the world. www.btexchanges.com has uk numbers.

Other directories – Crockfords (for Anglican priests), Medical Directory (for doctors), diocesan directory (for Catholic priests), council publications (for councillors), Spotlight (for actors and theatre – only theatricals can access Spotlight online). Your local library may have more directories. At a price, Crockfords (www.crockford.co.uk) is available online and the Medical Directory (www.themedicaldirectory.co.uk) as a CD-Rom. Your paper may be a subscriber.

Ask employers, colleagues, friends, officers of clubs and associations – who know the people you need or seek. The Data Protection Act has made it more difficult for data holders to help. They may need permission to give you details. You may then be dependent on them getting the person you seek to phone you. You might reach a Muslim through a local mosque or a Nigerian through a Nigerian association or church.

Electoral roll – This lists voters by the ward and street they live in. They can ask not to be listed. However, there should be a complete roll somewhere in the borough.

Publishers and agents – Anyone who has written a book can probably be reached through their publisher. Writers, performers and sportspeople may also have agents.

Websites – For companies, parishes, organizations and individuals. www.GroupsNearYou.com helps locate local community e-mail and online groups. www.linkedin.com lists professionals. It also includes a company directory.

www.journalismnet.com offers links – not necessarily free – for finding people, e-mail addresses and phone numbers. www.123 people.co.uk gathers references to people for free.

Twitter – When an aircraft crashed at Buffalo in the middle of the night, a broadcaster over the border in Canada found an eyewitness on Twitter. 'It's become de rigueur to use Twitter in any breaking-news environment,' writes BBC executive Matthew Ettringham ('The Future of Journalism', BBC College of Journalism, 2009).

Facebook – You can find some people on Facebook simply by putting their names in the search panel. Checking on their friends will indicate whether or not you have the right person. To find other people, you may need Facebook friends strategically placed in politics, music, entertainment, sport and other news-bearing fields. Through your friends you can contact their friends and the friends of their friends.

Google – People who have publicized themselves in some way, by writing a book, launching a website, selling paintings, running a company, even putting themselves on Facebook may be traceable on the internet via Google. It is easier to find those with unusual names. Some people's e-mail addresses appear on websites.

Advertising – You can advertise for people through your newspaper or through your blog, if it is well read.

Tom Ilube of the Garlik consultancy demonstrated at a Royal Society of Arts seminar that he could find a panel member's address in an hour (*FT*, 19 08 08). How does he do it? Here is his explanation:

- Open web search, particularly looking for clubs, organizations etc. that the person you seek might be involved in. This almost always gives a few clues on location.

- Search the online Companies House database, www.companies house.gov.uk. Millions of people appear on it. People usually think of company directors as men in grey suits. But the self-employed and anyone who is running a charity, or housing associations will pop up. (Companies House charges a small fee for company searches. Wealthy media can buy its database for £4,000.)

- Search the edited electoral roll at somewhere like www.192.com. The addresses of those on the roll will pop up. Even if people have come off the roll, they appear in older versions and will appear on 192.com. However, you need to figure out whether they are still at the same address. (For a fee, 192. com will search phonebooks, the electoral roll and Companies House directors reports and give addresses and phone numbers.)

- Search local authority planning permission sites. When someone submits a planning form, it often goes on the local council website.

- Search the social networking sites – Facebook, friendsreunited. These don't generally give addresses but often give good clues of where to look.

- Search blogs. People often give away location information in their blog posts.

- Sometimes, you need to look for a spouse. If the spouse is a company director, you can find the address.

The website www.Journalism.net will put you in touch with a detective agency. Remember that it is an offence to seek personal information about others from people who have no authority to give it to you. Information about people's private lives is protected by both the Human Rights Act and the Data Protection Act. Information relating to the working lives of public servants, however, can be obtained under the Freedom of Information Act.

In 2006 the then royal editor of the *News of the World* admitted conspiring to intercept royal aides' mobile phone voicemail. He was jailed for four months (the *Age*, 27 01 07).

The Freedom of Information Act

In May 2009 readers and viewers learned in embarrassing detail what MPs had claimed on expenses. This was from the *Daily Telegraph*'s leaked disc, the scoop of the year. The disc would not have been compiled but for the Freedom of Information Act and the dogged Heather Brooke, an American freelance journalist who, with other journalists, first requested details of 14 MPs' expenses and persuaded the Information Tribunal and the High Court that the public should know them.

Before that Paul Hutcheon, of the *Sunday Herald*, Glasgow, had already used the Freedom of Information Act to research the expenses of members of the Scottish Parliament. In 2005, he forced Tory leader David McLetchie to resign over his liberal use of taxis.

The FOI has proved fertile. Matthew Davis runs a news agency, Data News, on the strength of his FOI requests. At the time of writing, his website, Freedom of Information News, sports cuttings from the *Daily Express* (100 councils go through bins to try to fine you) and the *Daily Mail* (1000 police off work every day).

The Freedom of Information Act obliges 100,000 public authorities from government departments to schools and the BBC to disclose their written information to the public and the media. The Act also obliges them to have a publication scheme – a list of documents and information accessible on their websites. (Campaigners hoped that the Act would be extended to private companies providing public services, for example, water companies. By 2009 this had not happened.)

Reporters seeking information should first check what is in the publication scheme of the authorities they wish to approach. If the scheme does not help, Freedom of Information requests are easily made. Reporters simply need to write – by post or e-mail – to the authorities they believe hold the information they require, stating who they are and, as precisely as possible, what information they want.

The authorities should normally produce the information, if they have it, within 20 working days. Most do. If an authority refuses, a reporter can appeal to it and then, if still dissatisfied, to the Information Commissioner. There have been more appeals against the BBC than anyone else.

An authority can charge a fee. It can also refuse a request which would cost too much to pursue. (Reporters can then rephrase their requests in a less expensive form.)

Authorities are exempt from disclosing court records, information from or related to 12 security bodies, and information protected by laws including the law of confidence (*see* pp. 158–9). Some other information is partially exempt – but it should be released if there is a public interest in its release. These partial exemptions include government policy, information intended for publication, security information not related to the 12 bodies, communication with the Royal family, and information which could prejudice defence, law enforcement, commercial interests, international relations and relations between government bodies.

Jeremy Hayes, senior output editor at Radio 4's The World Tonight, reports that some civil servants are wary of pressure groups seeking information in order to get policy changed (*BJR*, September 2009). In mid-2009, Prime Minister Gordon Brown outlined plans to exempt Cabinet papers from disclosure, and a government paper can easily become a Cabinet paper. (Jeremy Hayes's report on the FOI, *A Shock to the System,* is at www.reutersinstitute.politics.ox.ac/.)

FOI in the provincial and suburban press

Release of environmental information is covered by the Environmental Information Regulations. Requests for it can be made verbally, not just in writing.

A *Manchester Evening News* Freedom of Information request disclosed that over 4000 alcoholics in Greater Manchester were on disability benefits, and this made a page one lead (18 03 09). The *Western Mail* (16 03 09) discovered what Welsh policemen did on the side. Their second jobs ranged from film extra to hypnotherapist.

Some people hoped the Act would bring to light dangers to health. A *Northern Echo* request disclosed the outcomes of inspections of school kitchens.

Figures obtained from the Crown Prosecution Service and the Metropolitan Police by Charlie Campbell of the *Wanstead Guardian* showed (24 01 08) that there were 50 rapes in the borough of Redbridge in 2006–7 but only two rapists were convicted.

One obvious question: why bother with a Freedom of Information request? Why not just ring up and ask, which could give you information immediately, not in 20 days? A report in *Kent on Sunday* (27 04 08) suggests one answer. It said that leaders of Swale Council had decided to dismiss its chief executive, after receiving an independent report into allegations in a whistle-blowing document. Given the public interest, a Freedom of Information request might have brought the actual allegations to light. A council cannot refuse to release a document because parts of it may be exempt. It must delete the exempt parts and release the rest.

Dave Collins, contributing to the Holdthefrontpage site (19 08 09), pointed out that a Freedom of Information request for details of councillors' expenses can disclose these without waiting for the 20 days in the summer when councils open their books after audit. (For further reading see *Your Right To Know*, by Heather Brooke (Pluto, 2005). There is an associated website at www.yrtk.org.)

Be alert

You need to be curious about and sensitive to the answers and material you collect. When 15-year-old Billy Cox was shot dead in South London, a card left with flowers called him 'heaven's new fallen soldier'. The *Independent* (16 02 07) assumed the card was from distraught teenagers. The *Daily Mail*, however, realized that the words 'fallen soldier' showed the card was from fellow members of a gang.

Ask questions until you have the story clear in your mind. The *Daily Mail* reported (13 03 09) that new Chelsea pensioner Dorothy Hughes *served with the Heavy Ant-Aircraft Battery on the South Coast to defend the country against V1 rocket attacks*. But which battery did she mean? There were probably several batteries of guns deployed. And V1s were flying bombs, not rockets. The rockets were V2s.

When the mother and mother-in-law of England football captain John Terry were cautioned for allegedly taking £800 of goods from Tesco and Marks & Spencer, the *Sun* (28 03 09) found out what goods – shirts, watches, sweets, leggings, flipflops and a green track suit. It led with the story under the headline *JT's mum nicked Pedigree Chum*.

Don't overlook the history

News often has a history which can be as interesting as the detail of the news itself. The second sentence of an article in the *Manchester Evening News* (17 03 09) read: *After a five-year battle with planners, Mark Boler, owner of Mere Golf and Country Club, has secured permission to build an 86-bedroom hotel.* The article continues with quotes from Mark Boler. But what happened in the five-year battle? Why was permission previously refused? How did Boler at last turn defeat into victory?

Covering controversies: finding the key fact

If you are covering a controversy, you need to know what allegations are being made and what evidence there is to support them. You must then offer their target a chance to reply. This is true also of allegations made in meetings and interviews and in stories brought to the paper by people with a point to make. You do not want to publish allegations and then have to withdraw some of what you wrote. Remember that you need a reliable note or record- ing of what people say to you. Ideally, the allegations of one informant should be backed up by another. Make sure you have a detailed grasp of the allega- tions, so that you cannot be fobbed off and your report lamed by a plausible but insufficient reply.

People arguing a case stress points which will appeal to the public. 'We are concerned for your safety,' they say. 'These people are needlessly disrupt- ing your lives,' replies the other side. Often, the heat and smoke and spe- cial pleading of the controversy obscure the facts. You need to ascertain the facts. Don't assume you already know. A controversy over racism blew up when Jade Goody verbally abused Bollywood star Shilpa Shetty on Channel 4's Celebrity Big Brother show. Dominic Lawson in the *Independent* (19 01 07) looked at what Jade actually said. He found she had attacked Shilpa for her wealth when most Indians are poor.

You will find confrontations easier to explain if you can identify the why – the fact or event which set the whole situation going. People always want more money. What has caused them to strike now, not last spring or next autumn? Ask ordinary strikers, not just leaders.

What makes a usable picture?

A picture, key to page layout, is said to be worth a thousand words. The task of taking that picture now often falls to reporters wielding mobile phones. This is not ideal. Photography requires time and space to get the telling image. It cannot be rushed. And reporter-photographers *are* rushed. One moment they are scribbling notes, the next they are picking up their phones and aiming at their subject. But that's life. Freelances have long had to take pictures if they wanted to make their articles more saleable. They have also known they must take pains with their pictures. Any old image will not do. Digital photography has made it easier to be sure of a good picture. You can see at once what picture you have taken. If it is not as you wish, take it again.

Many different camera-phones are on sale, with image definitions up to ten megapixels, which is as high as for an SLR camera. However, a camera with a relatively low pixel count can produce images superior to others with higher counts. SLR cameras score with their larger sensors.

Some camera-phones have flash. Others have light-emitting diodes – which they may call flash – to illuminate faces. Camera-phones may also have a useful mode for copying documents. They cannot normally zoom in on your subject. They can achieve a similar effect by reduc- ing the field of view. But this also reduces the density of pixels in the picture.

Here are some elementary rules for photography:

- Don't let your fingers stray in front of the phone or flash

- Get the focus right – you don't want fuzzy images. If your phone is self-focusing, give it time to settle on your subject. If you are snapping two people, it may focus on the background between them. However, you may be able to aim first at one person, hold the focus and then transfer your aim to the shot you want. Similarly, if you are taking a wide picture and want someone at the side to be in focus, aim at that person, hold the focus and traverse on to the wide picture.

- Get the lighting right so that readers can see the detail and expressiveness of faces – outdoors is usually better than indoors. Get the sun on people's faces. Have the lighting on your subject even, not a patchwork of sunshine and shadow. Indoors, keep windows out of the background. They can flood your picture with light.

- Get the people big in the picture, unless you are deliberately trying to make them look small. Big people have impact. Little people don't.

- If you are taking a full length picture, don't cut people's feet off.

- Frame your pictures. Get everything in that you want in. Leave everything you don't want out.

- Watch the background and any words appearing on it. Don't have something strange growing out of someone's head. (The background can make as well as mar a picture. The *Observer* (8 11 09) published a picture by Margaret Bourke-White taken in Kentucky in 1937. It showed black people queuing for poor relief, in front of a poster featuring a prosperous white family in a car under the headline 'World's highest standard of living'.)

The people and objects appearing in a picture usually need to form a unity. They can be in a group or a triangle, which is an interesting shape for the eye to wander round. But it is possible to create more subtle unities. Consider what you might have discarded as a no-hope image: seven speakers standing in a row at the Tory Party's 2009 conference. They are in a line, so this is a machinegun shot. They are seven so their faces are small and scarcely distinguishable. What makes the picture, and gives it unity and a certain humour, is that they stand behind a line of identical reading desks.

Take the readers into the story

Similarly, a picture of a press conference on Stanhope railway station in County Durham (*NE*, 28 06 06) was given unity by the platform, along which the speakers and journalists were strung out in a line of shabby, isolated figures. They were too busy, miserable or cold to see any joke. But the camera – from the opposite platform – saw one, at their expense.

Figure 2.1 One year on from the smoking ban

Asked for advice for reporters who have to take pictures, several senior journalists said: Don't do it. One, however, made an important point. Get pictures which take the readers into the story. Don't simply decorate it. Many of the best pictures, in fact, tell a story and the article accompanying such a picture becomes a lengthy caption. Figure 2.1 shows one from the *Westmorland Gazette* (4 07 08). It tells the story of the ban on smoking in pubs. The man on the left has had to leave the New Inn to smoke. He looks defiant but not very happy.

The photographer has probably asked him to look to the side, away from the camera. He has taken the picture from below the face but close to it, with a wide lens – the face is somewhat distorted and the vertical at the right of the picture is leaning in. The picture presents a puzzle. What does the man on the right, who has no visible cigarette, add to it? The face and the pub sign would have been enough to make the point about the smoking ban. Yet it is a better picture because the second man happened to be there, a counterpoint to the first. The second man, too, is fed up and looking off – silently – to the side. With so much sky, there is a sense of emptiness.

Interesting lines converge across the picture and unite it. One starts with the eyes of the man on the left, continues along the top of the pub sign and on to the eye of the man on the right. The other starts with the chin of the man on the left, takes in a bottom corner of the sign and goes on to the chin of the man on the right.

Types of picture

A face

News stories are about people, and most people's most expressive features are their faces. A picture of a face needs to capture that expressiveness. That means the face must be as large as possible within the frame. It must catch the

Figure 2.2   Down in the dumps: Silvio Berlusconi

face's features, which must be well lit. You may need to use flash to illuminate a face, even outdoors.

Within a face, the most expressive features are the eyes. The camera usually needs to see both of them. Faces in profile tend to lack life and impact, unless they are part of an alert and active body engaged in some task.

Children make good subjects because they look appealing and are less likely to be self-conscious. And, if they *are* self-conscious, that itself can be attractive.

If you are taking a face picture wider than a mugshot, the face should be a third of the way across it, not plumb centre. The eyes should normally be glancing towards the remaining two-thirds. If they are glancing the other way, the face conveys unease. 'Clinton calm' said a front-page headline (*FT*, 12 10 09). But the picture beneath murmured: 'Clinton troubled'.

Albrecht Dürer, in his fifteenth-century self-portraits, showed how powerfully a hand can enhance the expressiveness of a face. When Italy's constitutional court ended Prime Minister Berlusconi's immunity from prosecution, photographer Dario Pignatelli caught him with a hand – marked with raised veins – covering one eye (*FT*, 8 10 09). The other eye was cast down. He looked deeply miserable (*see* Figure 2.2.)

Bear in mind that a picture may only appear to tell a story. In reality, it captures a split second of a larger reality. Berlusconi may have been his usual ebullient self. But, just for a moment, he looked dejected. That was the moment Pignatelli wanted to capture. It is poignant that behind Berlusconi is the Italian flag, symbol of the nation he represents. The flag also gives the picture a simple background. Some of the best pictures have, like this one, only a few elements.

Hands also contribute to the *Big Issue's* image of actress Kate Winslet (2 02 09), an image so unusual you wonder if it is really her (*see* Figure 2.3). Her hands are drawing a lock of blonde hair across her upper lip, as if she were a

Figure 2.3 Foxy lady: Kate Winslet

moustachioed musketeer. The picture is dominated by her dark, unflinching eyes. It also shows a firm jaw. She seems to have a sense of humour. But she's not someone to meddle with.

Two faces

Adding a second face widens the range of your picture's expression. The two faces may be united in delight. If so, they need to be as close together as you can get them. A gap that appears small can look wide when published.

Besides unity, a two-face picture can express disunity and apartness. Russian President Medvedev and Prime Minister Putin rarely look as if they sing from the same hymnsheet. In the picture shown (Figure 2.4) (*FT*, 17 12 07), a serious Putin looks aside from the camera through partly closed eyes, asserting his nose and his independence. His lips are pursed, his jawline firm. His decisions are not open to debate. Medvedev, you suspect, is more malleable. His intent brown eyes seek contact. He wants to understand people. He has the suspicion of a double chin.

A Goff-INF image (*FT*, 16 06 07) took the discord picture a stage further. Not just the faces but the whole bodies of contestants in BBC TV's The Apprentice were in angular disharmony. Katie Hopkins looked archly off right. Simon Ambrose, facing slightly left, was slumped – arms folded – in his thoughts.

Figure 2.4   Who is the bigger of Russia's Big Two?

The group

A group of three faces can form an interesting triangle. They need to be close together or their impact will be diminished.

A group of four or more requires careful arrangement. The four boys in the *Wanstead and Woodford Guardian* (8 10 09) are unexpressive (*see* Figure 2.5). Their faces are not united in an interesting pattern. The two at the back have not been brought forward to form a single group with the two in front. There is no focus of interest, apart from the white collar of the boy on the left. The picture as published almost suggests the boys have been up to something, which was probably not the photographer's intention.

How might you get over this? Photographers commonly focus on one member of a group and have just that one looking at the camera. The other members look towards this dominant figure, as if taking part in a conversation.

It is risky to choose as the main figure an inanimate object but it did work in the *Yorkshire Post* picture (*see* Figure 2.6), dominated by a golden statue of the ballet dancer Anna Pavlova (28 06 06). Only the statue faces the camera. In shimmering white, the dancers from Billy Elliott the Musical look towards it. The long arms of the statue, encompassing the dancers, help unify the image.

A subtle Agence France Presse picture of Euroleaders (*FT*, 7 11 09) lacks this sense of singlemindedness. None of the leaders is looking at the camera. None is dominant. A dozen individual portraits are combined in a multiportrait. At the same time, prominent leaders are picked out: Gordon Brown (centre), Nicolas Sarkozy of France (front, second left), Eurocommission President Barroso (front, second right), candidate for the

Figure 2.5   A group without focus

Figure 2.6   Homage to Pavlova

Figure 2.7 We are what we wear

new EU presidency Van Rompuy (front right). A few leaders are chatting, others are isolated. What unites them and the picture is their uniform – their suits. Several have small lapel badges, suggesting membership of an exclusive club. The picture suggests that the leaders are all over the place, within a show of unity.

Face and object

A picture which combines a face and an object is relatively easy for non-photographers. It does not necessarily require skill in composition. All you have to do is get the face and object close together and in the frame. A face-and-object picture may be better if it suggests action: John Smith in his taxi or putting the finishing touches to his latest painting, not John Smith with his taxi or his latest painting. But do not let John Smith turn away from the camera.

Apart from the boy and his airgun, the picture (*see* Figure 2.8) from the *Northallerton Times* (23 06 06) shows only blue sky and a few treetops. By snapping the gun close-to and from underneath, the photographer exaggerates its size and increases its impact. The muzzle is in the top lefthand corner, which is where readers will begin to read the picture. Their eyes will travel down the barrel to the boy, intent on his aim. The size of his hand, also, is exaggerated. The gun displays an interesting contrast in colourings.

Figure 2.8   Eye on the target

If the airgun picture exaggerates, that of Damien Hirst and the zebra down-plays (*see* Figure 2.9) (*Sunday Express*, 21 09 08). They occupy only the central area of the picture. Hirst, seated square in front of his trophy, in rather too short a pair of trousers, is not glorying in his achievement. Like the public, he seems to be experiencing a moment of doubt. Is this striped fellow, preserved in his glass case, one dead animal too many? But, he looks defiant. He won't take a penny less than £5 million.

Monarch and realm

Many published pictures show someone powerful in front of the realm he/she dominates: the vice-chancellor in his study, the teacher in her classroom, the TV investigator with his library of videotapes, the Countryside Agency's deputy chairman sitting on Hadrian's Wall which stretches behind her into the distance.

In Figure 2.10 (*FT*, 27 09 08), an Italian shoemaker, Enrico Bracalente, stands in front of his workshop. Hs appears much bigger than the women who, with their backs to the camera, work behind him. His simple, short-sleeved shirt contrasts with the fussiness of the workshop clobber. The workshop's lighting provides a sloping line from top right which helps to unify the picture. It also helps that Enrico looks handsome and athletic.

The action shot

The *Observer* (8 11 09) wrote of *photography's unique ability to capture life spontaneously, beautifully happening*. Unfortunately, life happens at often

Figure 2.9   'I'll not take a penny under five million'

Figure 2.10   In his design centre, shoemaker Enrico

Figure 2.11   Here comes a fast one

unpredictable moments. Mobile-phone snappers are likely to turn up after the moment has passed. Even some famous war photographs were staged after the event. So most action shots in newspapers are taken at sports fields, where action is sure to take place. Photographers need to be in a position where they can get the action in the frame in the short time available. A *Grantham Journal* photographer has managed it well in this picture (*see* Figure 2.11) of bowler Andrew Mudie (30 06 06). Mudie is in full flight towards the crease with both feet off the ground. Unlike many action shots, from, say, rugby melees, this one is classically simple. It contains only Mudie and the stumps.

The arty shot

Occasionally, newspapers publish pictures which consciously try to be stylized and artistic. A simple way to give a touch of geometrical artiness to a

A quarter born of co-operation

Former railway storage yards are being transformed into Paris Rive Gauche, writes **Phyllis Richardson**

Paris Rive Gauche : the national library buildings, top, and one of the area's new walkways, above
4Corners/Roger Bertrand

Figure 2.12   Paris's bourgeois bohemia: strollers in the sun

portrait is to take your subject against a background displaying strong vertical lines. The obvious place for an arty picture is an arts page. Perhaps, the featured artist and the art object can be set apart from each other and sit inert like pieces on a chessboard.

A *Financial Times* article about Paris Rive Gauche (5 01 08) carried a picture which captures the stylish aspirations of this new bourgeouis bohemia (*see* Figure 2.12). Roger Bertrand of 4Corners caught people on a pedestrian walkway, against the sun. His picture exploits a limitation of digital photography – it cannot show detail in both highlights and deep shadow. The picture has detail in the highlit concrete, while the people walking on it are black silhouettes. Yet their outlines subtly show that this is indeed a well-heeled arty quarter, not Dagenham or Romford. The women wear smart coats. A trendy crosses the bridge on roller blades. There are no pushchairs or screaming brats.

The effect created here by sunlight can also be created by flash. You can hold a flash gun out to the side and highlight one side of a face, leaving the other side in shadow. Hard lighting gives a picture an edge. Flash can also make a figure stand out against a darkened background. The only splash of light on screen, an avuncular David Dimbleby's right cheek, made him a scary reteller of the story of Thomas a'Becket (BBC1, 10 02 10).

Animal pictures

Some readers look forward to the summer when politicians disappear from the news pages and make way for a touch of lightheartedness and endearment

Figure 2.13   Not one of us

captured by tiny piglets and other animals. If you take a picture of the Mayor in August, why not take her with her monster cat?

A humorous picture of four owlets, from Science Faction/Getty (*see* Figure 2.13), drew the eye to what was otherwise a humdrum *Times* feature on groups, cobbled together from clippings out of periodicals (6 11 07). The largest owlet, on the left, stands with open eyes, confident but lonely. The huddled three draw away from it, illustrating the feature's point that groups can be cliquey and gang up. This picture works well as a group shot. The large owlet attracts the eye. The others, less handsome, form a sort of chorus. With rounded heads and two eyes looking forward, owlets look like little people.

Buildings

Taken with a standard camera, buildings look as if they are falling over back-wards. This is because the distance from camera to top of building is much greater than from camera to bottom. You can often overcome this by taking your picture from upstairs in a building opposite. If you are taking people with a building, get them close to the camera, not to the building.

Maps and sketches

Make sure that spellings and information in a map or sketch coincide with those in the accompanying article (*see also* p. 61). The lettering in a published map or sketch needs to be at least 10pt in size for easy reading. This may mean it must be much larger in the original. For instance, if the dimensions of the published map are only half those of the original, the letters on the original must be at least 20pt in size. You can achieve this by sticking labels on the original. Or you may be able to delete the original lettering on the computer and substitute larger.

A note on captions

The easiest neat caption to write is a two-parter, with the parts usually separated by a colon, for instance, *Here from Korea: Min Hee Hwang* or *Where are they now? Cambridge Park Girls Brigade in the 1960s*. Captions should not be wordy, and they should add to the picture, not repeat what the picture already makes clear.

Questions

1. Where does your publication find stories?

2. Where have you found stories?

3. Have you pursued a story which turned out very differently from what you expected?

4. What successes have you had, and what pitfalls have you found, with research online?

5. What inquiries have you made/would you like to make, using the Freedom of Information Act?

6. Select a picture in a newspaper. What makes it effective?

3 Interviewing

Becoming a friend to the eminent

Interviewing people is pleasant. For a while, you are the friend and confidant of the eminent. Gavin Weightman, covering an election in 1974 for Westminster Press provincial papers, ended up in Downing Street smoking one of Prime Minister Harold Wilson's cigars.

It was shorthand that made interviews possible. The ability to record speech as it is spoken not only assists detailed, accurate reporting but lends immediacy and vividness to a report. Tape and audio recorders are an alternative but they can inhibit an informant. Listening to a recording takes at least as long as the interview it records.

Interviews can be related to the news. They can be part of a wider inquiry. They can be for profiles – accounts of the personality, life, achievements and ideas of someone in whom readers are likely to be interested. Reader interest is crucial.

Here are some of the people you might choose or be asked to interview:

- People who are, for one reason or another, in the news. They are opposing a supermarket or they carried out a rescue or they were on TV or they are campaigning against traffic or litter.

- People who are under attack. What is their reply to their critics?

- The manager of a firm which has developed a new product.

- Someone who suffers from a disease about which you are writing, or is engaged in treating it.

- A newly appointed trade union leader or head teacher or council official or company chairman or religious leader or footballer.

- A woman who has been awarded the British Empire Medal. (In the class-conscious honours system, the BEM is the humblest grade. Those who receive it must be unusual to have been noticed at all.)

- A celebrity who is visiting or in a new TV series or has written a book. Publishers are usually keen for their authors to be interviewed.

People who give you interviews are giving you valuable time and information. It is courteous to make an appointment to see them and to read, if possible, anything they have previously written on the interview's subject.

An interview should be a joint enterprise from which both sides gain something. You get copy. Your informant gets a chance to speak, to be heard and to be understood. You may get more help than you could reasonably expect. When David Ottewell interviewed Edmund Tan, a trainspotter whom a rail official stopped filming at Macclesfield station, Tan provided a video of the altercation for the website (*MEN*, 19 03 09).

Find out about your informants. The *Grantham Journal* (30 06 06) reported Dr Andrew Sutton's protest against a dispute disrupting his daughter's school, Kesteven and Grantham Girls. The report did not say whether he was a doctor of medicine or of science or philosophy. It did not tell us what he did for a living or whether he was prominent in local life. But readers would have been interested.

Find out about the subject you are asking about, so you understand the significance of what you are told. The *Evening Times*, Glasgow, interviewed Rizi Mohammed who took medical supplies to badly damaged Gaza (20 04 09). Israel was blockading Gaza at the time. So how did Rizi's lorries get in?

If you haven't much time

You may have time to arrange to see someone and prepare for the interview. More often, you need to find things out quickly. This could done informally, on the telephone or by e-mail.

Informally

Many interviews are conducted notebook in hand, at the scene of incidents or during breaks in meetings. Explain who you are, who you represent and why you are asking questions. This helps to establish your good faith. Be courteous but make sure you get your chance to find out what you want to know. Don't be put off with a promise to speak to you tomorrow. Tomorrow you may be brushed off.

On the telephone

These days, this is probably a mobile phone. The person you seek is more likely to have a mobile than to be near a landline phone. Not everyone will talk to a journalist who happens to ring up. Some may ask you to ring back.

In the meanwhile, they may have looked you up on Google. (See section below on People reluctant to talk, pp. 44–5.)

Before ringing, be clear in your mind what you want to ask and what you want to know. You will have little chance to gather your thoughts during your phonecall. If your informant finishes an answer and you are not ready with the next question, the interview will end. What might have been said is left unsaid.

When you ring, make clear who you are and who you represent. Explain why you want to know what you want to know. Inquire whether the person you called has time to talk to you. If at all possible, do not ring at awkward times – late in the evening, or just before someone leaves the office. Ask for an e-mail address, in case an important question occurs to you later.

Ask the simple and obvious questions to which readers, listeners and viewers want to know the answers. Such questions get people talking and explaining. All that talking gives them confidence to go on talking. Don't ask questions which invite the answer Yes or No.

Never overlook the obvious. A report in the *Independent* (8 11 06) had the headline *Superbug from Iraq casualties causing infections within NHS*. The report named the bug but failed to say how it affected patients. The *Daily Mail* (17 12 08) reported that tests showed up cancers on the left side of the bowel. But which is the left side of the bowel? Why should the side make a difference?

If you want to record a phone interview, ask your informant's permission.

By e-mail

E-mail is a flawed means of communication, prone to misunderstandings. But journalists use it increasingly to ask questions, preferably short, clear ones so that busy people can quickly understand them. E-mail is quiet in a busy newsroom. It is useful for making arrangements and gathering uncontroversial facts, less good if you want a straight answer to a question, not a diplomatic one. It is less intrusive than a phonecall – the person at the other end can finish what he/she is doing and then respond. It can put you in touch with someone whose phone is switched off.

If you are prepared to run the risk of misunderstanding, you can e-mail a complicated question to a stranger. If you then get no reply but ring, there is a sporting chance that the stranger knows what you want.

E-mail is good for communicating with people overseas. They may not speak English but they can surprise you with clear, e-mailed answers, probably written with the help of colleagues or friends. Even if they reply in, say, Spanish, e-mailed Spanish is easier to comprehend than Spanish on the phone. Simon Kuper (*FT*, 25 04 09) used e-mail to interview Angel Cabrera, the taciturn Argentine who had just won the US Masters golf.

'How do you feel?'

'Take me through the emotions,' said BBC Breakfast's Sian Williams to a man whose wife gave birth to sextuplets (27 01 09). Nowadays reporters ask people not just what happened but how they felt. At the Beijing Olympics, BBC reporters, brandishing microphones like coshes, demanded of athletes that they describe the experience, even before they'd got their breath back. Jermaine Mason, silver medallist in the high jump, was equal to the question (BBC1, 19 08 08): 'I feel like heaven,' he said.

The *Independent* got heartfelt replies from three England players who missed penalties in a World Cup quarter-final shoot-out (3 07 06): 'I have never felt this bad before as a footballer,' said Steve Gerrard, 'I just can't get the penalty out of my head.'

But to ask 'How do you feel?' of someone who just lost a relative or his home or tried in vain to rescue a neighbour from a fire is simply crass. Columnist Yasmin Alibhai-Brown criticized fellow journalists for asking the father of a murdered woman how he felt (the *Independent*, 18 12 06). He hadn't seen her since she was a little girl.

You can phrase 'How-do-you-feel' more diplomatically: Were you angry? Were you distraught? Was it bewildering? Are you bitter? Talk me through what happened. What went through your mind? To Miley Cyrus, Disney's Hannah Montana, the best question might have been 'What's it like being world famous at 16?'

Magnus Linklater, Scotland editor of *The Times*, paid tribute in the *British Journalism Review* (September 2008) to a former colleague at the *Daily Express*. Rita Marshall covered murder stories 'with such tact and sympathy that the people she dealt with remembered her with affection'.

Prepare well

Now for the more leisured interview which you have time to set up and carry out face to face.

The first task after fixing the meeting is to find what you can about the person you will see and the subject you propose to ask about. What has your paper written about him/her/it before? Your office library should help. If you are to speak to someone at all well known, Google on the internet may help also. It will tell you if your interviewee has written a book. Asked about his time in Africa, BBC newscaster George Alagiah said he had written a book about it. That was the end of that line of questioning.

Your interview may be about something complex: a controversial plan to close an accident-and-emergency department, perhaps, or build new houses on the site of an old house. You will need to find out all you can about the hospital or the old house, so that you can ask intelligent questions.

You may find you have missed a chance, if you are not well prepared. George John, a leading journalist for decades in the Caribbean, was asked to interview the visiting chairman of a Jamaican cement company. Cement is unexciting and the chairman was an elderly Canadian in a wheelchair. Only later did George discover that he had been a spymaster in the Second World War.

Conducting an interview

Be pleasant and friendly, look trustworthy and be interested in what you are told. Christopher Dobson wrote in *The Freelance Journalist* (Butterworth-Heinemann, 1994) that a friendly appearance, a soft voice, amiable chatter and an air of sincerity work wonders. TV programme-maker Bernard Clark said in an interview: 'Most of the best stories depend on finding the right person. You have to win their friendship and gradually they relax. You have to be yourself, a totally genuine person. People like to talk.'

Do not arrive late or shabbily dressed. Many people will feel that erratic timekeeping and dress presage erratic reporting. Be courteous enough to introduce yourself and explain why you want to know what you want to know.

If you want to record the interview, say so. It is possible these days to use an MP3 player with microphone. A separate microphone, not built into the recorder, gives better sound.

Don't be smarmy, or flippant. Flippancy might make you credible with a soldier but not with his brigadier. Some journalists have a natural ease with strangers. Some have a polite self-confidence which impresses the eminent. However, unless you are from an eminent publication, this is hard to pull off. With a complete stranger, it is best to be courteous and unassuming – not familiar, not patronizing, not servile. Look interested. If you interview an expert on clocks, you need to find clocks fascinating.

Challenge your informant's point of view with questions, but don't get involved in an argument and don't be rude. You are there to report your informant, not push your own points of view. Your informant will speak more freely if he/she accepts you as a friend. This is why, despite the noise of other lunchers and the difficulty of taking notes, it can be helpful to conduct interviews over lunch – though the office diary may be too busy these days to allow it. At the lunch table you are an equal, however celebrated your companion.

How did it all come about?

The best framework for questions is usually chronological. Ask first about what happened first and then move on through the story. 'Can you tell me what happened?' or 'How did you first get involved?' or 'Why did you think of trying this idea?' This also gives you your best chance of grasping what you are being told, if the story is complicated. Stories are much easier to understand if you can follow them stage by stage. *Take us through the story of how you beat your uncle in the local elections five years ago and why he hasn't spoken to you since,* said Moroccan TV hostess Nassima el Hor (*FT*, 6 07 10).

Listen – don't interrupt

Listen to what you are being told. Listen for the moments when the story takes an unexpected turn. Think of new questions inspired by what your informant is saying. Listen for quotes that will give life to your story. Ask your new questions when your informant stops speaking. Allow a few moments silence. Your informant may fill them by saying something fascinating.

At this stage, clear up the details you are not sure of. Try to get exact answers. When was 'recently'? What were the 'one or two difficulties'? How many were 'several'? Who were 'the people who helped'? Ask for explanations until you are clear in your mind what you have been told. If necessary, run through again the main points your informants have made, so that you know your understanding of them is the same as theirs. Don't make assumptions. They could be false.

Interviewing is like a lucky dip. You dip in with a question and it may bring up a prize. The longer the interview lasts, the more chance of a lucky strike.

Be patient with garrulous people. If you have to interrupt, do it kindly. Somewhere in all those words there could be valuable facts and lively comments.

Good reports and articles benefit from colour. What is your informant wearing? What colour is it? Is there anything to remark on in the surroundings? (On a famous comedian's sideboard were two mouldy oranges. They chimed with his lonely and sad frame of mind that afternoon.)

You may need to ask tough questions: 'How do you justify what has happened?' It is easier to ask tough questions if you have gained your informant's confidence. If an interview covers controversial ground, it will be useful to gather other people's points of view, particularly if these have not already been published.

Find out how much time your informant can spare. You do not want to be left with important questions unasked when a secretary comes in to announce the boss's next appointment.

What if your informant is unhelpful?

Most people you go to see for an interview will offer a cup of tea or coffee. This is a sign of welcome. No tea, and you know there is unease.

Your informant may limit what she is prepared to talk about, ruling out many questions you intended to ask. 'I will answer questions only about my book,' she says; and you were wanting to ask her about her life as the wife of a leading politician. Clearly, you need to have read the book and have questions to ask about it. Then, with the ice broken, you may be able to ask one or two of the questions you wanted to ask about her life.

Comedian Dave Allen agreed to an interview when his autobiography was published but then refused to answer any questions at all. In such circumstances, all you have to fall back on is your preparation. Allen's book described painful childhood experiences with religion and a hellfire priest. Asking him about his childhood might have got him going. Religion was prominent in his TV sketches.

An interview may take an unexpected turn, and you have to adjust your questions quickly. Sadiq Khan MP was invited to BBC1's Andrew Marr show (3 02 08) because *The Sunday Times* had reported that his conversations with a constituent in prison were bugged. It turned out that Khan did not know whether he had been bugged or not.

Some people will not speak to you readily. They do not see you as someone they wish to spend their time on. If they speak to you at all, it is briefly and guardedly on the phone. Freelance Mark Hollingsworth said in an interview:

> If you ring and say you know a friend, people are more likely to talk. You need to know how human beings behave. Why might they talk to you? People will talk to further their own agenda. Sometimes they have a grudge or they know they will benefit financially at some stage. People do ask for money… The British are private people. They don't talk to strangers. They don't trust the press.

Reluctant people may have a problem they are not mentioning. Two partners were running an innovative business that went bust. They were not keen to say they had resumed trading after buying back the company name. They still had former creditors sore about their losses.

From some people, you will need answers. You may have to phone them every day. Tom Bower, whose critical biographies of business moguls are based on countless interviews, rang one man 100 times. David Spark was unable to get a promised response from the comedian Ken Dodd. He travelled to his home in Knotty Ash and got an interview.

However, if talking could do people damage, you have to accept their right to refuse.

Reluctant people may agree to give their side of the story if told that others have talked to you. Nick Davies, a *Guardian* investigative journalist, needed to talk to delinquent boys, who had 99 reasons not to talk to an adult. He found two hanging around a public lavatory in Nottingham, looking for what they called business. He realized they wanted something to eat. 'Would you like to go for a McDonald's?' he asked. Half an hour later they competed to explain themselves to him.

If you get talking to a reluctant informant, keep talking. Tell stories. Your informant may come up with a revealing story in reply.

Nine Rs from the Chicago police

Steve Rhoads, of the Chicago police, suggested nine Rs to journalists at a workshop:

Receive – Ask open-ended questions. Don't interrupt. Receive as much information as possible.

Relieve – Be understanding. Relieve anxiety by changing the subject.

Reflect – Have you got the details right? You want the other person's view, not your interpretation of it.

Regress – Ask 'before that' questions, not just 'after that'.

Reconstruct – Going back to the scene can help.

Research – By this stage, you should be on good enough terms to ask the more stressful questions.

Review – Check the facts and quotes.

Resolve – Address any misunderstandings and discrepancies.

Retire – Give the other person the chance to add comments. Tell them how to contact you. End on a positive note.

Rhoads suggests you should be wary if answers don't match the questions. Is the truth being hidden? He says a good approach to people who do not want to say much is to ask several unthreatening questions before the one to which you want an answer.

'Don't say I said it'

If possible, try to persuade people to let their names be published with what they say. Words with a name attached carry more weight. And your report will be more believable. If they say their words are off the record, clear up what they mean. It may be they don't mind you using what they say provided you do not quote them as saying it.

People can deny saying what they said off the record or not for attribution. Tony Collins, executive editor of *Computer Weekly*, pointed out in an interview: 'If off-the-record briefers give you "facts" that prove not to be so, they know there is no comeback on them.'

The Press Complaints Commission says that reporters should try to obtain on-the-record corroboration if they get a story from unnamed sources. If allegations are not corroborated, the PCC will expect the target of the allegations to have had a suitable opportunity to comment (*The Editors' Codebook*).

In sensitive situations, it is better to have an anonymous informant than no informant. Perhaps you can agree together that part of your interview is on the record, part not.

People may fear a comeback if they are identified as your source. There are people you should not identify. In Tibet and neighbouring Xinjiang, Western China, anyone who speaks to a Western journalist is in danger of imprisonment and possibly torture ('Ethics in China's Wild West', Robert Barnett, *BJR*, 25 08 08).

If you have promised anonymity, you should keep your promise (see the section on Protecting sources, p. 195.) Contacts may not help again if you name them. But you also need to consider why you have received anonymous information – though, if the information proves good, you can still use it, even if the source's motives are suspect. Try to make it clear what sort of anonymous person you are quoting – a ministry official, a lawyer, an MP. There is no need to add 'who asked not to be named' or 'who spoke on condition of anonymity'. People can use anonymity to make a point or rubbish someone else's argument or character or abilities, without being seen to do so. In his book *The Control Freaks* (Politico's, 2001), former BBC political correspondent Nicholas Jones details the uses and abuses of off-the-record and not-for-attribution that were taking place around that time.

As a result a claim of 'off the record' no longer ensures anonymity. In the 2008 American presidential campaign, Samantha Power, visiting Britain to promote a book, had to resign as an aide to Barack Obama, after telling the *Scotsman*: 'She (Hillary Clinton) is a monster, too – that is off the record' (*Mail*, 8 03 08). The *Scotsman* printed what she said, arguing that she had agreed in advance that the interview, promoting a book, would be on the record.

Daily Express foreign correspondent Rene MacColl got a world scoop in the 1940s when President Truman fired former vice-president Henry Wallace for his pro-Soviet views (*BJR*, June 2007). Wallace went into hiding but MacColl reached him by phone. Then, as the interview ended, Wallace said it was off the record. He asked MacColl to promise not to use it. He didn't.

Being tough with public figures is one thing. Being tough with lesser and more vulnerable people is another. Lauren Pyrah, a *Northern Echo* reporter, got an interview from a Darlington market-stallholder about the visit of a famous TV chef. Then the stallholder rang back to say that, under his TV contract, he was not to give interviews. Lauren scrapped what he had told her.

The Press Complaints Commission speaks up for people not versed in media matters. They may not realize that they must make it clear from the start of a conversation that what they say is unattributable.

For some journalists who write repeatedly on the same subjects, off-the-record conversations offer invaluable inside knowledge. Hugo Young, political columnist at *The Sunday Times* and the *Guardian*, was one of these. He carefully noted down the candid views expressed, off the record, by top politicians, civil servants and judges from Mrs Thatcher's time onwards. The *Hugo Young Papers* (Allen Lane, 2008) shows what he gleaned.

If they ask to see what you write

This depends on your editor's policy and on the time available. If your editor does not have a hard-and-fast policy, you have to use your own judgment. Few journalists like other people looking over their writings. However, if the subject is factual and your informant is an expert, he/she will probably find two or three places where you have gone wrong. Your piece will be better for these corrections.

Again, if you have written a piece making allegations, you will need to give an opportunity for reply, though without necessarily revealing your script.

If you express forthright opinions and are confident they are soundly based, you do not want an informant to take the life and point out of them.

Some of the dangers of showing someone your copy are that:

1. Your informant seeks to make extensive stylistic changes. (If you do show an informant your article, insist that you will only correct errors.)

2. Your informant rejects your article as inadequate to the subject. If you think the criticisms may be justified, find another informant to give you an extra layer of facts. You could write a better article.

3. You are told that what you have written could seriously damage a worthy organization. If the organization is indeed worthy, your article becomes difficult to publish.

4. Your informant has cold feet about what he has told you and asks your editor to publish something blander. This is then up to the editor. (For the business awards magazine published by the Worldaware agency, a well-known designer gave a vivid account of the fume-filled realities of metal bashing in the Indian homes where his teapots were made. He was shocked to see in writing what he had said.)

5. Your informant takes such a dislike to you and your article that she tells the editor your piece is unacceptable and she is not willing to suggest changes.

6. Your informant rejects what you have written, finding it over-clever at his/her expense. This may be a sign your writing needs more humility.

Questions

1. What problems have you had with informants and interviewees?

2. How have you overcome them?

3. What problems have you had with informants who do not want to be named?

4. How did you handle them?

4 Newswriting: what am I trying to say?

In reading this chapter and the next two, reporters need to bear two things in mind. First, they must get the story written, even if the writing is not ideal. Second, they will be expected to follow their publication's style, which may vary from the advice here.

Learn from other writers

You can learn from the triumphs and errors of others. Read newspapers and magazines carefully, noticing not just the news but the ways in which it is expressed. Do news reports read clearly and, if not, why not? Are they succinct and sparing with words? Are they cluttered with minor detail? Do they employ overused words, phrases and approaches? Are there sentences that readers will not immediately understand, technical words that need to be explained? How do stories differ, in approach and in the details, from the same stories in other newspapers? Has the writer of today's report noticed last week's or last year's? Is today's report similar in style and format to the adjacent report, and several overleaf? Do reports fail to answer obvious questions? (A *Belfast Telegraph* lead story (4 05 09), about a children's food campaign led by Sustain, did not say who Sustain are.)

Everything flows from the opening

The intro or opening sentence is the key to a newspaper or broadcast report – from it everything else should flow. The intro should be crisp and clear; accurate, not just approximate. It should grasp the nub and what is new in the story, or its most graphic and unusual feature. Too often a report's best line is buried in the middle.

A report of a Football Association visit to Derby, to hear why it should feature in England's bid for the World Cup, could have begun: '*Derby can do it.* (Which could have led to a lively account of what Derby can do.) Instead, it began prosaically: *A delegation of VIPs from the Football Association have been impressed by Derby's can-do attitude during their first visit to the city* (*Derby Telegraph*, 21 07 09).

The *Sun* is good at intros. It caught what Gordon Brown was saying to the US Congress better than Brown himself: *Gordon Brown last night urged America to use the drive that put man on the moon to save the earth* (5 03 09). The *Daily Mail*'s intro was rambling in comparison: *Gordon Brown called on the US yesterday to shoulder its historic responsibilities by using its vast wealth to help stem the 'hurricane' recession battering the world.*

A simple idea usually makes a better intro than a complex one. The *Western Mail* (20 03 09) offered two different intros for the same story. The page one intro read: *Guaranteeing that there can never be a repeat of the 2005 e-coli outbreak is the only fitting tribute to Mason Jones, the five-year-old boy killed by the infection, the author of a major report urged last night.* The intro on page 2 read: *Serious failings at every step in the food chain allowed rogue butcher William Tudor to start the 2005 e-coli O157 outbreak, an inquiry has found.* The page 2 intro makes a clear statement. The page one intro struggles with a complex negative – that the absence of e-coli outbreaks in the future can be a tribute to the victim of the 2005 outbreak. Re-thought, it might read: *If there is no repeat of the 2005 e-coli outbreak, then Mason Brown, its five-year-old victim, will not have died in vain.* This, however, is a double-negative, and negative intros are best avoided.

Start with facts rather than comment

Normally, start your report with facts rather than a comment. This intro appeared in the *Westmorland Gazette* (4 07 08): *A father has praised his son's heroic attempt to halt the 'crazed' getaway of a supermarket would-be shoplifter by jumping on the bonnet of her car.* Here is a more graphic alternative: *A woman accused of shoplifting drove a car at up to 40mph away from the Asda supermarket in Lancaster – with a shopper clinging to the windscreen wipers.* A factual intro gives the headline-writer a better steer. A story in the same *Westmorland Gazette* was headed *Injured walker's claim could have 'major implications'.* But it could have been: *Woman walker trampled by cows sues for £1 million.*

Keeping the intro short

Traditionally, the intro of a story tells the reader who, what, where, when, why, how and even how old. *Roger Bannister, aged 25, today became the first man to run a mile in less than four minutes. His time at the Iffley Road track, Oxford, in the annual match between the Amateur Athletic Association and Oxford University was 3min 59.4s.* (*Guardian* 1954, reprinted 6 11 07).

But opening sentences can try to say too much. To avoid this and to capture the drama of events, many journalists cut their intros to a handful of words.

Most specific detail is squeezed out, leaving only the most striking, as here:

> *A bus driver who stabbed his wife 500 times was jailed for life for murder yesterday.* (The *Sun*, 6 02 09)

> *A grandmother who lost her voice 14 years ago has regained it after doctors injected her with Botox.* (*Daily Telegraph*, 6 11 07)

> *A man with a history of mental illness told a doctor he was a walking time bomb, hours before killing a teenage girl.* (*Daily Telegraph*, 6 11 07)

> *Pupils from schools around Scotland will compete in what they like to do – talking.* (*Evening Times*, Glasgow, 20 04 09)

In such stories, you have to read on to find who the story is about, because the names mean little to readers. You have to read even further to find out where the story happened. The *Sun's* TV mogul story, mentioned in Chapter 1, kept till the third paragraph the fact that he beheaded his wife in Buffalo, USA.

But don't let your intro be vague as here: *The end of traffic congestion has moved a step closer as the result of a pioneering trial in Reading* (*Reading Chronicle*, 25 09 08). The story concerned a new service, providing road and travel information by text or e-mail, and the intro could have reflected this.

Detail-free newspaper intros too often start with the indefinite article A. In normal life, no one talks or writes in this stylized way. This from the *Birmingham Post* (5 05 09) reads more naturally: *Randal Brew, the Tory who is challenging Mike Whitby to become leader of Birmingham City Council, has broken his silence by declaring: 'I'm the man for the job'.*

Since news is about people, there is a case for naming them in your intro, even if they are not as well known as the Birmingham councillors. The *Manchester Evening News* (21 03 09) began a triumph-over-despair story like this: *Eighteen months ago Lisa Daly was battling alcoholism, depressed and unemployed.*

Sun intros (6 02 09) used the names of people whom *The Sun* had previously featured: *Octuplets mum Nadya Suleman, Prince Harry's hero Marine Ben McBean, Soccer ace Micah Richards.* The *Sun* seemed to be saying to readers: 'You and we know about these people. We are members of the same club.'

Different ways to start

Here is a simple and straightforward narrative intro from the *Evening Times*, Glasgow (20 04 09): *This puppy has been branded Scotland's real Slumdog. Leo, a 12-week-old Akita-cross puppy, was found living rough on Scotland's biggest landfill site.*

Reports of court cases in which the main facts are not disputed commonly start with a narrative. So do health stories – they feature someone suffering from the disease or helped by the treatment in question.

The head of MI5 warned (6 11 07) that teenagers were being recruited into terrorism. Philip Johnston in the *Daily Telegraph* made his report different from everyone else's by starting with a narrative about a 17-year-old: *It was a terrorist case that excited little public interest. A few weeks ago, an Old Bailey jury found A– P– from East London guilty of possessing a document likely to be useful for terrorism. But what was remarkable was his age. When arrested he was only 17.*

Delayed-drop intros are popular in national papers. In these, the key point of the story makes a surprise appearance in the second sentence or later. Here is an example, from *The Times* (5 04 07):

> *Jonathan Rowan entertained friends with stories of being a professional ice skater, the heir to a hotel empire and a fugitive from an IRA hit squad. But he will be remembered for walking into the office of his ex-girlfriend and shooting her with a stolen .357-calibre revolver before turning the gun on himself.*

This opening has drama. In the first sentence, all seems well, even stylish. In the second, two people are dead. The detail about the revolver's calibre makes it the more chilling.

Delayed drops, however, do not suit stories online. These need to say from the outset what the story is.

Writers in the *Guardian* (6 11 07), used varied approaches. Duncan Campbell approached the Jill Dando murder appeal descriptively: *There was standing room only for the latest act in the drama that has surrounded the murder, more than eight years ago, of the television presenter Jill Dando.* Michael White was sardonic about Gordon Brown's plan to make youngsters stay in school or training till 18: *Fast-track student Gordon Brown was scarred for life by the sight of less able pupils falling by the wayside at school in Kirkcaldy. Forty years later, he now plans to make them do better, if necessary by fining them.*

It can help to look wider than the basic story. Here is how Barry McDonald began a piece in the *Evening Times*, Glasgow (23 04 09) about a new theatre seat being dedicated to the dog that played Toto in a production of The Wizard of Oz: *Michael Jackson, Alec Guinness and Sean Connery: they've all graced the stage of Glasgow's historic King's Theatre. For one woman, however, the biggest star to tread the boards was a little cairn terrier called Jenny.*

Awards stories can be dull. In the same *Evening Times*, Maureen Ellis livened this award story up: *Eastenders have taken the Glasgow Community Champion Awards by storm – by telling us about more than 140 of their local heroes.*

Finally, there is the portmanteau intro which gathers up several strik-ing facts. Here is how the *Guardian* began its report of a day at the Berlin Olympics of 1936 (reprinted 6 11 07):

> *This has been an emotional day for British supporters. They have exulted over HH Whitlock's victory in the 50,000 metres walk, glowed with pride as the crowd cheered DG Finlay's hurdling, watched with incredulous joy FR Webster pole-vaulting 13ft one and a half inches at the first attempt, and torn their hair at SC Wooderson's disaster in the 1500 metres.*

Putting the unfortunate Wooderson last gave the sentence punch.

Form a thread of ideas

From the opening sentence, the rest of a report should flow smoothly in an unbroken thread of ideas and fill the space allocated to it. This paragraph (*The Times*, 24 01 09) did not read as smoothly as it might have:

> *A voracious reader of sports books as well as the author of his own best-selling memoir, Jamie Carragher recently delved into* The Winner Within *by Pat Riley, the legendary basketball coach of LA Lakers fame. It is, the blurb tells us, a book about 'motivation, selfishness, teamwork, complacency, winning and choking'. A self-help manual for sealing championships, applicable to the west coast of England or the United States. Whatever your impression of Carragher, this is typical of the man, immersed in his work, seeking out knowledge, a self-improver who stumbled across Riley's book simply by scouring Amazon.com in search of inspiration.*

Here, the two sentences about the book are interposed between the two sentences about Carragher. The paragraph reads more smoothly if the fourth sentence – beginning *Whatever your impression of Carragher* – follows the first.

The second sentence of a story should not merely repeat the first in different words. It should carry the story forward with new information, as in this passage by Mark Tallentire for the *Durham Times* (28 03 08): *A major new woodland covering more than 150 acres is to be created on the outskirts of Durham. The Woodland Trust wants to transform Low Burn Hall farm into a publicly accessible forest, with woodland trails and conservation projects.*

You want the meat of the story in the first four paragraphs. These should show why the news is important and how it affects people.

Write as simply and directly as possible, dividing sentences like the next one from the Durham woodland story: *The trust, the UK's leading woodland conservation charity, revealed its plans for the farm, which lies between the A167 immediately south of Durham and the River Wear, after purchasing it at auction on Wednesday night.* Divided, this is easier to follow: *The farm lies between the River Wear and the A167 immediately south of Durham. The trust, the UK's leading woodland conservation charity, revealed its plans after it bought the farm at auction on Wednesday night.*

Give specific detail if you want to interest readers. A *Financial Times* book review (7 10 06) reported that the Tradescants, father and son, introduced many popular garden plants to England in the seventeenth century. Gardening readers would be keen to know which plants. The review did not tell them.

However, the detail you use needs to be telling. Don't hit readers with a surfeit of data like this: *A Sea King search and rescue helicopter from RAF Chivenor in Devon and the South Wales Police helicopter were sent to help the crew of Port Talbot's Royal National Lifeboat Institution D-class rigid inflatable vessel in the operation (Western Mail, 16 03 09).*

Normally, it is best to follow the intro with other related material and, if possible, a related quote, rather than head off in a different direction and return later. The *Northallerton Times* (23 06 06) led its front page with a report that a road safety campaign in North Yorkshire had cut road deaths and might be copied elsewhere. But the reader had to read several paragraphs, including a 48-word sentence, before learning that the campaign focused on motorcyclists.

The glider who crashed

The Northern Echo and the *Evening Gazette* (Middlesbrough) both reported (27 06 06) an accident in which a hang-glider (according to the *Echo*) or a paraglider (the *Gazette*) flew into the cliff close to the steep railway which leads from the small town of Saltburn down to its seafront. Neither knew the man's name and both went for the impersonal approach:

Echo: *A hang-glider pilot has been airlifted to hospital after crashing into a cliff face.*

Gazette: *A paraglider was airlifted to hospital after crashing into a Saltburn bankside before shocked onlookers.* (Why bankside, one wonders, why not cliff?)

Both papers then reported that the man was 52, that he landed close to the track of the cliff lift and that he suffered pelvic and spinal injuries. Both clearly picked up this last phrase from the ambulance service. (Otherwise, why not: He injured his pelvis and back?) And both now got bogged down in the ambulance men's story of how they climbed the cliff to get the man down. According to the *Gazette*: *Tees, East and North Yorkshire Ambulance Service area manager Dave Owen, paramedics Stuart Dack and John Smithson and emergency medical technician Harry Brown had to climb up a steep slope covered in thorn bushes to get to the patient who was about 40ft up the cliff.* A 46-word sentence drains the drama from a story. The ambulance men's various ranks and the clumsy title of their service got in the readers' way. Their names would have done.

Both the *Echo* and the *Gazette* had eyewitness accounts of the glider crashing. According to surf shop owner Nick Noble in the *Gazette*: *Three or four of us were outside the shop and were aware of this paraglider flying around. The next thing we knew he'd come down just the other side of the railings next to the railway. We called the ambulance and stayed with him, trying to keep him still. He was conscious and coherent but in a lot of pain. He was saying it was his back.*

Here is another go at the story, giving prominence to the eyewitness:

Ambulance men had to climb the steep cliff at Saltburn to rescue a 52-year-old hang-gliding enthusiast from Redcar. He crashed near the track of the cliff lift and was lifted off by helicopter.

'He was in a lot of pain. He was saying it was his back,' said surf shop owner Nick Noble. 'We called the ambulance and stayed with him, trying to keep him still. He'd come down just the other side of the railings next to the railway.'

The man was 40 feet up the cliff and Dave Owen, Stuart Dack, John Smithson and Harry Brown from the ambulance service had to climb through thorn bushes to reach him.

A rescue story in the *Western Mail* (16 03 09) contained a good, simple quote, from a lifeboat spokesman: *The man and his dog were swept into the sea but, luckily, there was a surfer in the water and he managed to grab hold of the bloke and get him to hold the surfboard until we got there.*

Be accurate and fair

Take the trouble to be accurate. Otherwise your credibility and that of your paper, service or broadcaster will suffer. Inaccuracy is unfair. Don't assume that the facts mean more than they say. There could be another way of looking at them apart from the way you or informants see them.

The basic requirements of fairness are that allegations should have some substance, and you should know who is making them. Those alleged to have done wrong should have the chance to reply and have their reply fairly and adequately covered in the report. This is also an important safeguard against a libel suit. Be wary of exaggerated, unprovable allegations, which can discredit your story. Give people under attack the benefit of any doubt there may be. (See the discussion of *Time*'s report on the Haditha killings in Chapter 12, p. 162.)

Establish the facts which both sides of a controversy agree on or, at least, cannot dispute. Clear, factual passages are hard to challenge. But they do have to be accurate. Even a minor error can be used to discredit your story. So do not include minor 'facts' if you are not sure of them.

In debate, forceful people present assertions as facts, which is why debates can confuse listeners. You need to distinguish what is fact from what is merely assertion.

Use crisp quotes

In reporting interviews, report first the most interesting things your informants said. Don't start with less interesting points just because they were said earlier in the interview. Direct quotations give reports life. They convey feeling. No report of more than 100 words is complete without one. Journalists need to recognize that the words in which an informant tells a story can be fresher, simpler and more moving than their own retelling.

Crisp quotes are the best: *Peter is a good-looking guy. He has a Bentley. He has a private plane. He's made a fortune, lost it, made it again. He is very inspirational* (*FT*, 16 06 07). Here is Michel Platini, president of the Europe football union, quoted in the *Sun* (6 02 09): *How can a guy cost 150 million euros? For me, it's ridiculous – from a football, social and financial point of view. If you want to buy a plane for 150 million euros, or a boat, you can do. But for a man?*

But not everyone speaks so memorably. John Richardson, Durham county's director of environment, said: *When you reach a situation where it costs us as much as £10 to £15 per passenger to run some subsidized services, there comes a point where we can't really justify using council tax payers' money to subsidize services which are only used by very few people* (*Teesdale Mercury*, 28 06 06). This calls for indirect speech: *John Richardson, Durham county's environment director, said some little-used services cost the county council £10–£15 per passenger, and it could not spend taxpayers' money on subsidy on that scale.*

It is a great journalistic gift to be able to sum up what someone said or did in a few phrases of indirect speech. This brief account of the bizarre aftermath of a murder appeared in a *Sun* court report (6 02 09): *As Glynis dialled 999 and fled to her back garden, Bailey trashed her house, even stabbing furniture, then sat down to watch TV.*

When you switch to indirect speech, you are switching from your informant's words to your own. So write carefully, so that you accurately represent what your informant wanted to say.

Quoted speakers may make references not immediately obvious to the reader. Journalists often fill out the sense with words in square brackets. *There's odd bits* [the government is doing] *at the edges* (*FT*, 25 08 08). Don't add words in square brackets if readers can grasp the sense without them. Square-bracketed additions can be clumsy, as in the next example: ...*Such great masters as [Joshua] Reynolds, [Jacques-Louis] David, [Jean-Auguste] Ingres, [Francisco] Goya, [Thomas] Lawrence, [Eugene] Delacroix, [Antonio] Canova and [Bertel] Thorvaldsen* (*Independent*, 31 01 07).

Always make it clear what speaker you are quoting and who the speaker is. If you switch to a different speaker, say who he/she is at the start of the sentence. Not every statement of accepted fact needs to be attributed to a speaker. But every comment and allegation should be. Journalists reporting several people are apt to return later to someone they mentioned early on without reminding the readers who he/she is. Who was Mr Northover in the fourth leg of a *Financial Times* article (24 11 08)? Readers had to look back to the second leg, or glance at a sidebar, to find he was head of policy at WaterAid.

Achieving pace

Reports benefit from pace. But how is it achieved? Here is a passage from a pacey report by Keith Dovkants in the *Evening Standard* (29 01 08), about Jerome Kerviel, a dealer who cost the French bank Societe Generale over £3 billion. It contains only two subordinate clauses, the who clause in the first paragraph and the where clause in the third. The quotes are brief and to the point. Every phrase adds a fact.

> *In Pont l'Abbe, Kerviel is remembered as a pack leader who played in goal for the junior football team, then became captain. He played a lot of football, sailed a bit and did judo to brown belt level.*

'*He seemed a bit more mature than the rest of us,*' *a contemporary recalled. His father, Charles, was a blacksmith and his mother, Marie-Jose, ran her own hairdressing salon, Chez Marie-Jo. The family was said to be comfortably off, close-knit, and went to mass together regularly.*

A studious teenager, Kerviel read Adam Smith for pleasure and secured a place at Lyon university where a staff member, Dominique Chabert, recalled: 'If he was a genius, we didn't notice it.'

But somewhere between leaving university in 2000 and the end of 2006, he acquired genius or at least a phenomenal level of expertise in manipulating the security systems of one of the world's biggest investment banks.

Explaining

Don't wait too long to tell readers the how and why of the news. How does the new treatment work? Why is it needed? Explain clearly. The *Wanstead Guardian* (30 07 09) mentioned that the government would not pay a £39 million house-repair grant till Redbridge Homes had a two-star rating. But what is a two-star rating? What must organizations do to acquire one?

Explanatory details can often be worked into the story as you tell it. If the story needs a longer explanation, keep it till the end. Here is an explanation of a cheap method devised by a Bangladeshi physicist to enable schoolchildren to make money by filling and selling ballpoint pens:

> *Dr Ibrahim's machine consists of an ink-filled cylinder with a piston operated by a springloaded handle. On the cylinder is a port for a pen to be filled, and a reservoir of ink in a tin. The handle pushes the piston into the cylinder and ink into the pen. Filled pens are put in four Ovaltine tins hanging from the ends of two crossed rods. An electric motor rotates the rods at high speed. Centrifugal force causes the tins to fly out sideways and pushes ink down into the pens, releasing any air bubbles. (Education Today, July 2003)*

Questions about numbers

In a finite planet, numbers decide between success and failure. Professor Richard J. Evans points out in *The Third Reich at War* (Allen Lane, 2008) that Hitler was defeated not just by the Allies but by the arithmetic. He did not have enough men and resources to win.

Some stories cry out for numbers. The *Evening Times*, Glasgow (20 04 09), reported a contractor pulling out of a £2 million housing-association deal because it could not guarantee workers' pensions. How much pension was at stake? How much money would a guarantee have required?

Numbers give precision. How many people work here? What are they paid? How large is the large *Daily Telegraph* newsroom? But don't use complicated numbers, unless they make a special point. *The Times* has a rule of three – 143, 378,129 will appear as 143 million, 1,433,781 as 1.43 million, 14,337 as 14,300.

Don't bore and confuse readers with too many numbers. Numbers should be telling. The *Guardian* (6 11 07) reported that firearm discharge residue, in the Jill Dando murder case, was only one two-thousandth of an inch long. Thus the case turned on a tiny speck.

Don't bamboozle readers with percentages. Fourteen per cent of seven is one and you might as well say one. Almost 60 per cent of 27 is 16.

Are they right?

Numbers, like other facts, need checking. Before accepting numbers, do a rough calculation. The *Financial Times* reported (14 02 09) that the average price of a typical house in the UK had dropped 16.6 per cent or £150,501 over a year. Since 16.6 per cent is a sixth, this puts the average price – before the fall – at six times £150,501 or over £900,000, far too high. It seems probable that the price had in fact dropped 16.6 per cent *to* £150,501, not *or* £150,501.

Here are a few errors which have appeared in the national media.

- *For every alcoholic drink a woman consumes, her risk of breast cancer rises 6 per cent* (BBC News, 12 11 02, quoted in *New Scientist*, 15 09 07). At this rate of increase per drink, few but abstainers would escape cancer.

- *The council said that it costs about £198 a week to provide for each youngster. While the government promised £140 it cut that to £100, leaving a shortfall of £5 a year* (Independent, 18 01 07). The shortfall is £98 a week, which is just over £5000 a year.

- *A crate of 20 half-litre bottles currently sells in one Berlin supermarket for £5.79. That's 5p a bottle* (Independent, 5 04 05). Actually, it's about 29p a bottle.

- *Boils up to three inches (10 centimetres) across* (Independent, 18 12 06). An inch is 2.54 centimetres. So three inches is roughly eight centimetres, not ten.

Do they make sense?

It's 60–40 against him being fit but he's got half a chance, said football manager Glenn Hoddle (quoted in the *Independent*, 28 12 06). Actually, he hadn't half a chance. The odds were three to two against.

The *Daily Mail* (25 10 08) reported that Prince William and Prince Harry were *ploughing their Honda bikes through rivers in temperatures of more than 100C*. At 100C, water boils. The writer meant 100F (Fahrenheit).

Do they prove their point?

Forecasts need care, even if they look precise. Treating obese people is forecast to cost the health service millions. Even so, obese people – like smokers – may save it money by dying early, avoiding expensive ailments of old age.

Prime Minister Gordon Brown told MPs (17 06 09): 'Current expenditure will grow every year to 2013–14 not just in cash terms but in real terms.' But, if you stripped out the higher forecast costs of debt, social security and other items, government departments' spending was clearly going to fall, not grow. Cuts were in fact planned for every year from April 2011 (*FT*, 17 09 09).

Numbers do not necessarily mean what they appear to mean. The French bank Societe Generale announced that rogue trader Jerome Kerviel had lost it £3.7 billion. Actually he lost £1.5 billion. The bank lost the rest when it quickly sold what he had bought on its behalf.

A query under the Freedom of Information Act revealed that North Yorkshire's chief executive received £128,000 in the year 2005/6 and just under £159,000 the following year, an apparent rise of nearly a quarter. However, he did not hold the job for the whole of 2005/6. Had he done so, he would have received £154,000. So his rise was only about 3 per cent (*NE*, 2 04 08).

Some numbers in newspapers are meaningless, for example, houses in Freiburg, Germany, use under 15 kilowatt hours of energy per square metre. But is this per week, per month, per year?

How significant are these numbers?

Are the numbers as significant as your informant claims they are? The government wants people to save fuel through insulation, low-energy light bulbs and so on. But what proportion of the fuel bill will these measures save?

Statisticians stress that numbers should be seen in their context. Michael Blastland and Andrew Dilnot wrote *The Tiger that Isn't* (Profile, 2007) to show that numbers are not as scary as they look. Researchers discovered that older women who take two or more drinks a day double their chances of endometrial cancer. But only one woman in 4000 contracts this cancer. Doubled to one in 2000, the risk is still small. To better understand risk, consult understanduncertainty.com, associated with Professor David Spiegelhalter of the Centre for Mathematical Sciences, Cambridge University.

Do they prove the opposite of what you say?

A former editor of Wisden (*Independent*, 27 12 06) gave three reasons why the Australian spin bowler Shane Warne was not the greatest cricketer ever. One of them was *As a bowler, his average runs per wicket has been less than that of others*. But to have taken wickets for fewer runs is a point in Warne's favour, not against him.

Be careful in distinguishing the letter O from the figure 0. E-coli O157, not 0157, is a deadly stomach bug.

Google to the rescue

If you are not great at calculations, the main Google site – www.google.co.uk – will crunch numbers for you. You want to multiply 41 by 39? Google 41*39 and you find out. Similarly 2–20 will give you two to the power of 20. The

Google symbols for add, subtract and divide are +, – and /. To find 24 per cent of 3000 write 24% of 3000. To find the square root of 625, write sqrt 625. Google can handle more advanced maths. It will tell you, for instance, the value of sine 30. But you must put your query in a form that Google understands. Google *sine 30* and you get –0.988031624, not the right answer in Britain at any rate. Google *sine 30 degrees* and you get the correct 0.5. Google also converts weights and measures. Google *8 pounds in kilogrammes* or *65 Fahrenheit in Celsius* and you will get the answer.

General knowledge

If you are not sure of general knowledge, check it. Errors sap your credibility. The *Independent* (24 05 06) wrote about *the marriage of Mary Queen of Scots and Philip of Spain.* Mary Queen of Scots married the Dauphin of France. It was Queen Mary of England who married Philip. The *Daily Mail* (23 02 09) wrote: *Each chunk of the ship will be sawn into lumps no bigger than an office desk – the maximum size for the blast furnace.* Blast furnaces extract iron from iron ore. They don't re-melt chunks of steel.

Here are a few inaccurate memories that have shown up in print: Iain Smith, for Ian Smith, leader of Rhodesia 1964–80; Martia Hunt for Marsha Hunt, Hollywood actress; Wollington for Willington, former Durham pit village; Gladys Alward for Gladys Aylward, who led Chinese children to safety in the 1930s.

Prices

Many stories about prices and purchases do not ring true with readers. Tim Harford wrote in the *Financial Times* (24 01 09): *Just think of the money most of us could save if we drank only tap water.* No doubt some people drink bottled water copiously. But most of us?

Many people find prices expensive that others can easily afford. Peter and Dan Snow presented a BBC TV programme about incomes in January 2008. They estimated that 90 per cent of wage and salary earners earned less than £46,000 a year. Many earned between £10,000 and £20,000.

Ending well

Reports should end, not just tail away. Their final sentence needs to say something. Ideally, it should also be short, like this by former Downing Street press secretary Bernard Ingham about a TV encounter between Tory leader David Cameron and interviewer Jonathan Ross: *In this empty world, Ross gets £6m a year; the Leader of the Opposition £121,840* (YP, 28 06 06).

In contrast this *Guardian* ending (22 05 08) went on a bit: *On this basis the Tories really need to be recording swings sometime someplace regularly in the range of 15%–20% to bring their average up to a level where they seriously threaten Labour for power.*

The rhythm of a final sentence makes a difference. You want to end with a strong point and a stressed syllable. This, in *The Times* (3 03 08), trailed away in an *if* clause: *The only person he told about the abuse was a psychiatrist who told him he would be placed in a mental hospital if he repeated the allegation.* Changing the order of the final clauses helps: *who said that, if he repeated the allegation, he would be put in a mental hospital.* (*Said* avoids using *told* twice.)

Daily Mail writers often achieve final punch by using a quote. This quote about pictures (24 10 08) is from actress Liz Hurley: *I now rely on nice photographers and a bit of retouching.*

Re-read what you wrote

The best way to make sure your report reads clearly and reads right is to re-read it. An article about the plight of women in developing countries summed up its message in 15 bullet points (*Independent*, 8 03 07). Unfortunately, the third and fifth points were the same. So were the fourth and seventh.

Re-reading is a safeguard against writing something you did not intend, for example: *Some 40 people were killed, which the pro-Musharraf MQM blamed for the worst of the violence* (*Independent*, 15 05 07). *Which* in this sentence should have been *with*. Re-read to spot any ambiguity in what you have written. If your report can be misunderstood by an editor, it will be misunderstood, as freelances know well. Re-read to make your report read better. If your mind stumbles while re-reading, a reader's mind will stumble at the same place.

Consider this awkward sentence: *Maurice Frankel said the fishing decision was part of a trend of departments opposing disclosure on the grounds it would deter officials from communicating freely with ministers* (*FT*, 6 01 07). It can be split in two. *Maurice Frankel said the fishing decision is part of a trend. Departments have been opposing disclosure on the grounds that it will deter etc.*

Re-read to make sure you have clearly explained your subject. The *Manchester Evening News* (17 03 09) told the moving story of a solicitor, father of a brain-damaged child, who provides instant cash for brain-damaged accident victims. The article suggested that he recovers the money through legal action. But it was not totally clear this was how he did it.

You may find you can make your report clearer, shorter and more cogent by reordering your material. Several chapters in this book have been reordered and this has helped keep the word count below the publisher's ceiling.

Check the illustration

The *Belfast Telegraph* (7 05 09) reported a family of Canada geese in Ballymena town centre. Only, the geese in the picture were greylags. Pictures, maps and charts often contradict the reports they illustrate. So check you are singing from the same hymnsheet as your colleagues. Colours can be dodgy. The grass is green, wrote Tom Lubbock, describing a painting by Monet (*Independent*, 16 12 05). In print, it was brown.

Writing colleagues can be as subversive as illustrators. The lead story in the *Western Daily Press* (1 10 08) concerned Hooks, 'a family-run furniture store' in Bridgwater. But a report and picture on page 5 showed that Hooks was an outfitters.

A man who took part in a disastrous drug trial was 28, reported the *Independent* (16 03 06). The picture caption said he was 23. The trialists were offered £2000, said the report. But Tom Edwards, who dropped out of the trial, told the writer of an adjoining story that it was £1100.

Writing corrections

Newspapers must correct what they got wrong. Since none of us is infallible, we all have to write corrections sometimes. They should satisfy those aggrieved but not give other people cause for complaint. Do not try to offload blame unfairly on to others.

If you receive a complaint about what you have written, tell your editor. Establish precisely what the complaint is. Be considerate but not apologetic. Being apologetic could prejudice your publication in a court action.

It may be you have a good note and are confident you have made no mistake. Or it may be the person complaining claims superior knowledge of what went on. If so, it is useful to find someone who can give you an independent view.

Quite often, the complaint will be about information given to you, and it will be against the supplier of the information as much as against your reporting. It is tempting then for the paper to publish a correction which says: 'We published in good faith information provided by so-and-so.'

If you are satisfied that the information was wrong and so-and-so provided it, this is fair enough. But first ask so-and-so for his/her side of the story, The published correction should not give so-and-so cause to complain.

Questions

1. What are the cases for and against omitting names and places from an intro?

2. How do you ensure readers can understand your reports at first reading?

3. Have editorial changes made your reports inaccurate? How do you guard against this?

5 Newswriting: choosing the words

Be clear at first reading and engage the readers

Readers like journalists to use clear, fresh words. Jeremy Butterfield, author of an Oxford book, *Damp Squid*, about disliked errors and clichés, told the *Daily Mail* (7 11 08): 'We grow tired of anything that is repeated too often – an anecdote, a joke, a mannerism.'

Journalists have plenty of words, imagery and sentence constructions to choose from, and some choose well. Here is imaginative language from Jeremy Warner, business and city editor, in the *Independent* (26 07 06): *Lord Browne had so many people spinning on his behalf that it would have done credit to a troupe of whirling dervishes.*

Words can capture a situation. TV comedian Tony Hancock volunteered to give a pint of blood and found an apt phrase for his dismay. It was, he said, 'very nearly an armful'.

Despite the wealth of choice, the same tired words appear in one media report after another. Everything and everyone is *iconic*, if not *most iconic*. A newspaper database recorded 45,000 uses of *iconic* in a single year. Nothing these days happens daily, annually, routinely, regularly. It happens on a daily, annual, routine or regular basis. People do not have fathers, mothers, sons, daughters, relatives. They have *loved ones*, a phrase which – in newspapers or on the air – radiates insincere compassion.

Redundant adjectives

Some adjectives and adverbs come too easily to mind: *abject* with poverty, *absolute* with premium, *big* with breakthrough, *bitter* with disputes, rivals, pills and blows, *bleak* with picture, *burning* with question, *clear* with message, *conspicuously* with absent, *daunting* with challenge, *deadly* with cargo, *deep* with trouble and disillusionment, *deeply* with flawed and humiliating, *devout* with Catholic and Muslim, *dire* with warning, *epic* with adventure, *grave* with doubts, *great* with inroads, *grieving* with widow, *gross* with exaggeration and ignorance, *groundbreaking* with treatment, *growing* with suspicion, *harsh* with truth and reality, *incredibly* with rare, *key* with project, *kneejerk* with reaction, *long* with overdue, *mammoth* with task, *massive* with increase, *narrow* with confines, *potent* with symbol, *precious* with cargo, *proud* with owner, *proverbial* with hot cakes, *sea* and *seismic* with change, *shock* with findings, *silent* with killer, *stark* or *timely* with reminder, *stark* with warning, choice or contrast, *sweeping* with reforms, *true* with potential, *unique* with insight, *unprecedented* with access, *utter* with poverty or failure, *vague* with notion.

Adjectives and adverbs need to do some work. If they fit too easily with their noun or verb, leave them out. Use words which capture exactly, vividly and succinctly the ideas to be expressed. Use active rather than passive verbs, and verbs rather than abstract nouns. Jail John Smith *for possessing firearms*, not *for possession of firearms*. Write about people being allergic to nuts, not having a nut allergy.

Words and phrases that readers may not previously have come across need to be explained, in an unpatronizing way. The *Financial Times* neatly explained liquefied natural gas as gas cooled into liquid for easier shipping.

The *Independent* reported (20 03 06) that women who have asymmetrical breasts could be more likely to develop breast cancer. The *Daily Mail* made the meaning clearer by writing: *Women with different-sized breasts may be more likely to develop breast cancer*.

Geography needs explaining, too. To write that a governor blamed Indonesian floods on *widespread deforestation in Puncak* (*Independent*, 5 02 07) immediately raises the question: Where and what is Puncak?

Use words right

The criterion for a new word or expression is usage. If people use it, then it is valid English. They use *blog* and *blogger*. So these are acceptable words. Usage takes sudden lurches. The American *train station* has replaced the English *railway station* in many people's vocabulary. The verb *sneak* has acquired a new past tense: *snook* or *snuck*.

But changes of usage, carelessly made, do not need to be accepted. Too often, words are used wrong. For example, in British English you cannot appeal or protest a conviction or impact something. You appeal or protest against or you have an impact on.

Here are some further examples of incorrect usage:

- *Tackling hospital infections is more complex than ministers anticipated,* reported the *Independent* (11 01 07). The right word is *expected*. The word *anticipate* has the sense of forestall, for example, *He anticipated the militia's attack by launching one of his own.*

- *Henry Hamman tells the story of his brush with this deadly bacteria* (FT, 9 08 08). It should be bacterium. Bacteria are plural.

- *Capitalism has grown to be the de facto arbitrary of global society* (*Big Issue*, 29 05 06). Arbiter is the word, not arbitrary. But driver would be better than either. De facto is redundant.

- *The Afghans – an unruly mix of Pashtuns, Tajiks, Hazaras, Uzbeks, Aimaks, Turkmen and a few others – have no such centrifugal force* (FT, 20 08 09). Centrifugal force pulls apart. The force that brings together is centripetal.

- *What England's departing manager meant to describe was his disillusionment with elimination in the World Cup quarter finals* (*Independent*, 3 07 06). No. What he meant was his disappointment.

- Not all adjectives ending in *ble* end in *able*. Discernible, accessible, divisible, deductible and submersible all end in *ible*.

- *The Birmingham Six became icons and celebrities. He was totally disinterested in this* (*Big Issue*, 29 05 06). The right word is *uninterested*. Disinterested means impartial.

- *An enormity* is something enormously bad. Enormity is not a synonym for enormousness.

- *Viewers have seen men foreswear gambling* (*FT Magazine* 7 02 10). This should be *forswear* (as in forgive). The prefix *fore* means before, as in foretaste or foresee.

- Strictly speaking it's *laissez faire* (an imperative, let do!) not *laisser faire* (to let do).

- *Access to alcohol symbolized terrifying lassitude to opponents* (FT, 28 04 07). Lassitude means weariness. Laxity would better fit the sense.

- *Less than 20 people.* Fewer than 20 people would be preferable. (Use *less* for a smaller quantity, *fewer* for a smaller number.)

- *Marshall Pilsudski* (*Independent*, 24 08 06). Marshall is a name. The army rank is *Marshal*.

- *The notion, perpetrated by the Russian authorities* (*Independent*, 3 07 06). Crimes are perpetrated. A notion could be promoted or perhaps perpetuated.

- *Mr Stumpf quashed repeated speculation* (FT, 25 08 08). No, he ended speculation. *Quash* is a legal term meaning annul.

- *Lily Allen emerged in 2006 with her retinue of infectious pop songs* (*MEN*, 17 03 09). A retinue is a group of followers. A group of songs could be a repertoire.

- *He sank, he shrank, he sprang, he span.* These are the past tenses of sink, spring, shrink and spin. As the rebellious peasants of 1381 put it:

when Adam delved and Eve span, Who was then the gentleman? However, in cricket reports 'he spun' is correct.

- *The downpours did little to improve the water shortage* (*Independent*, 1 06 06). You can end or ease a water shortage. You cannot improve one.

- Either poorest or worst would be better than lowest in the following sentence: *A Unicef study says that the welfare of British children is among the lowest in the developed world* (*Independent*, 22 02 07).

- *Wracked* (*FT Magazine*, 23 11 08). The word is *racked*, from the rack on which prisoners under interrogation were stretched before the invention of waterboarding.

Prefer the simpler form of words: preventive not preventative, education-ist not educationalist, dissociate not disassociate, disfranchise not disenfran-chise, disillusion not disillusionment, oriented not orientated, transport not transportation, best-heeled not most well-heeled.

Use one word rather than two or three: *fetch* not *bring back*, *sped* not *drove quickly*, *climbed* not *headed upwards*, *shocked* not *sent shockwaves through*.

You may even get away with inventing a word. Metal-detectorist, used by a treasure expert on the Antiques Roadshow (BBC1, 26 10 08), filled a gap in English vocabulary. Charity canvassers who waylay shoppers have become chuggers. In the Oscar-winning film *Slumdog Millionaire*, a telesalesman is a phone basher.

Be wary with words that imply a judgment – terrorist, extremist, fascist, racist, martyr – or can be seen as disparaging (for example, ethnic).

Keep jargon at bay

Jargon fails to engage the readers' minds. Sir Arthur Quiller-Couch, famous Cambridge University language pundit of the early twentieth century, saw writing jargon as shuffling around in a fog of abstract terms. So don't let the jargon of your informants get into your copy as here: *Care bundles are groups of interventions that when carried out together result in better outcomes for the patient* (*Western Mail*, 16 03 09). Better get straight to the point: *Care bundles include better hygiene, better administration of drugs and better checks on patients. These improvements are more effective if made together.*

Jargons speak of interactions between people, rather than of what happens when people meet. They speak of the agricultural sector when they mean farming, social services instead of social workers, human resources instead of staff, entertainment talent instead of entertainers, added police presence instead of more police.

For jargonistas a college is an educational facility, a factory a production facility, a health centre a health facility, a port a port facility. Disabled toilet facilities have not, as it would appear, been put out of action by vandals. They are toilets for disabled people. Jargonistas love technical terms and initial letters. In your reports, you need to tell people what the technicalities mean and what the initials stand for.

Professionals use jargon to communicate meaning to fellow pros and, sometimes, deny it to proles. The Plain English Campaign gave a Golden Bull Award in December 2007 to Virgin Trains for its answer to an inquiry about prices. This began: 'Moving forwards, we, at Virgin Trains, are looking to take ownership of the flow in question to apply our pricing structure, thus resulting in this journey search appearing in the new category matrix format.' The answer ended: 'I hope this makes the situation clear.'

In the reassuring jargon of government, problems are mere challenges, and passengers have issues, not complaints. Everything is on track or in place. But, outside Whitehall and the TV studio, outlines are not put in place. They are drawn. Laws are not put in place. They are introduced. 'In place' is commonly redundant. According to the *Financial Times* (23 10 08), the International Energy Agency said that *higher prices would be in place*. What the IEA meant was *prices would be higher*.

As for 'on track', trains and trams are on track, not health reforms. Whatever is *on track* may be just starting, well on the way or due to start at the end of next year. Columnist Roula Khalaf writes (*FT*, 10 09 09): *Expect a big yawn if the president [Obama] promises another 'peace process' buttressed by 'confidence-building measures' and operating on several 'tracks'.*

Journalists need to grasp the facts obscured by the jargon and present them to their readers.

Cliché

When he strolled into New York's Brill Building in the summer of 1958, it was a classic case of 'love at first sight', reported the *Sun* (6 02 09). *Love at first sight, master of all it surveys, rogue elements, tip of the iceberg, drop in the ocean, slip through the net* and *pull out all the stops* slide effortlessly into print. The appropriateness of *pull out all the stops* depends on the context. In the following sentence, it strikes a useful, sceptical note: *The 21st February Movement, a state youth wing whose sole purpose is to prepare for President Robert Mugabe's annual birthday festivities, has pulled out all the stops for his 83rd bash* (*FT*, 24 02 07).

Clichés can be imaginatively transformed. Columnist Matthew Engel described President Sarkozy of France as *a politician who can never pass a can of worms without reaching for the tin opener* (*FT*, 30 06 07).

Clichés found a stout defender in 2008 – Julia Cresswell, author of *The Cat's Pyjamas: The Penguin Book of Clichés*. In the *British Journalism Review* (December 2008), she pointed out that Homer gave us *bite the dust*, Dryden *blaze of glory*, Hitler *heads will roll*. (She could also have mentioned *cloud cuckoo land* from Aristophanes.) It is hard to speak without using clichés, she suggested.

They are a well-established shorthand. *The tip of the iceberg* is neater than *a tiny part of the true scale of the problem.*

But, if you use a cliché, remember it is an image and the image has to work in your sentence. Two clichés in the same sentence make a mixed metaphor. The *Daily Mail* (20 11 08) quoted a BBC reporter saying: *However she cuts the cake, she has a huge mountain to climb.* Also, clichés get flogged to death. The *Concise Oxford English Dictionary* reported that *case* is the 18th most commonly used English noun (*Mail*, 22 06 06). Almost a century before, Sir Arthur Quiller-Couch tried to drive it out in his book *On the Art of Writing* (Cambridge, 1916). He failed. But it is worth making a resolution to shun *the case* and its well-worn brethren the problem – 24th in the OED list – *the move* and *or otherwise*. *Suitability or otherwise* means *suitability or unsuitability*. Why write *otherwise* in place of *unsuitability*?

Besides overused clichés, there are useful idioms. If you feel that bash, geek, food chain, hot potato, lose the plot, lunatic fringe, sacred cow, sleeping giant or take for a ride is a useful idiom in the context of your article, use it boldly – do not put it in quotes, which suggest you are ashamed of it.

Put quotes round a word only if you want to be ironic or to stress that this is the actual word spoken. Robert Verkaik, the *Independent*'s law editor, wrote (26 01 07) about *guards accused of torturing captives in the 'war on terror'*. His quotation marks made it clear that the war on terror was not something whose wisdom he believed in.

Journalese: downturn hits tax loophole

❛ All this was set to change with the hostile bid surge in the tougher climate, vowed the 55-year-old. The media-savvy entrepreneur would not back down from unveiling his pledge of a shake-up and crackdown but the likes of the security services would clamp down on a regular basis on the ballooning risk factors associated with putting food on the table. Meanwhile, the sage of Kirkcaldy, drumming up support while battening down the hatches, was stepping up to the plate in an escalation of the stand-off. It was a perfect storm. The magic bullet had backfired. ❜

No one actually printed this but some come close.

Clichés dear to journalists are journalese. Those in fashion in 2008 included 'the likes of', 'the duo', 'put food on the table', 'step up to the plate', 'going forward', 'at the nexus of', 'the elephant in the room' and 'a perfect storm'. In what sense the storm was perfect never got explained. The year 2009 kicked off with kick-starts of the economy, and problems at the cusp of going viral.

But why copy the overused imagery and vocabulary of other journalists, when you could use fresh images of your own? Columnist Jonathan Guthrie wrote (*FT*, 22 11 07): *Small businesses were going belly up like goldfish in a pond laced with Paraquat.*

Journalese infects not only journalists. A research manager remarked that obesity 'is an avoidable risk factor. It's a cancer time-bomb' (*Independent*, 21 05 07).

One odd feature of journalese is the patronizing use of *child* or *children* to refer to school pupils under 18, especially if they are victims of or involved in some crime or incident. Scarcely anyone in real life uses *child* for a boy or girl over 13, let alone a burly 17-year-old. At 13, they become teenagers or young people or students. So why not describe them as such in the media?

Journalese can obscure realities. Take the phrase *security forces*. It is abstract and feels reassuring. In many countries, however, the security forces are violent, operate illegally and use torture. The Anna Politkovskaya murder hearing (*FT*, 19 02 09) showed that, in Russia, security agents and criminals work together.

Elegant variation

Last year the 55-year-old retail mogul paid £60,000 at a charity auction to lock lips with the supermodel (*Independent*, 1 05 07). Sir Philip Green and Kate Moss are locked in this sentence in a literary conceit known as elegant variation. Elegant variators fear to repeat a word or name and seek an alternative. Charles Darwin in one sentence becomes the great scientist in the next.

Here's another example. *The biggest exodus was from Newham, which suffered a loss of 9,910 people. Other boroughs with large outflows included Brent, where 7,780 residents left, Ealing, which lost 7,200, and Lambeth, which suffered a 5,890 drop* (*Evening Standard*, 24 08 06). All this means is *Newham lost the most people – 9,910. Brent lost 7,780, Ealing 7,200 and Lambeth 5,890.*

In *The Art of Writing*, Sir Arthur Quiller-Couch (Q) mocked elegantly varied sport reports: 'Hayward and C.B.Fry now faced the bowling, which apparently had no terrors for the Surrey crack. The old Oxonian, however, took some time in settling to work.'

Nowadays, elegant variation has spread far beyond the sports pages. It not only replaces names. It also replaces pronouns. Why, some seem to think, use drab he, she or it, when you can write *the 46-year-old* or *the chancellor* or *the illicitly smoked plant extract?*

Q, who expected an undergraduate's essay on Byron to mention Byron several times, found instead that half way down the page he became 'the gloomy master of Newstead'. Overleaf he was 'the meteoric darling of society'; 'this arch-rebel', 'the author of Childe Harold', 'the apostle of scorn', 'the ex-Harrovian, proud but abnormally sensitive of his club-foot', 'the martyr of Missolonghi', 'the pageant-monger of a bleeding heart'.

Q's undergraduate has hundreds of imitators in twenty-first century media. Instead of Tom Jones they write *the Pontypridd singing legend*, instead of the Pope *the Bavarian theologian*, a scorpion *the arachnid*, lace *the diaphanous fabric*, Viagra *the circulation booster*, East Timor *the half-island nation*, Hugh Grant the Oxford-educated star, President Yar'Adua of Nigeria the former chemistry lecturer, North Korea the reclusive Communist state, soya the protein-rich bean, GlaxoSmithKline the pharma titan, Faust the classical German tale, St Pancras Station the King's Cross landmark, the Champions League the cash-rich tournament, St Albans the prosperous Hertfordshire commuter town, Parkinson's disease the degenerative disorder, Indian prime minister Manmohan Singh the Cambridge and Harvard-educated former management consultant, YouTube the user-generated internet site and Wallace and Grommit the clay character and his faithful dog. Even the no-nonsense Sun referred to Melanie Slade, footballer Theo Walcott's girlfriend, as the understated bookworm (6 02 09).

One plus for elegant variation is that it can strike arresting contrasts, between, for instance, the master of ravaged flesh (artist Lucian Freud) and the English landscape painter (John Constable) (FT, 7 03 09). But, mostly, it is an overworked mannerism. It can compromise clarity. Who was the Birkbeck philosophy lecturer (Independent, 9 03 07), who the Boundary Park club (Mirror, 17 02 09) and who the Critics Choice award-winners' eponymous front-woman (FT, 14 02 09)?

It weakens sentences. The Daily Mail reported (21 02 07): 'Tens of thousands of workers and their families face a painful death from the untreatable condition. This would more powerfully read: Tens of thousands of workers and their families face a painful death. The cancer is untreatable.

And elegant variation wastes words. The Independent reported (10 01 07): First Great Western bowed to pressure yesterday by increasing fast services between Oxford and London. The company's new timetable had sharply cut fast trains between the two cities. The second sentence could have been half the length: Its new timetable had sharply cut them.

Many elegant variants can be omitted. The waiting list for the product is running at 50,000 could read The waiting list is 50,000.

Writers often use elegant variation to inject details into their copy, as in this passage (FT, 23 03 08) The shaven-haired former policeman with razor tracks carved into his eyebrows, fired by Sugar in only the second week of last year's series, spells it out: 'I am an all-out businessman. I am a businessman.' The 37-year-old dressed in a sharp black suit, shirt and tie.... A straightforward version is possible: Thirty-seven year-old I. C. is a shaven-haired former policeman with razor tracks carved into his eyebrows. He wears a sharp black suit, shirt and tie. Last year Sugar fired him in the second week of the series, etc.

Elegant variation can raise a smile. Is the influential striker an adviser to the sage of Kirkcaldy? How many children has the prolific psychologist? Does the blunt-talking Mississippi native – also known as Ken Lewis of Bank of America – wear a feathered headdress on Sundays?

TV personality Claudia Winkleman wrote in the Independent (31 01 07) of Winnie, a Ugandan child: She wears a green dress and has the most enormous eyes. She lives in a tiny hut – the roof is falling in. If she had written The ill-nourished two-year-old wears a green dress, she would have turned Winnie into just another cliché.

His and their

We care about people's feelings. So lepers are now sufferers from leprosy. Pensioners became senior citizens and then older people. Those who formerly were educationally subnormal now have learning difficulties. Bear in mind that changing the word does not change the reality. As Abraham Lincoln pointed out, you can call a dog's tail a leg. But the dog will still walk on four legs, not five.

'Companion animals' are pets. The disadvantaged are still poor; and it does handicapped and disabled people no favours if the reality of their situation is hidden in a euphemism. Visually impaired people are people who do not see well or have poor sight.

Edward Stourton of the Today programme (*FT*, 8 11 08) quoted the BBC's disability correspondent, Peter White, who is blind, as saying that over-sensitivity about language can stop people talking about complex subjects that need to be addressed. Stourton also says people should have the right to decide for themselves how they want to be described.

There is no need to tiptoe around sensitive subjects. A *Manchester Evening News* report (16 03 09) about an award-winning film featuring children with disabilities would have had greater impact if it had said what the disabilities were. Unexplained, the phrase 'children with disabilities' is social-services speak.

English usage has yet to fully accommodate sensitivity to women. Is a heroic woman a hero or a heroine? The *Daily Mail* (27 08 08) described Olympic gold-winning swimmer Rebecca Adlington as a hero.

The *Guardian's* stylebook prefers actor to actress. But this has its pitfalls – one article described Italian film producer Carlo Ponti as 'a man with a good eye for pretty actors' (*BJR*, March 2008).

Since the eighteenth century the words *he* and *his* have referred to people generally, as in the phrase *Everyone to his own taste*. It is not easy to replace this male domination with something even-handed. Emma Jacobs (*FT*, 3 10 08) captured the difficulty in a sentence: *Someone finds something out about himself or herself that makes them stronger.*

Everyone to his or her own taste is clumsy. Everyone to their own taste is better. But *one juror had time off after hurting their foot treading on a golf ball* (*Mail*, 10 09 08) reads as if the injured juror shared the foot with someone else.

The fact is that *they* and *their* still feel plural, even if used as singular. *A patient would be compelled to take their treatment* (*Independent*, 9 01 07) sounds awkward. The sentence is better plural: *Patients would be compelled to take their treatment.*

A 2009 TV advertisement showing a woman having a stroke included the line: Is their speech slurred? It sounded like a condescending conversation between doctors at a patient's bedside.

Tim Harford, *Financial Times* economics columnist, used she rather than he in this sentence (19 05 07): *Every time a person chooses to live in a city, she is preserving the environment for the rest of us.* In contrast, McNae's *Essential Law for Journalists* sticks to tradition, using he to include she.

There is no single right solution. Ask yourself if what you write sounds right. If it does not, rephrase it. The juror who hurt their foot would better have hurt *a* foot.

Credit crunch price cut war

British journalists have enthusiastically adopted the German practice of stringing nouns together. Thus, in German, Star (starling) and Kasten (box) make Starkasten – speed camera. A more ambitious German coined Neuwagenverweigerungsproblem (the problem presented by motorists who refuse to buy new cars).

In English, noun-stringing has given us bear hug, climate change, road deaths and *The Times* crossword. The *Daily Mirror* (17 02 09) managed a nine-worder: *TV property guru Phil Spencer's crumbling home-finding business.*

Postcode lottery, speed camera and carbon footprint convey complex ideas in two words. But noun strings are overused. Some replace more straightforward language. *The airline will introduce in flight mobile phone capability* means the airline will enable mobile phones to be used on its planes.

Too often, stringing nouns together results in journalese: *body parts, collision course, David-and-Goliath court battle, death leap, death crash, gold medal glory, kneejerk reaction, knife crime, miracle cure, murder bid, nightmare scenario, paradise island, peace process, pension pot, quality time, rogue elements, security services, strike/travel chaos, wake-up call, wonder drug.*

'Peace process' signifies lots of process, to enable clever people to justify their salaries and lobster thermidor, but precious little peace.

How unique is unique?

Something is unique or it isn't unique. It cannot be almost unique. If there are two, it isn't unique at all. Similarly, none is none. Three is three or scarcely any, not *almost none*.

Many adjectives cannot be qualified – legendary, groundbreaking, hemisphere-shattering, renewable, internationally known. Optimal means best. Conditions can be less favourable but not less optimal.

Negatives are just that – negatives. One country cannot be more impotent or powerless, one dispute more intractable, one enemy more implacable, one factor more unimaginable, one government more illegitimate, one resource more inexhaustible, one voter more disfranchised than another. If a jungle is impenetrable, it can't be penetrated. There are no degrees of can't. A jungle can, however, be less penetrable, a problem less tractable.

Misfortune is an exception. It is possible to be more or even most unfortunate. And if 'most internationally known' is awkward, there is an alternative: best-known internationally.

Questions

1. What single words could replace the word-groups in italics? (In the first example, the answer could be *intended*.)

    The way *it is supposed to*
    Will *make every effort* to
    The report *printed next to it*
    Adding new rooms to a hotel
    Is a stark illustration of
    He *unearthed the fact* that
    This *brought to light the fact* that
    He *advanced menacingly* towards
    The addition of a third face
    A front page *of an issue of the Independent*
    Move to another country
    Building societies *transformed themselves into* banks

2. Which of these words are misspelled? Accessible, discernable, protestor, adviser, descendent.

3. Rewrite these passages without the mixed metaphors.

    a. Ghana has navigated a scenario that could have tipped less stable countries into turmoil (*FT*, 6 01 09).
    b. Asia's inflation troubles are not taking place in a vacuum. From Washington to Frankfurt, central bankers are banging the drum on rising prices. Leading emerging markets have followed suit.

4. 'The condition' is often used as an elegant variant for all manner of diseases. Rephrase these sentences (from *FT*, 10 01 09) without using 'the condition'.

    a. India now has perhaps 32 million diabetics, most of whom do not know they have the condition.
    b. In Egypt, one in three people with very severe hypertension didn't even know they had the condition.

6 Newswriting: getting the words in order

> We have an obligation to put ourselves in the reader's place. It is his comfort, his convenience we have to consult ... The more difficulties we obtrude on him by obscure or careless writing, the more we blunt the edge of his attention ... You see, then, what an obligation we owe to him of order and arrangement.
>
> Sir Arthur Quiller-Couch, On The Art of Writing, 1916

Related words should be close together

It is not just the choice and number of words that matter. As Q points out above, how they are arranged matters, too. Sentences, long or short, need to say what they mean. Here is one that might not be elegant but said what it meant: *The UK music industry's big problem at the moment is getting to grips with the fact that more music than ever is getting into the hands of its consumers without them having to pay for it* (FT, 14 02 09).

A sentence needs to make clear which words are to be read with which. Unintended relationships between words can raise a smile. *Joe F. was serving an indeterminate sentence for possession of firearms at Wormwood Scrubs prison* (*Independent*, 9 01 07). Did he keep them under his prison mattress?

This sentence from the *Evening Times*, Glasgow (22 04 09) has got *to mark World Earth Day* in the wrong spot: *Scots are being urged to take action to reduce the amount of food waste they generate to mark World Earth Day*. Better, and shorter, would have been: *Scots are being urged to mark World Earth Day by wasting less food*.

This sentence from the *Big Issue* (2 02 09) got into trouble because the final phrase strayed three lines from the verb it qualified: *Not many articles on the topic cite the media's creation of a climate in which many people are scared to visit their local for fear of being glassed as part of the problem*. This reads as though *as part of the problem* is to be read with *glassed*. Actually it should be read with *cite*.

Sentences need to be tidily organized. In the sentence that follows, the repairs are mixed up with the renewals: *New windows and door, an entire new roof and structural repairs were carried out as well as new plastering to indoor walls and a new boiler in the kitchen* (*Teesdale Mercury*, 28 06 06). This could read: *The pavilion has a new roof, new windows, a new door and, in the kitchen, a new boiler. Its structure has been repaired and the inside walls have been replastered.*

Ordering the clauses

The simplest sentence to write well is a short sentence, making a single statement. *The Campbells are coming. There's going to be war.* If you're afraid of the Campbells, these two short sentences tell you all you need to know. It's time to get out.

News reporting can be short and to the point. But it also needs some flow to it. Varying the length of sentences makes a report read more smoothly. You may want to put last in a sentence the words you want to emphasize. *He went to his office next door and returned with a set of false teeth.* Apart from this, it is usually best to put the main clause before subordinate clauses and phrases.

The *Reading Chronicle* reported (25 09 08): *While the housing market is in decline, signs have emerged of the pent-up demand for homes in and around Reading.* This would be better the other way round: *Many people are seeking homes in and around Reading even though the housing market is in decline.*

However, putting a phrase first can avoid a false linkage. The *Belfast Telegraph* reported (1 05 09): *The Education Minister said it was important for disadvantaged children to be given priority during an interview this morning on the BBC. During an interview in* this sentence belongs with *the Education Minister said* not with *given priority.* So this word-order would have been better: *During an interview this morning on the BBC, the Education Minister said it was important for disadvantaged children to be given priority.*

'If' clauses are often better placed first because they can trail away at the end of a sentence.

Written words can have a ring and a rhythm, which makes them easier to understand. The following clause is hard to read: *how artificial the struggle these cartoons illustrated actually was.* A more rhythmic word order helps: *how artificial was the struggle these cartoons illustrated.*

Was, is and will be

Standard English normally requires that the verbs in the main and subordinate clauses of a sentence should be either in a present tense or a past tense. You should not write: *While I was away, she has had to learn to drive.* It should be: *While I was away, she had to learn to drive. Or she has had to learn to drive while I am away.* (Present tenses include the perfect *she has had* as well as the present *she has* and the future *she will have.*)

Look at this sentence: *Small-scale gold mining has been transformed into a large-scale industry as the junta sold off concessions* (*Independent*, 10 01 07). The sequence of tenses requires *has sold off*. Or a participle could have avoided the problem: *... large-scale industry, the junta selling off concessions*.

Conditional tenses – *should, would, might, ought to, were to* – can serve as both past and present. After a present tense, *may* and *might* are both possible, *may* expressing a stronger likelihood than *might*. *May* cannot be a past tense. A *Manchester Evening News* feature (21 03 09) read: *Jeff feared he may not live to enjoy either marriage or family.* 'May' here should have been 'might'.

In newspapers, it is better to avoid the compound tenses – *had given, will have given, might have given* – even though strict grammar may require them. More important, the present tense *I give* has an impact which other tenses lack.

In reported speech introduced by a verb in the present tense, any tense can follow. So you can write *He says* [present] *they came earlier* [past]. But, if the introductory verb is in the past, the following verbs should strictly be past, too – *He said that gold mining was ruining a protected valley*.

Nevertheless, you can often use the 'historic' present in place of a past tense in reported speech, particularly if you are describing a present situation – *He said* [past] *that gold mining is ruining* [historic present] *a protected valley. Gibbons are no longer heard there.*

Write succinctly

Reports, even in the best newspapers, commonly waste space by saying the same thing in different words in consecutive sentences. There was no need for a columnist to write: *Gordon Brown's views are no easier to define. Indeed, in some ways they are even more difficult to establish* (*Independent*, 4 01 07). He could simply have written: *Gordon Brown's views are in some ways even harder to define.*

It is surprisingly easy to cut a 700-word report to 500. Little is lost if the second and fourth sentences, shown in bold, are deleted from this report in the *Daily Express* (22 09 08):

> *Eastenders actor Phil Daniels had the dubious honour of being the first celebrity to be booted off the new series of Strictly Come Dancing last night.* **The star was voted out by the judges after his performance with Italian-born Flavia Cacace.** *He was a surprise choice. Betting men would have backed a hasty exit by the former BBC political editor John Sergeant.* **The 64-year-old had been favourite to go home first.** *But on the night he put in such a charming and elegant performance that he won the chance to dance again.*

Reports commonly contain wordy and redundant linking phrases such as *The problem stems from the fact that* or *Another problem is that* or *One example of the latter category is.* Such phrases as *it is advisable to* may also be redundant, and slightly pompous.

However, for easy comprehension, some sentences require more words than the writer has allowed them. With two 'thats' omitted, this phrase is harder to follow than it need be: *a relevance surveys suggest viewers prefer* (*FT*, 1 09 09)

Simpler, less clichéd writing: some suggestions

Going forward	In (or for) the future
Part of a package of	One of several
No fewer than three	Three
The extent to which …	How, or how far
Availability crisis	Shortage
Gunshots	Shots
Gunshot wounds	Bullet wounds
Meet up with, face up to, lose/miss out on, free/head/open up	Meet, face, lose, miss, free, head, open
Potable supplies	Drinking water
This could be about to change	This could change
Treatment facility	Clinic, treatment centre
Production facility	Factory, plant
A state-guaranteed credit facility	State-guaranteed credit
Clean-up operation	Clean-up
Roads infrastructure	Roads
Building development	Building
In the coming weeks	Soon
Vowed to abandon music	Said he would abandon music
The reason was due to	The reason was
Comes in the shape of	Is
The ban remains in place	The ban remains
How long the ban remains in place	How long the ban lasts
Put in place revised services	Revise services
Emergency services	Police, fire and ambulance crews
Moved swiftly to scotch the rumours	Swiftly scotched the rumours
Many are in the £10,000–£20,000 a year bracket	Many earn £10,000–£20,000 a year
Suffered from the effects of smoke inhalation	Suffered from inhaling smoke
To change people's perceptions of the condition	To change how people see it
Because of the continued absence of a regular ferry	Because it still has no regular ferry
This is not the case	This is not so
If this were to be the case	If this happened

Than would be the case if	Than if
In the case of the NHS	In the NHS
In other cases, children were	Other children were
There are many more cases of this type	This has happened to many more
One case of a child being forced to be a servant was reported	One child was forced to be a servant
In both cases those who were arrested	Both of those arrested
In many cases, women are the only breadwinners in the family	Women are the only breadwinners in many families
To spend more money more quickly than would otherwise have been the case (Independent, 21 11 06)	To spend more money more quickly
In the case of building societies there was little accountability to owner-customers (FT, 29 09 08)	Building societies were little accountable to owner-customers
Human resources	People, staff, workers
Energy resources	Coal, oil and gas
Coral conservation	Saving coral
Environmental protection	Protecting the environment
Most well-known	Best known
The lobster population	Lobsters
The desertification situation	The spread of desert
Due to the fact that	Because
Shrouded in a cloak of anonymity	Shrouded in anonymity
In her absence	While she is away
Help from online assistance	Help online
Teenagers committing anti-social behaviour	Teenagers behaving anti-socially
It includes the likes of Gap and Nike	It includes Gap and Nike
Put enough food on the table	Buy enough food
There are lots of alternatives out there that are	Lots of alternatives are
The extent of the problem can be discerned from the OECD's figures which forecast that	The OECD has forecast that
Patients in life-threatening situations	Patients whose lives are at risk
Placing management in the position of having to choose	Forcing managers to choose ...
Designed as a wake-up call to (FT, 25 11 08)	Designed to wake up
There is strike action by pilots today (BBC Breakfast, 17 11 08)	Pilots are on strike today

The pithead baths is a typical example of one of the buildings (Independent, 11 07 06)	The pithead baths is typical of the buildings
There has been a reduction in the number of bloodstream infections associated with patients who need intravenous medicines or fluids (Western Mail, 16 03 09)	Fewer patients have picked up blood infections from injections and drips
Cabs for tourists arriving by air were unobtainable (Independent, 4 07 06)	Tourists arriving by air could not find cabs
Another problem in modern smog is the presence of tiny particles (Independent, 13 06 06)	Modern smog also contains tiny particles
With its new, fuel-efficient aircraft, Ryanair produced 50 per cent fewer emissions and 45 per cent less fuel-burn than long-haul airlines with ageing fleets (Independent, 7 11 06)	Ryanair's new, fuel-efficient aircraft emitted 50 per cent less exhaust gas and burned 45 per cent less fuel than the ageing fleets of some long-haul airlines
IT and skilled engineering continue to be areas where there is a shortage in the skills base of the workforce, while nursing and care are other areas where there is a need for new workers (Western Mail, 19 03 09)	There are not enough skilled engineers and IT staff New workers are also needed in nursing and care

Avoid muddled thinking

A notice at Whipps Cross Hospital, London, in 2007 read: *Over 250,000 people attended outpatients last year. Of these, 48,181 did not arrive for their appointments.* (So presumably the attendance was only 202,000.) Not only hospital notices display muddled thinking. Here is some from newspapers:

- *Subsidy cuts, which prop up unprofitable services* (Teesdale Mercury, 28 06 06). It is subsidy which props up the services, not subsidy cuts.

- *The trend of declining import prices now seems to be over and to be contrib-uting to higher inflation* (FT, 10 06 06). Declining import prices do not contribute to inflation: they reduce it. More direct language would solve the problem. *Prices of imports no longer seem to be declining and this is contributing to higher inflation.*

- *The penalties are as good a place to start as any, and another debilitating collapse of nerve* (Independent, 2 07 06). An essential word is missing from this sentence. Missed penalties are not a collapse of nerve in a football match, but they can *show* one.

- *There the lobster population seems to be thriving unlike further south which has been devastated* (Independent, 5 07 06). This should read ... *where it has been devastated.*

- *A spokesman for the district council was unavailable for comment* (Mail, 23 05 06). If he wasn't available, he wasn't a spokesman. Better would be *No spokesman was available.*

The hanging participle or hanging nominative still raises a smile, as in this sentence about apparently towering visitors: *Measuring an impressive 7ft 8in long, visitors to Tinker's Gardens were encouraged to accept that this particular cucumber was the greatest curiosity of its kind* (MEN, 19 03 09).

It's a shame about the hanging participle in this lively passage about the actor Richard E.Grant: *Looking like he's about to kiss every single person in the auditorium, arms windmilling extravagantly, near-manic euphoria spilling out in every direction, it's like witnessing the benevolent version of his character Withnail* (Big Issue, 29 05 06). The participle *looking* requires that Grant, not it, be the subject of the sentence.

Both of them hit each other

The *Daily Mail* (20 11 08) quoted cycling commentator Phil Liggett as saying: *This is the steepest part of the course and I'm afraid it gets steeper later on.*

Here are more mistakes with comparisons:

- *Crumbling buildings in the North are twice as likely to suffer further deterioration than in the South* (Independent, 11 07 06). This should read *as in the South.*

- *The number of claims has risen at more than double the rate as actions launched against directors about other misconduct* (FT, 4 05 09). This should read either *double the rate of* or *twice as fast as.*

- *Muslims suffer similar disadvantages as other excluded groups* (Developments magazine, 43, 2008). This should be *to other excluded groups.*

- *The French work fewer hours than in almost any other country* (FT, 6 01 07). This requires *people* after *than.*

- *Israeli settlers take six times the water as local Palestinians* (Independent, 9 11 06). Israeli settlers take six times as much water as local Palestinians.

- *Compared to the war in Vietnam, US losses have been comparatively light* (Independent, 18 05 06). The word *comparatively* is not needed. We know a comparison is being made.

The words *both* and *each* also cause problems, as here: *Both men swore at each other* (FT, 31 08 09). This should read: *Each swore at the other or they swore at each other. None of the doctors who treated her were able to access each other's notes* (*Independent*, 25 05 07). None of the doctors who treated her was able to access the others' notes.

Punctuation

The purpose of punctuation is to make meaning clear.

A sentence in an article about Wangari Maathai, Kenyan Nobel prizewinner, read like this: *As a child, she played by a stream spurting from a fig tree's roots, sheltered from the rain under the arrowroot's giant leaves and trailed her fingers in frogspawn* (FT, 24 02 07). The problem word here is *sheltered*. Who or what is sheltered? Is it Wangari, the stream, the roots? Better punctuation makes for clarity. *As a child, she played by a stream that spurted from a fig tree's roots. She sheltered from the rain under the arrowroot's giant leaves and trailed her fingers in frogspawn.*

As here, the most useful punctuation mark is the full stop, followed by a capital letter. It shows that one thought has ended and another is about to begin.

Commas help to unite words to be read together as a phrase and separate words which are to be read separately. A comma after *projections* would make this sentence easier to follow: *Even on Gordon Brown's projections growth in the public sector as a proportion of the economy is coming to an end* (*Independent*, 21 02 07).

Notice how the comma changes the meaning of this sentence: *Investors marked down its shares by 2 per cent, more than the index* (FT, 20 02 10). This means that 2 per cent is more than the decline in the index (for all shares). Without the comma, the sentence would mean that the mark-down was 2 per cent in addition to the index's decline.

A comma before the relative pronoun *which* can make it clear the *which* relates not to the previous word but to an earlier word or to the whole previous clause. *He said he would come tomorrow, which is fine by me.*

If there is a comma at one end of a clause or phrase, there should also be one at the other end. *And* and *but* are often followed by a phrase ending in a comma. There should also be a comma after, not before, the and or but. *He wrote swiftly but, I would add, accurately.*

Deploy commas with care. Here is a sentence from the *Financial Times* (30 01 09): *Ford will not benefit, and may even suffer from, its foresight.* The comma after *from* is misplaced. The sentence should be *Ford will not benefit, and may even suffer, from its foresight.*

Commas sometimes make possible a different shade of meaning. *The books, which are red, are on the table* means that all the books are red and are on the table. *The books which are red are on the table* means that the red – as distinct from the yellow or blue – books are on the table.

Longer sentences may require something stronger than commas to show that a phrase is to be read separately from the rest. In news reports, dashes are preferable to brackets for this purpose. Brackets interrupt the flow of the eye over the sentence. Dashes do not. If you do use brackets, use them round a whole sentence or round a phrase at the end of a sentence, for example, *He said Yes (whereas others might have said No)*.

Possessives, using apostrophes, can cause trouble. The *Daily Mail* (25 10 08) wrote about *the princes's aides*. The possessive formed from princes is princes', with no added *s*.

Whether you write St James' Church or St James's Church depends on your publication's style.

If something belongs to two people, both require an apostrophe plus 's', e.g. John's and James's pencils. Similarly, write India's and China's carmakers, not India and China's carmakers.

The Smiths and the Joneses do not require an apostrophe. These are not possessives.

Long sentences

Newspapers prefer short sentences but publish many long ones, some more puzzling for the reader than others.

This 66-worder introducing a story by Brian Lee (*Western Mail*, 17 03 09) has a thread that is easy to follow despite the detail clinging to it. It helps that the 'when' clause follows the main clause: *Dead or Alive, a six-year-old bay gelding owned by Cardiff bookmaker David Lovell and trained in the Vale of Glamorgan by Abbi Vaughan, wife of National Hunt trainer Tim Vaughan, landed one of the biggest betting coups seen at a point-to-point in years when winning a division of the maiden race at the recent Flint & Denbigh meeting at Bangor-on-Dee.*

Piling on the facts can cause trouble, however, if you delay the main verb, as here: *Winstone's performance as the foul-mouthed Frankie who, with his amoral football agent son Martin (Danny Dyer) feathers his nest with underhand deals at the expense of the club he claims to love, was literally breathtaking (Mail, 12 05 06).* (The sentence would better start: *Winstone gave a breathtaking performance as the foul-mouthed Frankie, etc.*)

The next sentence staggers under the participial phrase beginning 'featuring' which is stuffed in front of the verb 'exudes': *Tonight's documentary is just as clear through editing and, featuring by now near-legendary figures from Merrill Lynch, Bank of America, Barclays and the rest, exudes a sense of occasion (FT, 10 09 09).*

Sometimes, what over-postpones a sentence's main verb is a long subordinate clause: *Whether that was the real reason or whether it was because Sir Ian had failed to ask the right questions of his officers before he went on air to broadcast what turned out to be an untrue account of Jean Charles de Menezes' conduct on the day in question, one thing is clear (Independent, 13 06 06). One thing is clear* should have come first. The sentence could also have been simpler: *One thing is clear, whether that was the real reason or whether Sir Ian had failed to discover the truth before broadcasting an inaccurate account of what Jean Charles de Menezes did.*

Here are other reasons why many long sentences do not work:

1. Ideas are ill-connected. *The collapse of the ITV Digital pay-television service in 2002 left them all with much less television money than they were expecting and has been a big factor in many clubs struggling to survive (FT, 16 04 08).* The second idea would be better as a new sentence: *This has hindered many clubs in their struggle to survive.*

2. They end weakly with an afterthought or unrelated idea or detached phrase. *Every other university in the country has embraced longer terms, where the workload is more spread out and students have more time to prepare work rather than cram the night before – which is, more often than not, what ends up happening (Independent, 21 02 07).* The sentence would not end so weakly if it finished more actively ... *what they end up doing.*

3. The main clause is split by a lengthy parenthesis. *To the north the waters are low – thanks to the huge green pipes sucking out what the neighbouring kibbutzes and moshavs use to irrigate their farming land – but crystal clear (Independent, 19 10 06).* This would better read: *To the north the waters are crystal clear but low, thanks to, etc.*

4. They contain lists and handle them poorly. A list is easier to read if the shortest items are listed first. *London Lite* reported (6 10 08): *Windows were blown out sending shards of glass over the rooftops below and doors forced off their hinges.* It would read more easily like this: *Doors were forced off their hinges and windows blown out, sending shards of glass over the rooftops below.*

Items linked together in a long sentence should preferably be in the same grammatical form. *Various items of folklore have been repeated over the years about Stevens' time in Fleet Street, from the time he supposedly threw a fashion editor's filing cabinet out of a window, to reportedly firing a company secretary via the office intercom (Independent, 15 06 06).* The final phrase would have been better in the same form as its predecessor ... *to the time he reportedly fired a company secretary, etc.* Or a new sentence could have begun after Fleet Street: *He is supposed to have thrown a fashion editor's filing cabinet out of a window and fired a company secretary via the office telecom.*

Sometimes ideas flow too quickly for the mind to organize them, like this: *Even without such unfortunate consequences, as is the case with most people simply touched by the suffering of other people, indulging in too many thoughts of 'what if ...' is a sort of perverse anti-luxury because, despite the almost inconceivable ill-fortune of the McCann family, and despite widespread declarations that one knows just how they are feeling or, more honestly, cannot begin to imagine it, there is next to no likelihood, statistically, of quite such a calamity ever befalling anybody else (Independent, 9 05 07).* If thoughts pour on to your keyboard in this way, send them back into your mind and insist on one at a time.

Split infinitives

There are four main ways to qualify a present infinitive. Here they are in four sentences:

1. Smith decided to boldly go about his task.

2. Smith decided to go boldly about his task.

3. Smith decided to go about his task boldly.

4. Smith decided boldly to go about his task.

To boldly go was made famous by Star Trek. For decades, journalists dreaded to split infinitives, lest they be thought uncouth. Split infinitives are now returning to favour. They disrupt the rhythm of a sentence less than the 'boldly to go' construction (4), popular with many writers. A front page caption in the *Birmingham Post* (5 05 09) read: *Randal Brew is to openly oppose Birmingham City Council leader Mike Whitby.*

Split infinitives can add emphasis. Thus a nineteenth century missionary, Joseph Booth, aimed *to firmly, judiciously and repeatedly place on record the great wrongs inflicted on the African* (Harry Langworthy in *Christian Missionaries*, James Currey, 2002). A split infinitive is also useful when verb and adverb merge into a single meaning as in *to rudely interrupt, to swiftly go* or *to unquestioningly support.*

There is no logical case against split infinitives. If it is permissible to write *in dramatically increasing* why outlaw *to dramatically increase?*

The *boldly to go* construction runs the risk of attaching the adverb to the wrong verb. *He failed successfully to go about his task* is nonsense. No one fails successfully. The *Guardian* (18 10 08) wrote about truth being concealed *in order fraudulently to get government insurance cover.* This could have less painfully read *to get government insurance cover fraudulently.*

Even pedants have no problem with splitting more complex infinitives. *None could be said wholly to have succeeded* (FT, 23 12 06) could have read: *None could be said to have wholly succeeded.* Similarly, *Two women still to be formally identified* is acceptable English. It does not have to be *Two women still formally to be identified* (Independent, 13 12 06).

Only and mainly

Only should be as close as possible to the word it qualifies. The *Daily Mail* reported (25 09 08): *Other local authorities are also understood to offer only weekend burials to Jews and Muslims.* What it probably intended was: *Other local authorities are also understood to offer weekend burials only to Jews and Muslims.*

Words akin to only, such as mainly and chiefly, should also be close to the words they qualify. *The rain in Spain falls mainly on the plain,* as My Fair Lady puts it.

Relative clauses

The constructions *and which* and *but which* are clumsy. Putting one relative clause inside another may also be clumsy, but you can introduce one of the clauses with *which* and the other with *that:* for example, *which came to a conclusion that I regretted.*

This sentence (*FT,* 14 07 09), with two relative clauses one after the other, is a jumble of words: *Subsidence is one of several water-related crises Jakarta is facing that are combining to make severe flooding increasingly frequent.* It can easily be reordered and simplified: *Subsidence is one of several water-related crises that are causing increasingly frequent flooding in Jakarta.*

Do not be misled by Microsoft Word's pedantic insistence that *which* must always be preceded by a comma, and *that* cannot be. This is not so.

Winston Churchill is supposed, possibly erroneously, to have protested against *up with which I will not put* (as opposed to the more natural *which I will not put up with*). Prepositional phrases do sometimes need to come before *which,* not at the end of the clause. The *Financial Times* (13 02 09) wrote about racially motivated attacks *of which 97 people died as a result.* The better order is *as a result of which 97 people died.*

Questions

1. Write in simpler English

   a. I think we are heading towards a period where it is probably the case that we will be able to secure the best entertainment talent for less than we have been able to do in the last few years. (Mark Thompson, BBC director-general, *FT,* 3 11 08.)
   b. More widely, public health consideration needs to be given to preventing music icons promoting health-damaging behaviours amongst their emulators and fans. Where popstar behaviour remains typified by risk-taking and substance use, it is unlikely that youths will see any positive health messages popstars champion as credible. (Report quoted in *FT,* 4 09 07.)
   C. The extent of the problem can be discerned from the forecast that by 2030 the UK will have 1.9 taxpaying workers for each jobless person over the age of 65. This compares with a support ratio of more than 3 to 1 in 2005.

   (Continued)

2. Rephrase this sentence, getting rid of the what has been/has been construction:

   The car itself has changed relatively little, but what has, however, been revolutionary has been the changes that it has made possible in the physical fabric of our cities. (*Independent*, 31 01 07.)

3. Make the lists in these sentences easier to follow

   a. He highlights further public sector reform, such as more vocational education, international terrorism and economic challenges. (*Independent*, 20 02 07.)

   b. The next step would be to get the UN team that's now in place in Burma to start talks with the junta about improved humanitarian access to tens of thousands of displaced people in the country's east, the fight against HIV/Aids, reconciliation with Ms Suu Kyi's party, which has been shut down, and other issues. (*Independent*, 25 05 06.)

7 Newswriting for the internet

Readers must want to read what you write

Straits Times Interactive in Singapore was launched in November 1995 with a constantly updated account of the court appearance of Nick Leeson, the trader who ruined Barings Bank. Here was a website doing what the printed *Straits Times* could not do and what broadcasters struggled to do: report the news the moment after it happened.

More and more people read and write online, while fewer, outside India and China, read newspapers. Online is more versatile and less costly. Printed newspapers rely on unreliable advertising to cover most of their increasing costs, and most charge their readers an increasing sum per copy. Online sites offer near-free distribution. From most, the reader gets something for next-to-nothing, though some charge.

The first essential for writing online, as for newspapers, is material – like the Leeson case – which readers will want to read. The readers can be anywhere in the world. A journalist with a special, even if limited, interest can build up a sizeable audience. Hordes of cyclists clicked on to a site about maintaining bicycles.

But readers won't read even the most attractive story if they – or Google – do not rate or know about the website on which it appears. News websites needs exclusives, to attract audiences. After Robert Peston, the BBC's business editor, secured scoops about the 2008 credit crunch, his blog reached a readership of 650,000.

The Drudge Report pushed itself to the front by breaking the story of President Clinton's flirtation with Monica Lewinsky. During the American presidential election campaign of 2008, Google's chief executive remarked: 'Virtually all of the most important stories have been broken in the blogosphere' (*FT*, 12 09 08).

Online technology imposes constraints on stories and layout but not the printed page's constraint on the space a story occupies. Tom Whitwell, assistant editor of *The Times*, has explained how he lengthened a story on Times Online when the Drudge Report linked to it (*BJR*, March 2008). With tens of thousands of Drudgers about to arrive, he added a picture and links to other reports and restored 11 paragraphs cut from the printed version.

Online, stories constantly develop, as the news develops. They have a life of their own, promoted by the interest and comments of readers. In the *Daily Telegraph* newsroom a display shows which are attracting interest and which are not. So bright young writers may become new stars while old stars wane. This could be a bad thing. News of great import may attract few viewers. A story on the *Telegraph* website (8 06 09) that simply listed comedian Sacha Baron Cohen's five funniest lines attracted many.

Getting online: html

Online content and writing need to be attractive and high standard. If you lose readers' interest, they can easily move elsewhere or switch off. News sites try to make their copy easy to read by keeping paragraphs short and leaving a line of white space between them. Readers may read only what they can easily see. So conciseness – and an ability to get the main facts into the first few paragraphs – are valuable, even though a story online can be any length.

The easiest way to get online is to blog. Go to www.blogger.com/start and follow the instructions. In a few minutes, you can be blogging for free. A successful blog is a recommendation for a job in journalism.

Setting up your own website is also straightforward. For this, you can find instructions in *The Rough Guide to the Internet* by Peter Buckley and Duncan Clark (Rough Guides, 2009). If you plan a site of any complexity, Mike Ward advises you how to plan it (*Journalism Online*, Focal Press, 2002). You can find his book online.

Writing online must be in html – hyper text mark-up language. Html is a series of pairs of commands or tags which tell a browser how to recreate your page on someone else's computer. <HTML> </HTML>, at the start and end, show a story is to be in html. <BOLD>and</BOLD> tell the browser that **and** should appear in bold.

Websites are famous for their hyperlinks, usually set in blue and underlined. A reader who clicks on to a link is transported to further relevant information on another page on your site, or to some other site of your choice. For instance, to link a reference to MPs' expenses to Heather Brooke's Your Right to Know website, the html command is <a href=www.yrtk.org>MPs' expenses<a>. To link to an explanation, on your own site, of how MPs have 'flipped' houses in their expenses claims, the commands can specify the file name (in the place of the website address).

Using Notepad on a PC or Text Edit on a Mac, you can compose a web page with all the html commands necessary for its re-creation elsewhere. However, there is normally no need for this. With Microsoft Publisher, for instance, you can save your copy as 'web page filtered' in html.

Microsoft Frontpage and Macromedia 's Dreamweaver are Wysiwygs – what you see is what you get – programmes which convert text to html. In newspaper offices, the click of a mouse converts text for printing into text for the website.

Stories on a news site

The opening page of a typical news site presents to the reader a list of stories each represented by a headline and a standfirst (which could also be called a teaser or long lead body). There may also be pictures. Click on a headline and the reader is transported to the main text of the story. Click on a picture and readers may be similarly transported, or they may find themselves watching a video.

All this is brought about by the site's content management system. The CMS presents a questionnaire to whoever is putting the story online. This may call for a headline, a standfirst and the main text. Newspapers tend not to put hyperlinks in the text but they do use headline hyperlinks linking to other stories on their site.

They can also link to the full version of an interview, rather than just an edited version. They can link to source documents of a story. Channel 4's account of the government inspectors' report on MG Rover and the Phoenix Four linked to the report in full (11 09 2009).

In print, newspapers do not normally advertise one another's work. Online, linking to other sites builds up the audience and the chance of appearing high in Google's response to a search. Some sites – the Drudge Report, digg, reddit – contain little but links to other sites.

A journalist putting a story online may be able to select 'tags'. These are words linking related stories. If a story is tagged MPs' expenses, headlines hyperlinking to other stories tagged 'MPs' expenses' will appear on the website near the story. If the system does not include tagging, journalists have to hunt out and link to related stories themselves.

A further possibility is to put in meta data. This indicates the sections of the site where it should appear. A story about jobs at Jaguar Land Rover might be sent to sections for employment, motors, companies, the West Midlands and India (where JLR's owner, Tata, is based).

Sites often ask readers to write in comments. Or, in an election report, you could get readers to select the results they want to read.

One surprising feature of web news pages is how similar many are to one another. They typically present a single news story in a broad column, with – on each side – links to other stories or sections of the site, plus advertisements. The reason for this is that the layout of a web page is laborious to change. You can replace one story with another and one picture with another. But changing the shape of the elements in a page requires much writing of computer code.

Headlines and standfirsts

Whereas readers of a newspaper can see the whole layout of a story and scan headline, captions and subsidiary headlines, readers online may at first see only a headline. If they are to click on it to see the story, the headline needs to grasp their interest. Usually, it needs to sum the story up – many website layouts allow for quite long, two-line headings.

A clever but vague headline will not do. However, you may get away with an intriguing headline. *Here is the story that everyone is reading.* The Sun online follows the printed *Sun's* punning headline style. An online headline should probably not include a placename, since it could be read anywhere in the world.

Both headline and standfirst must come within a stated number of characters, perhaps 140 for the standfirst. Since this standfirst will have the headline above it, it should amplify, not simply repeat, what the headline says. Some news sites use as standfirst the story's first paragraph.

Headline and standfirst also help persuade search engines to list your story above other people's. Shane Richmond of Telegraph.co.uk points out that names of people, businesses, teams and places do well in search engines (*BJR*, December 08). So, it seems, does the word terrorist.

Search engines can pick some unexpected winners. Google made the *Deccan Herald* in India top of its list for a story about a Panorama report on illegal immigrants in Southall, London. The *Age* (Melbourne) came out top for the jailing of the *News of the World's* former royal editor (*see* p. 22).

BBC News online

The BBC's is typical of technology-constrained national news sites. (For something quirkier, look at The Sun online which reflects the printed *Sun's* tabloid style.) On the evening of 5 June 2009, the BBC's lead story – on a cabinet reshuffle – ran to about 1000 words, down the centre of a long page. It appeared with links to many related stories. On other pages, other major news was similarly displayed. Stories on websites usually carry a date and probably a time. They don't use the words yesterday, today and tomorrow. The BBC's reshuffle report was illustrated with pictures of Prime Minister Gordon Brown, Tory leader David Cameron and Liberal Democrat Nick Clegg. You could click on the pictures to see videos of interviews and of Brown's press conference. An hour later, the page had been updated, Clegg giving place to possible future Labour leader Alan Johnson. Associated with the reshuffle story were panels setting out the new cabinet and also the county council election result, plus an invitation to readers to have their say. Also close to the reshuffle were the headlines of three related pages which readers could click on to. One of these pages gave the full video of the Brown press conference with, below it, a timed list of updates of cabinet and election news. Another comprised pictures of cabinet members. To the left of the cabinet reshuffle were links to other sections of the BBC site. To the right were click-on headlines for

14 more stories connected with the reshuffle and the council elections. There was also a link to political editor Nick Robinson's blog and to seven more video interviews.

How the internet is changing reporting

There is more to writing for the internet than satisfying a content management system, using much the same copy as has appeared or will appear in the newspaper or magazine.

Reed Business Information found that viewers of websites attached to its 45 magazines were growing more slowly in number than those of the internet as a whole. RBI was losing market share. It appointed Karl Schneider, former editor of *Computer Weekly*, to be editorial development director and do something about it. He believes that the internet is bringing change as great as the development of printing. Before printing, people got news by word of mouth, possibly from several people. Printing transferred power to the individual reporter, writing in a back room and passing printed copies to the public. The internet has now broken the reporter's monopoly. Members of the public can again provide news. They can write it themselves in a blog or they can contribute to websites. Reporters gain a new and different status as the central actors in networks of viewer comment.

In 2007, the story of foot-and-mouth disease in Surrey broke on a Friday evening, a bad time for journalists heading home for the weekend. Isabel Davies of *Farmers Weekly* didn't head home. Having seen a reader's tip about the outbreak, she confirmed it with the relevant ministry, Defra. Then she did not wait to construct a complete story. She put what Defra had said on the Farmers Weekly Interactive website. Readers responded. One gave news of an exclusion zone around the stricken farm, restricting movement. Readers asked: 'Does it include cattle under a year old?' Isabel went back to Defra and posted a reply on the website.

This is how Reed websites now handle breaking news, even though it challenges the tradition that no writer's work should be published till checked by someone else. Journalists put on to a Reed site what they know when they know it. Readers respond, enriching and perhaps correcting the story. After the story has run an hour or so, a journalist gathers all this material together in a report.

Reed websites are aimed at communities of readers – farmers, aircraft enthusiasts and so on. More and more content is created by these communities. The wisdom used to be that web reports should be short. But a 3000-word blog for the Flight website about a three-day visit to Boeing's aircraft factory attracted more interest than any other Reed story. So length is now flexible.

Interactions and links

The web can speak in illustrations as well as words. A Contracts Journal map allows building contractors to click on their town and see if any contracts notified to the European Community are on offer there. Reed receives the contract information through an RSS feed.

Illustrations can form part of a package of reports on a common theme. Each report appears on the web with links to the other reports in the package.

Packages covering important or dramatic events often include a timed account of how they unfolded: 12.30 Aircraft seen approaching the runway 12.32 Aircraft crashes. And so on. With the help of dipity.com, this can be put on an interactive timeline. Click on 12.32 and see what was then happening.

Much news is now published in blogs. A blog can publish a series of news stories on, say, progress on the site for the 2012 Olympic Games. As well as interplay between writers and reader-communities, there can be interplay between bloggers. A blogger outside Reed comments on a Reed article and puts in a link to it, so readers know what he/she is commenting on. So more readers look at the Reed site. Such links have an additional benefit. They register with Google's search engine and improve a web page's chances of appearing at the top of Google's responses to search queries.

Links can be mischievous. When George W. Bush was president of the United States, Google searches for the words 'miserable failure' used to give top place to Bush's home page.

Bringing in the cash

Websites now bring in 60 per cent of Reed Business Information's revenue, far above the 11 per cent of revenues reported by researchers Outsell in July 2009 as typical for news organizations' websites.

Not all the 60 per cent is from advertising. Some is from selling information. Karl Schneider is doubtful about the potential for selling general news, but expert information can be sold. For instance, the site XpertHR sells human resources managers information on how to fire people, if they need to.

Karl Schneider is now seeking to harmonize work on printed magazines with that on websites, to reduce the effort required. For instance, instead of a straightforward article, a magazine could use one built from web contributions and comments.

Straight news is best covered on websites. But print still has strengths. Magazines and newspapers are portable (though mobile phones with web access are portable, too). Print can publish bigger and higher-definition pictures. In summer 2009, the *Guardian* published a double page aerial photograph with boxes showing progress at different places on the Olympic site.

The development of the internet means that journalists have a lot to learn. The technology is constantly changing. Journalists wrestle with it, to get it to do things it does not do readily. Reed encourages staff to share their discoveries with one another. Every Thursday it holds 'Elevenses', when they meet to discuss a particular topic. Reed also has Yammer, which allows staff to ask one another for help.

Video reporting

Moving video pictures make news on the web more attractive and so also attract advertisers. Reporters, therefore, are commonly expected to bring back video from their engagements, shooting and recording it either with a mobile phone or a video camera. (They may also record audio, using an MP3 player with microphone and downloading it to Windows Media Player. For advice on audioreporting, see *Journalism Online* by Mike Ward (Focal Press, 2002).)

News websites garner video in several other ways. They interview people in their own studios. They receive video from agencies. They receive video from mobile-phone users.

Mobile-phone video

This provides pictures and sound together, though the sound may be poor. It can capture a sudden happening, such as a police officer pushing over doomed news seller Ian Tomlinson at a demonstration near the Bank of England in April 2009. A website can use mobile-phone video soon after it arrives.

The *Birmingham Mail* (May 2009) equipped reporters with Nokia N96 mobiles, which can take still and video pictures. They normally downloaded stills and video on to laptops. Then they added captions and sent the pictures on to the office by e-mail.

Making a video report

It is possible to put video camera and studio interviews straight on a website. More often, video camera pictures are used to construct a video report or podcast lasting, say, three minutes.

You can get an idea of what is involved if your computer has Windows XP and the Movie Maker programme. To try this, you need to download some audio and pictures on to your computer. (For the audio, you could select music on YouTube, get its web address and download it through mediaconverter.org.) Then open Movie Maker. This will divide your screen into two, with a menu on the left and a timeline beneath. Click 'import audio' on the menu and a folder will open in the left-hand screen. If this does not contain the audio you want, change the headline to the right folder. Click on the catchline for the audio and a symbol for it will appear in the screen. Drag the symbol down on to the audio timeline.

You can drag down pictures similarly on to the video timeline, above the audio. Normally, a still picturte will run for a second but this can be extended. When you have finished marrying pictures to audio, your completed video will run in the right-hand screen.

Colours look different in different lights

Birmingham Mail reporters, in May 2009, were using Sony A1E video cameras, which are light, and Sony Z7s, which are heavier but easier to adjust.

Adjustment is important. The focus and sound level must be right. The pictures must not be over or underexposed. People being interviewed should be a third of the way across the screen, looking into the remaining two-thirds.

Colours look different in outdoor light from indoor. But, on screen, a red coat needs to look the same whether outdoors or indoors.

High-quality video requires the camera to be on a tripod. So news reporters need a car to carry all their equipment: mobile phone, laptop, video camera, tripod and headphones.

They use video cameras mainly to shoot interviews. To make the interview footage into a video report, they also need additional video pictures, to accompany the voice-over – their account of the story. Voice-overs should not be wordy. They should let pictures tell the story when possible. Story-telling sequences of video are therefore useful.

A reporter's first task back at the office is to download – ingest – the video into a computer. If they spent half an hour interviewing and taking pictures, ingesting the video will also normally take half an hour.

Avid, which works on PCs, is a long-established computer programme for producing video reports from raw video. The *Birmingham Mail*, however, has moved on to an Apple Mac programme called Final Cut. Like Movie Maker, Final Cut displays two screens plus two timelines running across the screen, one for sound, the other for video accompanying the sound. The reporter can run the video he/she has taken on the left-hand screen, picking out passages or quotes for the video report (by typing i for in at the start of a passage and o for out at the end). These quotes can be dragged on to the video and audio timelines. (An alternative approach is to divide the whole of the video into identifiable clips and sub clips, a selection of which can be placed on the timelines later.)

The reporter then needs to record the voice-over, put it on the audio timeline, and construct from voice-over and interview quotes the audio component of the report. (This could also include music.)

Visually, this audio component can be seen stretched across the screen on its timeline. The interview quotes will have video attached. The final task is to attach appropriate video clips to the voice-over (and/or recorded music, if a musical soundtrack is being used). The natural pauses of speech divide the voice-over into sections with which video clips can be matched.

There is a simpler alternative. The reporter can set up the video camera to record himself/herself narrating the voice-over. So the voice-over is recorded with pictures attached to it. When all is finished, the end result will run on the right-hand video screen.

An editor turns the video report into a file for the website by using the CMS (content management system). The CMS puts on the screen a questionnaire. At the *Birmingham Mail* this asks for the report to be given a label, a headline, a teaser text (or standfirst), a small teaser picture, a larger picture, and tags.

Viewers who go to the website will see the headline, the teaser text and the two pictures. If they click on the pictures, the video will run. The tags will put on screen a list of headlines of related stories bearing similar tags.

A Manchester United tag, for instance, will bring up headlines of other Manchester United stories. By clicking on a headline, viewers can see the story to which it refers.

It is wise to be sure that anyone who appears in your video has agreed to appear in it (given the privacy protections of the Human Rights Act and the Data Protection Act). McNae suggests that people may be more reluctant to be shown on video than in pictures in the paper.

Video reporting is an art

Video takes reporting into the field of art and artifice. What looks life-like may be contrived to give a lifelike impression. What comes first may not have come first in reality. The BBC got into trouble in 2008 for showing the Queen apparently leaving a photo shoot when, in fact, she was arriving.

If you watch the news packages carefully which appear in TV bulletins, you will notice that – generally speaking – the message of a package is what the voice-over says it is. This is because the voice-over provides the context within which interviewees are seen and heard. If the voice-over text sounds hostile to them, they may not be 'heard' at all – viewers will discount what they say.

This does not mean that the reporter is personally hostile. He/she may be reporting someone else's views in the voice-over. These views are news and this is why the package is on TV.

So video presents new challenges to fair, even-handed reporters. In a written story, the quotes from those interviewed are permanently there to see. In video, the quotes are shorter and have come and gone in a moment, leaving only an impression behind. It is important that impression is fair, and that voice-overs on controversial subjects reflect the differing views.

The views that frame stories shape their message, writes former Reuterman Daniel Simpson (*BJR*, September 2009). Many reports, not only video reports, have a frame of received and possibly inaccurate wisdom.

The *Daily Telegraph* newsroom

Editor Will Lewis designed the *Daily Telegraph*'s newsroom at London's Victoria Station to integrate the printed and online Telegraph. In the old Canary Wharf office, they ran separately. The vast room, 37.5 metres by 37 (123 feet by 121), has a conference table at its centre. From this hub radiate spokes, seating staff covering news, home affairs, features, business, sport, comment. Reporters each have two screens, one for their writing, the other for the internet. They write for the online Telegraph or the printed *Telegraph* as the occasion demands.

Research has shown a spike of interest in the online Telegraph between 9.00 and 10.00am. People have read the morning paper and arrived at their offices, keen to know how the news has moved on. So the *Telegraph* produces an updated paper online. Preparations for this begin with a conference at 6.00am.

Research has also shown growing interest in news illustrated with moving pictures. These may come from the Press Association or Independent Television News. They may come from the *Telegraph*'s own TV studio. Telegraph TV brings in money, from advertising and sponsors. The *Telegraph* newsroom is an integrated production hub, gathering up material from all sources and delivering it to print and the website.

Andrew Currah of Oxford University suggests in *What's Happening to Our News* (Reuters Institute, 2009) that this we-can-do-everything approach may be too complex, too costly, too difficult to manage and too hard to train for, given the small size of training budgets. With a repeated need to train for the latest technology, the *Financial Times* rowed back a little in 2009 from complete integration. It uses different sub-editors for print and website.

Peter Horrocks, head of the BBC World Service, suggests in 'The Future of Journalism' (BBC College of Journalism, 2009) that media fortresses seeking to cover and provide everything are doomed. He hopes for greater co-operation, with different organizations concentrating on different strengths.

Google News, digg and reddit save effort and money by sorting out their copy by computer. Tom Whitwell, assistant editor of *The Times*, said (10 06 09) that Times Online, too, was seeking an automated process to analyse and classify text.

Daylife, a fully automated website, organizes news into clusters offered to other sites. Thus, USA Today's Cruise Log uses a Daylife story-cluster about cruises.

Blogs

'If blogs are boring and non-partisan, no one reads them,' wrote political blogger Guido Fawkes (www.order-order.com, 19 11 08).

What makes a good blog? San Francisco-based Merlin Mann, of 43Folders.com, suggested (19 08 08):

1. Identify your audience.

2. Have an individual voice. What is your personality like? What obsesses you? Good blogs reflect focused obsessions.

3. Good bloggers think about something a lot. They can't stop reading and writing about it.

4. Good blogs are written, not defecated.

5. Good blogs are weird.

6. Good bloggers try a little harder.

One way to success is to have an absorbing interest shared with other people, who could be anywhere in the world. Ruth Gledhill on Times Online has had great success exploring current controversies in Anglican Christianity. Her blog has won her more space than a newspaper could ever give her. She plays host to a vibrant and argumentative forum which can attract over 100,000 words of comment – more words than there are in this book.

Political blogs can make news. In 2009, Guido Fawkes broke the story of Downing Street adviser Damian McBride providing smears by e-mail about Tory leaders for a new Labour blog. In June, Guido disclosed more embarrassing e-mails, concerning Prime Minister Gordon Brown. They had been written the previous year by Lord Mandelson, who had since become Brown's chief lieutenant.

Guido Fawkes is the pseudonym of Paul Staines, an opinionated Right-Winger with a jaundiced view of politicians. Guy Fawkes, he has said, was the only man to enter Parliament with honest intentions. Guido told the *Guardian* (9 07 07) that his best sources were probably younger, savvier journalists whose stories had been discarded. Of course, they might have been discarded because they were unfounded or could not be verified. Bloggers do not necessarily adhere to journalistic standards.

Another leading political blog, Iain Dale's Diary – www.iaindale.blogspot.com – was anti-Brown like Guido Fawkes but more measured, publishing short comments such as you might find in the leader column of a serious, Right-leaning newspaper. It was popular (over 70,000 readers a month to Guido's 100,000) and, for people who live and breathe politics, it could provide essential information. During a government reshuffle in October 2008, Dale reported ministers' coming and going minute by minute (*BJR*, March 2009). Dale wrote in the *British Journalism Review* (December 2008): 'I saw blogging as a platform for me to give my views on politics. I could do it when I wanted and write what I wanted with no media filter.'

Not only Right-Wing bloggers have drawn blood. Brian Coleman, Tory Mayor of Barnet, was censured for calling music producer-cum-blogger Roger Tichborne 'poisonous' (*Barnet Times*, 10 09 09). Coleman faced paying £10,000 for his defence costs.

The rewards of blogging

Mark Kobayashi-Hillary, who writes on computing, technology and globalization, told a Commonwealth Journalists Association meeting in London (27 01 10) that he makes a living from blogging. This was something new. In 2008 Iain Dale's Diary, though popular and influential, did not make Iain Dale a living. But, even then, blogging gave Dale and others a high profile, which helped secure broadcasting and writing work. A service called MessageSpace sells advertising on blogs.

In the United States, blogging has paid well. Bloggers were making 75,000 dollars a year from a blog with 100,000 readers a month, according to Slate.com (*BJR*, December 2008). The US-based Daily Beast, which gives space to many bloggers, is published by Tina Brown, former editor of the *New Yorker* and once a journalist at the *Sunday Telegraph* in London. She told Andrew Marr (BBC1, 7 06 09) that The Beast has two million readers. Its main features are heavyweight blogs by leading writers and experts on American politics and world affairs. Comment, The Beast's mainstay, has proved popular online, and this popularity has boosted the status of commentators at British newspapers as well.

News at The Beast is represented by a 'Cheat Sheet', with tasters of major stories in other publications. The Beast thus follows the advice of Prof Jeff Jarvis, of the City University of New York: 'Cover what you do best. Link to the rest' (quoted by Peter Horrocks in 'The Future of Journalism', BBC College of Journalism, 2009).

In Britain, the *Guardian*'s Comment is Free features *Guardian* stalwarts but is also a platform for bloggers throughout the world. Editor Alan Rushbridger writes: *Comment is Free publishes more than 1000 pieces a month by a wide range of people, not many of them traditional journalists. They are politicians, doctors, lawyers, priests, rabbis, teachers, soldiers, businesswomen, academics* (BJR, September 2009).

The law online

In 2008 more than half the complaints received by the Press Complaints Commission concerned stories online. Online publication carries the same legal hazards as other publication. In April 2008 the chief executive of a Sunderland housing company won £100,000 for defamatory allegations on an anonymous website called Dads Place (*NE*, 4 04 08). Then Mathew Firsht won £22,000 from a former schoolfriend who put a false profile of him on Facebook (*FT*, 25 07 08).

Gina Ford – who advocated letting babies cry themselves to sleep – launched a suit against the Mumsnet website which she accused of 'vicious libels'. (One message accused her of strapping babies to rockets and firing them into South Lebanon.) The action was settled, Mumsnet paying part of Gina Ford's costs and urging members to be civil and fair in their comments (*Mail*, 10 05 07).

Every websurfer's hit on a website counts as a new publication under the law. So anything actionable should be deleted from a website quickly. Newspapers have had to pay damages for what they printed and for the same story on the website.

In two respects, English law is kind to websites. It requires libel claimants to show that people in England actually accessed the website they are claiming against. Also, section 1 of the 1996 Defamation Act may absolve sites of responsibility for the comments that outsiders post without their knowledge. However, if they receive a complaint about a comment, they must either delete it or be prepared to defend it in court.

Mr Justice Eady decided in July 2009 that, since Google's search engine is automated, Google is not liable for the defamatory material it may list in response to users' queries.

Sites may have to delete earlier crime stories when a suspect is arrested and contempt-of-court restrictions come into play. (For a fuller discussion, see McNae, Chapter 37.)

The courts' power over websites is, however, limited. Under the law of confidentiality, the *Guardian* was ordered to remove from its website leaked documents from Barclays Bank about tax avoidance (17 03 09). But websurfers could still find the documents on the wikileaks and techcrunch websites. Tweets on US-based Twitter undermined a UK court injunction against reporting a Parliamentary question about waste-dumping in the Ivory Coast (*FT*, 14 10 09).

Copyright is important to writers for the web as for writers for print. Websites and bloggers can be cavalier, not only publishing links to other sites but reproducing whole articles. The writer of an article so reproduced has little hope of redress, particularly if the reproducers are abroad.

Questions

1. How have you handled readers' comments online?

2. How have you won an audience for a blog?

3. Why do people read blogs?

8 Sportswriting

This has been our Achilles heel which has been stabbing us in the back all season
David O'Leary when at Aston Villa (*Independent*, 28 12 06)

Die schoenste Nebensache der Welt (The most beautiful side issue in the world)
Football, according to *Der Bund*, Bern (29 05 08)

A straight, simple kick was all that was needed and the rest was delirium with women screaming in all directions, odd ones fainting, more weeping, and the entire Blackpool team 'imparadised in one another's arms'.
Guardian, 1953: Matthews wins the cup
for Blackpool (reprinted 6 11 07)

TV has amplified the hunger for sports news

It seemed impossible to make a hospital appointment. The appointment-making call centre in Milton Keynes was engaged, morning, noon and night. But the evening that Manchester United played Chelsea in Moscow, a call got through. Everyone but the caller, it seemed, was watching the football.

Sport grips the imagination of people of all ages, as the *Guardian* passage above about Matthews shows. It inspires glorious mixed metaphors like O'Leary's. It inspires even teenagers to buy newspapers.

The Moscow match in May 2008 left few unstirred. This may be sad. Professor Daya Kishan Thussu, in *News as Entertainment* (Sage, 2008), sees growing sports coverage as part of a shift of attention away from public issues such as poverty. Was the cup final in Moscow important in any real sense? Within weeks, Euro 2008 had driven it from the sports pages. But enthusiasm for sport and sportspeople is a fact of British life. For many, it is their main encounter with real-live drama. Could fate be more cruel than to Chelsea stalwart John Terry? He had only to drive home a penalty to win the cup. Instead, he slipped on the rain-soaked grass. Prime Minister Gordon Brown at any rate thought that was important. He sent Terry a letter of condolence.

The French novelist and philosopher Albert Camus remarked: 'What I know most surely about morality and the duty of man, I owe to sport' (*FT*, 21 03 09).

Unfortunately, sport has become so important that it can be immoral, too. Harlequins' director of rugby, Dean Richards, was shamed for his part in faking an injury so that a goal kicker could take the field in a cup match in place of the 'injured' player (*Evening Standard*, 18 08 09). Sporting heroes attract admirers. In 2009, the golfer Tiger Woods fell from grace by engaging in an affair.

Sport always gripped a great many. But Matthew Engel, well-known for his stint writing about cricket for the *Guardian*, points out that it is television which has made sport an obsession for people of every social group. When football first appeared on TV, the days of writing about it seemed numbered. People could see what happened – so who would want their newspaper's fanciful descriptions? In fact, TV created a demand for more sportswriting. Sports fans were eager for their paper's view of the game. Rob Steen points out (*Sports Journalism*, Routledge, 2008) that they want to read about their team every day.

Reporting the play is only part of sportswriting. There's the history and statistics, the what happened last week, last year, back in 1902. There are the injuries, and the manager's son's operation. There are the interviews. There are the celebrity interviews. There are the drugs. There are the incidents on the pitch, in the stands, in night clubs and hotels, even on the Strictly Come Dancing floor.

There's the business of sport – betting, club finances, transfer deals, sponsorships, agents, the colourful people who own and manage clubs and players and racehorses, and the spats and intrigues and jealousies and corruption that go with all these. According to Italian author Umberto Eco (*FT*, 20 02 09) most sports fans prefer sports chatter to sport itself.

Off-field news and allusions crowd bewilderingly into match reports. *The goal elevated City back up to third place in the Barclays Premier League after their 6–0 drubbing at Stamford Bridge and, to put it in a historical context, it is the first time since 1902 that they have won their first seven home matches in all competitions, even if it was overshadowed slightly by an aggravation of Michael Johnson's groin problem and news of a similar injury suffered in training by Nelson Onuoha (The Times, 6 11 07).* The English sentence struggles to tell it all in a single breath.

A week in the life

Dave Evans covers West Ham United for the *Ilford Recorder*. That means writing, designing and sub-editing five pages of copy a week about West Ham. He also writes for the Recorder website. Colleagues cover Leyton

Orient, and Dagenham and Redbridge. The sports staff spend Monday to Wednesday filling the sports pages, 15 or 16 in all, several of them with match reports sent in by minor clubs. On Thursday mornings, West Ham's manager gives a press conference about Saturday's match. This is too late for the *Recorder* in which Dave has already written a match preview. However, the press conference feeds the *Recorder* website. Friday is a day off. Then on Saturday comes the match. By midweek when the *Recorder* appears, other media will already have described it. So Dave writes a comment rather than a shot-by-shot report. *This was a dour, disappointing game, short on quality and lacking in attacking ideas, decided by a controversial goal that probably should not have been allowed* (28 02 08).

He will chat to a player for a few minutes after a match. This is Dave's one chance for an interview for next week's paper. The club does not want him talking to players after the weekend. In fact, the club is his chief competitor. It runs its own website and wants to be first with any news. It may steal away for the website the player whom Dave wants to interview after a Saturday match.

North-East journalists covering Newcastle, Sunderland and Middlesbrough are in a similar situation. They get chances to interview players on the record only at the pre-match press conference and after the match. If there is only one match in the week, this can leave several days with not much to write about.

The end of the 2006/7 soccer season was memorable for West Ham. The Hammers faced relegation from the Premier League but clawed their way towards safety. They needed a win from their final game, against Manchester United at Old Trafford. Dave recalled (4 03 08): 'We decided to try to galvanize the West Ham support with a simple campaign. In our final edition before the game, we mocked up a huge picture of manager Alan Curbishley sitting on Steve McQueen's motorbike in the poster from the film *The Great Escape*. The campaign really took off. Apparently he was really pleased with it, more so when the Hammers won at Old Trafford. The response we got from the public was phenomenal.'

In the summer, Dave Evans covers bowls where he finds 'lots of characters. They are better to talk to than footballers.'

Covering a match

Sportswriters need to know a great deal about the sport they are covering. Their readers know a great deal. A match is part of a history, or series of histories, of teams and their players. Watching the match carefully is vital. You have to concentrate. In the chaos of a rugby union game, it is not always easy to see why players are penalized. You need to be a pleasant and helpful colleague for other sportswriters, for you will need their help.

You can find out before a game who are the team members and who the officials. You then have to identify them on the field. This is easier now players wear numbers and even their names. Cricket scoreboards may tell you who (what number) is bowling and who took a catch.

Match reporters now generally write on laptops. There are often wireless links at the ground to transmit copy to the office. Laptops can also be plugged into a phoneline, for a fee. Few reporters need to shout into a mobile phone above the roar of the crowd.

Do not be in a hurry to leave. There can be incidents and clashes when the match has ended. There may also be managers, coaches and others offering their views. Keep records of who played and what they scored.

Match reports

This was a short, simple and neat summary of a tennis match by Reginald Brace in the *Yorkshire Post* (28 06 06): *You had to feel sorry for Katie O'Brien at Wimbledon yesterday. Halfway through her opening match against the Italian Tathiana Garbin she looked to be in charge – a set and 3–1 up and thumping the ball with the zest you would expect from a sturdy product of North Humberside. Then it all began to go awry for Yorkshire's only representative in either singles event at the championships. Garbin moved up a gear. Katie started to look increasingly anxious after standing a tantalizing two points from victory at 6–5. The tie-break spilled away 7–2, and the final set was all Italy. Joy for Garbin, anguish for O'Brien.* This starts with a short, crisp sentence followed by a longer one which captures the hard-hitting O'Brien's supremacy in the first half of the match. Then, in only a few more words, we learn how it all went wrong. A six-word coup de grace brings the misery to an end. All this lacks is the score, 2–6 7–6 6–2, published on a different page. Brace also had a quote from O'Brien to sum up her misfortune: 'In my eyes I should have won today but my nerve gave way.'

Good match reports like this grasp the shape of the game and interpret and comment on it. In team games, they identify the players who made the greatest contributions to the result. An account of, say, a 0–0 draw at soccer can be boring if it simply describes the ball hitting the side-netting. The readers want to know who were the stalwart defenders and how they kept the strikers at bay.

Matthew Engel says he is awestruck by the ability of ex-professionals to read a game. He is himself a shrewd judge of what makes a match go one way or the other. He can also manage an imaginative turn of phrase. Women tennis players, oohing and aahing their way through Wimbledon, were *like owls calling to each other across a moonlit farmyard* (FT, 3 07 09).

Engel sees in good sportswriting a special skill: that of seeing, recalling and capturing in words a sudden incident on the field of play. Perhaps this, by Tom Dart in *The Times* (3 03 08), is an example of what he has in mind: *He was too smart for his own good, too unlucky for words. As two Milton Keynes Dons dawdled, Stephen Brogan, the Rotherham United player, sneaked in to pick up the loose ball, Willy Gueret, the goalkeeper, charged out, body met body and Brogan's left leg was broken in two places – a 50–50 challenge that will cost him 250 days of his blossoming career.*

A related skill is the ability to see what makes some players outstanding. Here is *FT* arts writer Peter Aspden's comment on Wimbledon star Roger

Federer: *Spectators watch in hope that they will see unimaginable angles, ridiculous rallies, inconceivable winners* (14 06 08).

You may need to mention some players' shortcomings. But criticize deftly and kindly. Professional players depend on their game for their living and they have to live with what you write. You may think that one of your media colleagues is a lazy, lousy writer but you would not say so in print. Rather than *Smith is a hopeless defender*, write *Smith mishit the ball in his own penalty area, allowing Jones to score the winning goal*.

Study the tactics and techniques that players and teams use. Informed comment on them can enhance your report.

Cricket writers these days have reverse swing to write about, a phenomenon discovered by Sarfraz Nawaz, a Pakistani bowler, in the 1970s. It can turn a game when the batting side seems to be heading for a big total. Swing always used to be associated with a shiny new ball. But a much used, unshiny ball will also veer on its way through the air, if it is rougher one side than the other and the seam is tilted towards the rougher side. Sarfraz found he could surprise batsmen by swinging an old ball in the reverse direction to his new-ball swing. Reverse swing is controversial because a ball can be roughened on purpose. An England v. Pakistan match in 2006 was abandoned after umpire Darrell Hair alleged during the England second innings that the ball had been tampered with.

Don't forget the crowd

The abandonment of the 2006 England v. Pakistan match affected thousands of spectators who lost the cricket they had paid for. Matches involve spectators as well as players. Matthew Engel, in his Test match reports of the Ashes series in 2009, always noted what the spectators were up to, singing raucous songs or booing Australian captain Ricky Ponting to the crease.

The final, twenty eighth paragraph of a somewhat somnolent local cricket report recorded that a six hit a boy in the face, causing a seven-minute delay. Who was the boy? Who went to help him? How badly was he hurt?

An attractive, off-beat approach in *The Northern Echo* to a Wimbledon match (29 06 06) recognized that tennis is also about those who watch: *She was almost persuasive but, for Maggie Barton who made a 250-mile round trip to be here, her blind faith proved just that. Tim Henman has more than his share of fifty-something superfans but, as Roger Federer ended his Wimbledon in straight sets yesterday, they were already looking to a future without him. 'Maybe I'll feel the same about Andy Murray one day but I can't see it,' said a dejected Maggie whose long, cold night on an SW19 pavement repaid her with nothing but problems with her sciatica.*

Different approaches

Match reporters face a decision. Do they concentrate on a match already reported on TV? Or do they raise other issues such as the situation the match has created? Do they keep it simple? Or do they weave a complex web to fascinate the knowledgeable? Two contrasting approaches appeared on opposite pages in the *Daily Mail* (28 04 08). Here is one opening, which went for complexity: *Steve Watson spoke of ringing his former West Bromwich Albion team-mates, begging them to perform the favour of a convincing win at the Hawthorns tonight. The veteran Sheffield Wednesday midfielder's only problem could be finding a telephone line not engaged by the hordes of people with a vested interest in the outcome of the game. Tonight's fixture between West Bromwich and Southampton has suddenly become crucial in determining the glory and heartbreak of the Championship.* This opening by Ray Matts ignores the match in which Sheffield Wednesday has just beaten Leicester. Instead, Matts switches to the match tonight between West Bromwich Albion and Southampton. Matts's approach is designed for readers who know about the promotion and relegation battles and also know that The Hawthorns is West Bromwich's ground.

The report opposite Matts's began in a more straightforward fashion: *Hull captain Ian Ashbee admitted his late winner was the most important goal of his 14-year career. With five minutes to go, it seemed that his side would have nothing at stake at Ipswich on Sunday, their play-off place having already been secured and automatic promotion ruled out. But Ashbee's headed goal changed everything, keeping alive Hull's chances of finishing in the top two.* (Hull won promotion through the play-off.) Arindam Rej's report on the Hull game captures its dramatic moment, while still catching the significance of another game to come. The report later features a tackle that seriously injured Hull striker Windass.

Though Saturday matches are covered on TV and in the Sunday papers, a sharp, vivid description of the drama on the pitch lifts a match report even on Monday.

'We only just got away with it'

Broadcaster and columnist Carolyn Hitt used a light-hearted style to describe on Monday a Saturday rugby match between Italy and Wales (*Western Mail*, 16 03 09). Her intro read: *We came, we saw, we only just got away with it.* She went on: *It was the uncharacteristic errors and fumbles that lingered most in the minds of the relieved* (Welsh) *supporters as they headed for the Piazza del Popolo for the post mortem. How could Hooky have missed that sitter? How scary was Mark Jones's scramble with Rubini on the tryline? And what was that crab-dance in to touch from Andy Howell? And why, why, why so much kicking? Not just from Wales. This Six Nations is turning rugby into the European Aerial Ping Pong Championships.* She also gave a taste of Rome outside the Stadio Flaminio, featuring a sing-in involving Welshmen – led by entertainer Max Boyce – and pupils from a French school.

Do match reporters strive too hard for effect? Iain Dale's account of West Ham v. Portsmouth (15 11 08) in his blog West Ham Till I Die was conversational and low key, while picking up the match's salient features. It began: *Let's start off with the plus points. The main one was that, for the first time in*

25 games, I think, we kept a clean sheet. Defoe had a couple of chances but, apart from that, we were fairly safe. The second plus point was the performance of Valon Behrami, especially in the first half when he was buzzing around everywhere, tackling everything that moved. He was hacked to the ground late in the first half and wasn't quite the same afterwards. Dale is a popular blogger. Might some readers prefer his simpler style?

An evening at the cricket

Here is an unpublished report of a 20/20 cricket match between Surrey and Hampshire at The Oval on 18 June 2008. The figures in brackets refer to the comments below.

Three sixes in an over (1), in a 90-run partnership between Abdul Razzaq who hit 65 and ex-Test batsman (2) Mark Ramprakash (60), were not enough. Surrey scored 175 runs but lost to Hampshire by four wickets in a 20/20 match at the Oval last night.

A quick 45 from Michael Lumb – before he went down the wicket to Saqlain, missed and was bowled (3) – took Hampshire to 53 in five overs (4). They maintained their run rate and, in the end, had an over to spare. This win put Hampshire on six points alongside Kent and Essex in the 20/20 championship (5). Middlesex has won all its four matches and leads the southern division with eight points.

Surrey missed James Benning (5), who hit 50 not out against Middlesex but has a problem with his hip. His replacement as opener, Ali Brown (6), was out first ball. However, Surrey's bowling, opened aggressively by Chris Jordan, looked better than Hampshire's, which included seven wides. Surrey also held catches more securely and slow bowlers Schofield and Saqlain, brought into the side as substitutes, took five wickets between them. But every time they winkled out a free-scoring Hampshireman, there was another to take his place (7).

This was not cricket as it used to be. For one thing, much of the sizeable crowd regarded it as primarily a social occasion (8). There was constant standing up and sitting down in the stands as city workers arrived or went to buy pints at £3.30 each in biodegradable starch beakers from young men with beer-laden backpacks (3). In the Hampshire innings, the crowd essayed a few Mexican waves and booed the spectators in front of the pavilion for not joining in. Big hits and the fall of wickets were greeted with triumphant music on the loudspeakers.

On the pitch, the players – like the grey clouds above – looked rather drab, Hampshire in navy blue, Surrey in grey tops and brown trousers. Unkind observers might have thought they had wandered into a match between Dartmoor and Pentonville (9).

Surrey started and finished quietly, with only two runs in their first two overs and one in their last. In between, Abdul Razzaq hit four sixes. Ramprakash, a fleet-footed winner in Strictly Come Dancing (2), hared between the wickets and hit Nantie Hayward out of the ground. Hayward caught and bowled him next ball.

Hampshire, however, had their hundred up in 11 overs (4), two fewer than Surrey, and when they weren't hitting boundaries they were running quick singles. They reached 155 in 16 overs (4), leaving only 21 to score in their last four. Within three hours of the start of play, Greg Lamb hit a final boundary and they had won (10).

Table 8.1   Surrey v. Hampshire, The Oval, 18 June 2008

Surrey

S.Newman b Taylor	15
A.Brown c Harvey b Hayward	0
M.Ramprakash c&b Hayward	60
U.Afzaal c Benham b Lamb	19
Abdul Razzaq c. Ervine b Harvey	65
T.J.Batty c Carberry b Harvey	4
C.Jordan not out	1
M.Spriegel not out	0
Extras	11
Total (6 wickets)	175

Bowling Hayward 4-0-41-2; Taylor 4-0-38-1; Riazuddin 4-0-36-0; Harvey 4-0-20-2; Lamb 4-0-36-1

Hampshire

I.Harvey lbw b Collins	1
M.Lumb by Saqlain	45
M.Carberry st Batty b Schofield	45
C.Benham c Schofield b Saqlain	6
S.Ervine c Brown b Saqlain	46
N.Pothas c Jordan b Schofield	0
G.Lamb not out	22
M.Dawson not out	3
Extras	9
Total (6 wkts)	177

Bowling Jordan 2-0-25-0, Collins 3-0-40-1; Razzaq 4-0-28-0; Saqlain 4-0-24-3; Spriegel 3-0-25-0; Schofield 3-0-33-2

In the bowling, the first figure is the number of overs the bowler has bowled, the second the number of maiden overs, the third the number of runs conceded and the fourth the number of wickets. In 20/20 a bowler is allowed to bowl only four overs. The Daily Mail's published scorecards usefully include how batsmen got out, for example, caught at short leg.

Commentary

(1) There was no match winning or losing moment to highlight, nor a tight finish as in the Kent/Essex match the same evening. The three sixes seemed the next best thing for the intro.

(2) Tells the reader about Ramprakash's claims to fame.

(3) Give detail when possible.

(4) The rate of scoring is crucial in a 20/20 game. Both sides lost six wickets but Hampshire scored faster.

(5) These put the match in the context of the 20/20 championship and Surrey's previous game.

(6) It is important to know who the players are, especially if there are changes in the published side. The loudspeaker said that Chris Schofield had come in in place of opener Benning. But it was Ali Brown, number 3 on the scorecard, who opened the innings.

(7) This paragraph assesses the play and why Hampshire won. Details of who scored what are in the scorecard.

(8) The spectators are part of the action. Always find something to mention about them, though obviously you would not be able to mention the beer again in another 20/20 match report. You could, however, comment on the relentlessly upbeat tone of the man on the loudspeaker. Where did they find him?

(9) Don't be afraid to tell it as you see it. Readers who went to the match may have thought something similar.

(10) The piece ends strongly, on a stressed syllable.

Where match reports go wrong

They are overloaded with historical and off-field detail

Sportswriters do go on a bit sometimes. They ramble. Better choose the most striking historical parallels than unload into your report the whole record book. The golfer scoring 69 yesterday may be a former amateur champion who played in the same tournament last year, shone alongside Vijay Singh in Miami, hit an opening 65 in the USPGA and is ranked 28th in Europe and 112th in the world (*NE*, 4 04 08). But yesterday's 69 would have been a five-under-par 66 if the golfer had not dropped three shots at the last three holes. The lapse makes him more than a series of entries in the record book. He is a human being kicking himself for messing up a wonderful chance to win an international tournament.

They contain too many long sentences

Sport is action. Long sentences bog action down. Putting separate pieces of action into the same sentence can result in a jumble: *David Villa had given the Spaniards a 28th-minute lead from the penalty spot after Lilian Thuram had bundled over Pablo inside the area before Franck Ribery equalized shortly before half-time* (*NE*, 28 06 06).

The record book can be to blame as here: *Garbin is ranked 68 in the world compared to O'Brien's rating of 235 but the fact that she had lost six successive first-round matches at Wimbledon gave her 20-year-old opponent from Hessle, North Humberside, genuine grounds for optimism* (*YP*, 28 06 06). Sorted out, this could read: *Twenty-year-old O'Brien from Hessle, North Humberside, had real grounds for hope. Garbin had a higher world ranking but had lost six first-round matches in a row at previous Wimbledons.*

Too much elegant variation

Elegant variation – the use of a description rather than a name – has been popular in sportswriting for more than a century. But it sets puzzles to less knowledgeable readers. Which cricketer is 'his fellow Australian'? Not everyone would know that New Zealand rugby league player Vainikolo and 'the Bradford winger' were one and the same. But a writer who named England defender Rio Ferdinand as Ferdinand every time could be confident that everyone knew who he was writing about.

Sportswriting through the week

Much sports reporting is not of a particular match. It interviews players. It discusses the fortunes of clubs and managers, and business deals. All this benefits from a simple, fluent, humorous approach.

> *Waiting for the return of Craig Bellamy has been almost like waiting for the second coming. There have been one or two moments, like when he was reported to have played in a behind-closed-doors friendly, when you thought it was only a matter of time before you saw him in the flesh. But, alas, his followers still wait patiently, and the latest news suggests that they will have a while to wait yet. Dave Evans, Ilford Recorder (21 02 08)*

Steven Howard (*Sun*, 13 03 09) managed a tongue-in-cheek simplicity: *Strike up Land of Hope and Glory. Wave the cross of St George. The Big Four are all through to the Champions League quarter finals. The English are the toast of Europe. Or are we?* (He goes on to point out that the four clubs fielded only nine English players out of 44.)

The *Sun* (6 02 09) contained several short intros: *Joe Calzaghe has bowed to family pressure and hung up his gloves; Tony Adams insists the Portsmouth boo-boys will not force him to quit; Shay Given says he was ready to quit football – because Newcastle had become such a shambles; Michel Platini is ready to ban crazy-spending Manchester City from European competitions.*

In the last of these, *crazy-spending* catches the nub of the story. Reporter Antony Kastrinakis's piece continues with five paragraphs of UEFA president Platini's actual words, not just a summary of his campaign to curb the English Premier League.

The *Daily Mail's* intro – which did not focus specifically on Manchester City – was flaccid in comparison with the *Sun's*. It read: *Michel Platini put himself on a war footing with the Premier League yesterday by pledging to curb the power of their big-spending clubs with stringent new financial regulations for European competitions.*

Here are two more rather pedestrian intros:

1. *Lewis Hamilton says he does not read the papers. This must be true. How else can you explain his demeanour as he faced the press at the launch of his book* Lewis Hamilton, My Story, *yesterday? The British Formula One driver looked like a man fresh from a three-hour yoga session rather than one who has been the subject of sneers and sarcasm over his decision to leave behind his fans in the United Kingdom and live in Switzerland (The Times, 6 11 07).*

2. *There can't be many better qualified than Daley Thompson to give their observations on the present state of British athletics – and the double Olympic champion pulls no punches on the subject (NE, 29 06 06).*

In intro 1, the first three sentences are superfluous. The piece could have begun: *Lewis Hamilton looked like a man fresh from a yoga session when he met the press yesterday about his book* Lewis Hamilton, My Story. Intro 2 told readers nothing, and the following paragraph told them only of Daley Thompson's past exploits as a world-beating decathlete. So what was Daley actually on about? We finally learn in the last seven paragraphs of a 24-paragraph story – clearly, he got more persuasive as he went on. He wanted sports, he said, to 'drag the kids through the doors'.

❝ Now the kids say: 'Hold on a minute. I'm not going to go down there and sweat and do all that running around. I'm going to be a world champion rally driver in half an hour on the PlayStation' … Ninety per cent of all sports coverage is football. Other sports have to buck up their ideas and start marketing themselves. ❞

Daley also reminisced: 'It was different when I was a kid. We were running around. We walked to school. We walked back. We hardly ever got on a bus and most of our parents didn't have cars.' The interviewer had done well to get Daley to say what he did. It was a shame not to have brought the lively material up to the top of the piece. It might then have avoided the lame, negative headline *Daley has no instant fix for nation's problem*.

Many sportswriters seem to expect little of the sportspeople they interview. So they write down what they said, how they said it, rambling from subject to subject and back again. Yet maybe there is a glint of gold amid the dross. The writer's task is to get the best material to the top of the story.

Seek out the sports stars who are, in some way, out of the general run. Whereas most leading golfers look prosperous and athletic, Angel Cabrera, the Argentine who won the US Masters in 2009, was overweight and began life poor. He went to the local golf course, as a caddy, because he needed a job.

Try to achieve impact by using your material well, rather than by exaggerated language. Sports metaphor can become overblown, as here: *The first duty for Bishop must be to impose a structure to the juggernaut that is Hamilton's public persona (The Times, 6 11 07).*

If you are imaginative, it is possible sometimes to get beyond the routine of sports reports and interviews. A Swiss paper, the *Baseler Allgemeine Zeitung* (31 05 08), heralded the Euro 2008 footballfest with a scientific analysis of the vulnerable limb which makes football possible, the human leg.

Looking it up

The sports reference books that were once the bibles of sportswriters are consulted less these days. Sportswriters turn instead to the internet:

- www.soccerbase.com has the basic information about footballers, teams, managers, transfers and so on.

- www.cricinfo.com does a similar job for cricket. There is also www. golftoday.co.uk.

- www.bbc.co.uk/sport is a wide-ranging site. Apart from football, cricket, rugby, tennis and golf it features boxing, athletics, snooker, racing, cycling, sport-for-disabled-people, the Olympics, squash, netball, darts, bowls, basketball, baseball, American football, ski-ing and ice hockey.

- www.telegraph.co.uk/sport is also well thought of. Like the BBC site, it has running stories about matches in progress.

Questions

1. Write a profile of a sportsman or woman whom you admire.

2. Who is your favourite sportswriter? What do you admire about his/her work?

9 Reporting the courts

Justice in the United Kingdom must be seen to be done. Therefore courts are open to journalists and the public, and absolute privilege protects fair, accurate and contemporaneous court reports against libel actions. If journalists are excluded or their reporting restricted, there must normally be an Act of Parliament which requires or empowers the court to exclude or restrict them.

These restrictions grow ever more complex. To fully grasp what you can and cannot safely report, you need to read McNae's *Essential Law for Journalists*. What this chapter attempts is to suggest how, given the way the courts work, the many stories told in court can best be presented to readers.

The media-law section of www.holdthefrontpage.co.uk publishes topical articles about the courts and media law.

Shining a light on life

Courts and tribunals cast light into dark places: corruption, cruelty to children, bad behaviour in City firms, deaths on active service and even (*FT*, 19 02 09) the co-operation between Russia's security men and criminals. They also illumine the stories and struggles of some of society's least noticed members.

- A young woman at Redbridge magistrates court admits assaulting an exasperating former friend. Her explanations carry a ring of desperate truth. She gets a 12-month supervision order to help her sort out her life.

- An elderly Sikh denies that he was disorderly while drunk. He lives next to a school and complains that schoolboys ring the police about him on their mobile phones.

- A young man has been arrested because he failed to appear in court after being bailed on a charge that he assaulted his girlfriend. On the court day he was in North Cyprus, with the girlfriend, looking after his sick mother. He vainly relied on his brother to tell the court where he had gone. The magistrates fine him £50 for failing to appear, or one day's imprisonment. He has been in the cells overnight and so has already served the sentence.

Fairness and accuracy are essential

There is no fundamental difference between court reporting and other reporting. The requirements are the same: to understand what has happened and to report it fairly, accurately, clearly and in a manner to catch the attention of readers. Fairness and accuracy are essential to ensure your paper or website has the defence of privilege against a libel action and to avoid injustice to the accused, witnesses and people mentioned in the proceedings but not involved.

Outsiders against whom allegations are made in court may ask your publication to publish a reply or rebuttal. This could suggest a witness has been lying. The wording of such a reply needs to be cleared with a lawyer.

Before a crime becomes a court case

Do not imply that a named person may be to blame, when you report a crime, fire or accident. Cars collide with trees but are 'in collision with' other cars. The classic, safe crime story reads: *Police chased two young men yesterday after a bank hold-up. Later a man was arrested.* This account does not say if the man arrested is one of those chased.

Again, you might report: *Police inquiring into a bank raid issued a description of a man they would like to interview. He is George Smith.* You should not say Smith is a suspect.

Many crime stories run for days before anyone is arrested and criminal proceedings begin. For a year after the three-year-old Madeleine McCann disappeared in Portugal nothing much happened. Newspapers filled this void with speculation and allegation. As a result, Madeleine's parents and a local man, Robert Murat, won six-figure damages for libel.

Criminal proceedings begin with an arrest or the issue of a warrant or summons. From that point, reporting is subject to the law of contempt of court (unless the arrested person is released without charge and without being bailed). You can still write about the incident that led to the arrest but, under the Contempt of Court Act 1981, your report must not create a substantial risk of serious prejudice to forthcoming court proceedings. The *Sunday Mirror* was fined £75,000 in 2002 for publishing an interview with the father of a victim of assault.

A crime story should not appear near a report of a court appearance relating to the crime. Papers should not publish pictures of people whose identity will be an issue at a trial. However, no one has been charged with contempt for publishing a police wanted-person appeal.

As a result of a *Sunday Times* victory at the European Court of Human Rights, the Contempt of Court Act allows comment on public issues raised by a court case, provided any effect on the court hearing is merely incidental.

The courts' interpretation of the Contempt Act, with its proviso that the risk of prejudice should be substantial, have made the law less rigorous. Judges have considered reports published a long while before a trial as unlikely to seriously prejudice it. The desire for impact does cause newspapers and broadcasters to publish arguably prejudicial stories (*see* p. 194).

Magistrates courts

Magistrates courts sit regularly in just about every English town. The police ought to inform newspapers of any special additional hearings. (In Scotland, local councils run district courts. These are being replaced with justice of the peace courts run by the court service.)

Magistrates are unpaid and have a legal adviser. They have a chairman who sits with one or more fellow magistrates. Or a district judge may sit alone. If the chairman is not present, another magistrate will preside. If his/her name is Hilary Smith, he/she will appear in reports as Mr/Mrs/Ms Hilary Smith, presiding. It is important to identify who the magistrates are. Magistrates cannot keep their identities secret.

Anyone accused of a serious offence is likely to be represented by a lawyer. The case against the accused will probably also be presented by a lawyer, from the Crown Prosecution Service. In Scotland, the counterpart of the CPS is the Crown Office and Prosecutor Fiscal Service. In Northern Ireland, it is the Public Prosecution Service.

Courts have duty solicitors, to advise accused. They also have probation officers and other specialists whose advice may help with sentencing. You can clear up queries with any of these people when the magistrates are not in court. The legal adviser sits in front of the magistrates, with the lawyers opposite. Probation officers and other specialists probably sit at the side.

Court lists are likely to give the names of the accused, their addresses and the offences alleged. In July 2009, court staff were advised to provide these lists by e-mail. You need to check what the list says with what is said in court. The legal adviser will ask accused people their names, dates of birth and addresses, and whether they plead 'Guilty' or 'Not guilty'. Witnesses are not obliged to give their addresses.

The accused may well not be tried straight away. What can be reported of adjourned, remand, bail and legal-aid hearings is normally restricted to the court's decisions, the charges, bail arrangements, the names of the people involved and the accused's name, occupation and address. Arguments for and against bail cannot be reported. On no account should you report any reference to previous convictions.

In court, the prosecutor may accept a guilty plea to, say, driving without due care, and drop a more serious charge – dangerous driving. A man accused of attempted murder found the charge reduced to common assault. Such changes must be reported.

If an accused pleads 'Not guilty', the prosecutor calls witnesses to prove the accused's guilt. It is better to report the first-hand stories of the witnesses than the prosecutor's second-hand, if polished, account.

Magistrates can protect witnesses with *special measures* – for example, they can allow them to sit behind screens or give evidence by videolink. Under section 25 of the Youth Justice and Criminal Evidence Act 1999, they can exclude all but one reporter when they hear evidence from a vulnerable witness in a case concerning a sexual offence or where the witness might be intimidated. Special measures must not be reported.

Under the 1999 Act, section 46, magistrates can also prevent identification of a vulnerable witness. However, the law lords, at least for the present, have decided that courts need to know who witnesses are. They cannot rely solely or mainly on anonymous witnesses. In Scotland, a new Vulnerable Witnesses Act has become law. The magistrates may break for lunch or till another day. Reports of the case before the break will probably contain more of the prosecution than the defence. Report defence challenges to what prosecution witnesses say. Give a fair account of the defence after the hearing resumes.

Requests and restrictions

When you are covering a court, someone may ask you not to report a case. Refer the request to your editor. Tell your editor also about any request or order from magistrates. If they make an order, find out under what section of what Act. Journalists have successfully challenged magistrates who exceed their powers.

Complainants in many sex cases must not be identified in the media. But the courts have generally resisted efforts to protect accused adults from identification.

Under section 39 of the Children and Young Persons Act, magistrates can order you not to identify an accused or witness under 18 in adult court. (If you leave the court, make sure no such order has been made while you were out.) But they should not make a section 39 order automatically. They should first weigh the case for open justice against that for protecting a young person. They cannot forbid you to identify a dead child, unless they have a special reason.

The Press Complaints Commission upheld a complaint from a woman witness whose local paper reported her mentioning her schoolboy son's mental health problems in court evidence (PCC Report 41).

Section 4 of the Contempt of Court Act gives courts power to postpone – but not ban – reporting if it would prejudice court proceedings.

Section 11 of the Contempt Act empowers courts, if justice requires it, to ban publication of a name they have directed should not be mentioned in court. The case might involve blackmail, or an accused might face another trial in another court.

Magistrates can exclude press and public if they believe that justice cannot be done with them present. Perhaps, secrets are being disclosed.

Court cases can raise public issues. For example, the accused may complain about their treatment. There is a public interest in reporting this.

Beyond the hearing

After one case, a man was carried shoulder-high from the court that acquitted him. Some people are keen to make statements and comments when their case is over. But don't seek a statement from someone who is anxious.

Any pictures must be taken outside the court precincts. Television has narrowed the definition of precincts. It commonly shows people going into or coming out of the court building or making a statement on the court steps. However, photographers can be in trouble if witnesses complain they were hassled.

Youth courts

Magistrates hear cases against offenders under 18 in youth courts, unless they are charged jointly with adults. The public are excluded but media representatives have a right to be there under section 47 of the Children and Young Persons Act.

In reporting a youth court, you must not give name, address or school or in any other way identify the accused or any witness under 18. Any other way includes hairstyle, clothing, home village or even a tell-tale sequence of events given in evidence. You must also avoid reporting a detail which, with details in other newspaper reports, can identify the accused or a young witness.

The magistrates can release you from these restrictions but only in the public interest or to avoid injustice to the young accused. The restrictions also apply if a young offender appears in a crown court for sentence.

In reporting youth court, avoid the words conviction, sentence and charge. A young offender is accused, not charged, and found guilty, not convicted.

ASBOs

The purpose of an anti-social behaviour order is usually to stop someone from doing something. It tells people what young Jimmy is not supposed to do. This conflicts with the principle that young offenders should not be named.

There is no automatic ban on naming young people in ASBO proceedings, either in a magistrates' court or youth court. Magistrates can impose a ban under section 39 of the Children and Young Persons Act but must have a good reason. In youth court an accused cannot be identified in an account of a criminal case related to the ASBO, unless the court decides he/she can be. So, if you name the accused in reporting the ASBO, you cannot report the criminal case. If young accused are before a youth court for breaking ASBOs, an Act of 2005, quoted in McNae, allows them to be named unless the court decides they cannot be.

Crown court

Criminal offences are of three types. Summary offences are tried by magistrates. Indictable offences such as rape and murder must go to crown court (or, in Scotland, the sheriff court). Triable-each-way offences can be tried by magistrates but accused may choose trial by jury at crown court if they risk jail. You should report it if someone elects to go for trial. Don't just say they were committed for trial.

Magistrates can commit to crown court for trial without hearing witnesses, unless the accused has no lawyer or the defence submits the evidence is insufficient.

If an accused is committed or sent for trial, reporting of the committal proceedings is restricted (*see* McNae). In essence, the restrictions mean that charges but no evidence can be reported. The restrictions will be lifted if the accused or all the accused request this (perhaps because they hope witnesses will come forward). If the magistrates decide to try one of a group of accused themselves and not commit him/her to the crown court, the trial before the magistrates can be reported.

If an accused is committed for trial or sentence, tell your chief reporter or news editor so that the crown-court case will be covered. Fairness requires this. A report of the committal, giving the charges, is inevitably damaging. At crown court, the accused could be cleared.

Crown court hearings follow a similar pattern to those in a magistrates' court, with two important differences. Before the jury considers its verdict, the judge will sum up, reviewing the law and the evidence. This is helpful to reporters unable to attend the full hearing. Second, if the jury finds an accused guilty, the judge will pass sentence, explain his/her decision and make comments.

As already mentioned, complainants in rape and many other sex cases must not be identified in newspaper reports. The Press Complaints Commission upheld a complaint against a rape trial report which included the victim's hobby and what she was wearing when attacked. From these details, people could work out who she was (PCC Report 41).

In incest and other inside-the-family cases, the PCC advises that newspapers should name the accused but not use the word incest or state the accused's relationship to the unnamed victim(s).

The case of Baby P, a child who died from injuries sustained in his Haringey home, raised several issues. At first, he and his abusers were not named although there is normally no bar on naming accused people or a dead child. A bar was imposed in part because Baby P's stepfather was also accused in another case but, more importantly, to protect Baby P's brothers and sisters. However, in August 2009, the bar was lifted.

If crown courts seek to restrict reporting under the Contempt of Court Act or the Children and Young Persons Act, newspapers can appeal. Anyone seeking an injunction to restrict media reporting should tell the Press Association, which runs an injunction alerts service.

Telling the story

Court cases have a story to tell. It is important to tell that story, despite the reporting restrictions and the flood of comment from all and sundry that court cases can evoke. The *Derby Telegraph* (21 07 09) reported the jailing of three former executives of Derby County football club for conspiring to defraud the club of up to £375,000. One said he had received a legitimate payment for brokering a £15 million loan. The *Derby Telegraph* story began, reasonably enough, with a comment from the judge, that the three thought themselves above the law. But it never quite got round to explaining what had happened. What was the situation at Derby County in 2003, when it was taken over by a new consortium? Where did the three accused come in? Where did the £15 million loan come from, what was it for and what happened to it?

A trial at Snaresbrook

Here is a report of a case heard at Snaresbrook Crown Court in London in June 2008. The names of accused and victim have been changed. Ali A, the accused, was a short, wiry man in a black leather jacket. He was a waiter who aspired to be a taxi driver. He had a wife and two small children and they lived with his parents and other relatives in a crowded house in the East End. He could not read English well. He was proud of his car, his one expensive possession, which his mother had helped him buy. The numbers in the text refer to points discussed at the end of the report.

> *Road rage (1) led to a 25-year-old Leytonstone waiter (2) and father of two being sent to prison for two years yesterday. A jury at Snaresbrook Crown Court found him guilty of assault causing actual bodily harm (3) to an off-duty bus-driver. His black Polo car worth £2000 (4) was confiscated. He was also given three months for driving while disqualified, to run concurrently (5) with the two-year sentence.*
>
> *The waiter and the bus-driver agreed (6) the incident began with the black Polo pulling in front of the bus driver's car in the Mile End Road and 'cutting it up'. They also agreed it ended with the bus driver on the ground in nearby Hannibal Road after being hit with a steering-wheel lock. He suffered a two-inch cut to his scalp and found blood pouring down his face.*

The bus driver said he was attacked not just by the waiter but by a taller passenger, one of three in the Polo. The waiter, Ali A, of Red Street in nearby Bow, said he was scared of the bus driver (7) – 6ft 2 to his 5ft 3 – and hit him in self-defence. He denied anyone else got involved. He pleaded 'Not guilty' (8).

Judge Brasse (9) said a prison sentence was inevitable, though this was A's first conviction for violence. Road rage was an aggravating factor.

Anthony R, the bus driver, of Blue Street, Whitechapel, told the court that, after the Polo cut him up, he flashed his lights and both cars stopped at traffic lights leading into Stepney Green (10). The other driver shouted at him and tried to open his (R's) passenger door.

He turned into Stepney Green and then into Hannibal Road where he saw the Polo again. He started to write down its registration number. 'By this time, the driver and tall passenger caught up to me (11). He put his hand through the window and grabbed me by the throat. The tall guy shouted at him to get my keys. I sped off but a car was coming the other way. I got out of the car. He was standing there with the Krooklok (12). Then I was hit from behind and landed on the floor, and I got a blow to the head from the Krooklok. I was shouting: "Somebody help me."'

Mr Henry Valance, for A, told the court that A was married, with a daughter now two and a half and a son 16 months. He had passed a test for a taxi licence (13).

A, a slight but wiry man in a black leather jacket (14), told the court (15) that he pulled in front of R to avoid parked cars. At the traffic lights, R started shouting and screaming and swearing. 'I started swearing back at him.'

R followed him into Hannibal Road, revving his engine and flashing his lights. 'I parked. He started running towards me, carrying a metal rod about 18 inches long. I got out. I saw him swinging the rod towards me and I used my fist. He hit me three times on the back. I was so scared I had to use it [the steering wheel lock]. The third time I hit him, he fell to the floor.'

A was cross-examined about his earlier defence statement (16) in which he did not mention R coming at him with a weapon. The passengers in A's car did not give evidence (17).

(1) Road rage makes the case topical.

(2) Nothing to be gained by naming the waiter in the first sentence.

(3) The report must include the charge. Actual bodily harm is the least serious of the bodily harm charges. The most serious is wounding with intent, followed by wounding and by assault causing grievous bodily harm. Within the first few sentences, a court report should normally tell the reader who was accused, where he, she or they live, what they were accused of, whether they pleaded 'Guilty' or 'Not guilty' and what the court decided.

(4) The value of the car is worth mentioning. It was not an old banger.

(5) Concurrently. The waiter will serve the second sentence at the same time as the first. It is not an additional three months.

(6)   Grasping what the two accounts of the incident have in common, before going on to the differences, helps tell the story.

(7)   This sentence sums up A's defence and shows how much smaller he is than the bus driver.

(8)   If someone pleads 'Not guilty', a report must say so.

(9)   This seems a good place for a few of the judge's comments and explanations.

(10) This helps the reader to understand the geography.

(11) R's graphic story is best told in his own words.

(12) Krooklok. You would not usually use a trade name but Krooklok is the word R used.

(13) This explains more of A's circumstances.

(14) A description is worth giving, if you can work it in. However, A's reading problem has been left out. To mention it in a paper circulating in his home area could be unfair.

(15) Court reports must be fair to the accused. They must explain their defences and report points made in their favour. They must give them the benefit of any doubts there may be.

(16) Defence statement. Accused people no longer have a full right to silence. Before trial, they must make a statement setting out their defence.

(17) The failure of A's friends to give evidence was important.

Make the most of what you have heard

Court reports commonly fail to take full advantage of the evidence. A report in the *Northallerton Times* (23 06 06) began: *The condition of Billy, a seven-year-old Shetland pony stallion with rotting face wounds shocked a court on Friday and led to a digger driver being banned from keeping animals for three years.* The intro could have read, even more strikingly: *A Shetland pony called Billy had putrid face wounds from a blue nylon head collar embedded in his face, when a vet and an RSPCA inspector went to see him.*

It is better to avoid an abstract start. One court report (*NE*, 27 06 06) began *The treatment of a grandmother and devout Christian provoked an outcry last night after she was led away in handcuffs to begin a jail sentence.* This would better read: *Supporters called 'What a load of rubbish' from the public gallery of Derby magistrates court yesterday when a grandmother was led away in handcuffs to begin a jail sentence.*

Don't reduce the impact of your intro with unnecessary words. A *Yorkshire Post* report (30 06 06) began: *A Sheffield schoolgirl has been convicted by a jury of wounding a classmate in an incident where she used a razor to repeatedly slash her across the face.* It reads better in two sentences and without *in an incident where*.

Olinka Koster's report in the *Daily Mail* (22 07 08) of the jailing of Blake Fielder-Civil was simple and straightforward. It began:

> *Amy Winehouse's husband was yesterday jailed for viciously assaulting a bar manager and plotting to buy his silence. However, Blake Fielder-Civil, 26, will be free by Christmas because of the time he has already been locked up. He admitted assaulting James King, 36, outside a pub and then plotting to bribe his victim in a £200,000 deal not to testify in court. Yesterday Miss Winehouse, who has blown kisses to her husband at previous hearings, failed to show up for his sentencing at Snaresbrook Crown Court, East London. Her spokesman said: 'I think it will be a relief because there is a release date now. 'Judge David Radford told Fielder-Civil: 'You behaved in a gratuitous, cowardly and disgraceful way.' He said Mr King's cheekbone had been broken in the attack, requiring 'the surgical reconstruction of his face' with a metal plate behind his cheek and eye.*

This report answers the major questions: When will Fielder-Civil get out? What, in brief, was he accused of? What were King's injuries? It also gets in an innocuous but human comment from Amy Winehouse's spokesman. Normally, newspapers should not name relatives of accused people. But Amy Winehouse was mentioned in evidence and by the judge.

The report later details what Fielder-Civil's barrister said on his behalf, gives a short account of the assault and conspiracy and says what happened to other accused. When there are several accused, you can leave the detail of charges and sentences to the end of the story or put it in a separate panel.

This report has the advantage of dealing largely with undisputed facts. When an accused pleads 'Not guilty' and disputes the allegations, you must attribute them to the people who made them. Otherwise your report may not be protected by privilege against a libel action.

Features after the trial

When a major court case ends, newspapers commonly publish features about the people concerned or the issues raised, possibly including evidence not put to the jury.

One striking feature concerned not a person but a gun. In *The grisly history of a pistol known as Exhibit RS1* (*Guardian*, 18 10 08), Sandra Laville showed that a pre-war Czech semi-automatic, which a mother found in her son's toy safe, had been used in several shootings including the murder of a drug dealer.

You may get maps, pictures and witness statements for after-the-case features from the Crown Prosecution Service and the police (*see* McNae). Witness statements will be important if you decide to investigate a complaint that a conviction is unsafe. They may contain something not mentioned in court. Compared side by side, they may show up differences in what witnesses have said.

County courts

Civil justice provides damages and court orders for those who suffer loss or injury as a result of the fault of, or breach of contract by, others. Plaintiffs make complaints against defendants. People may lose in court but they are not convicted or found guilty.

Local county courts now handle most civil claims in England and Wales. (In Scotland, they go to the sheriff courts.) Only the complex cases go to the High Court.

A county court judge may reserve judgment at the end of a hearing. You should be able to arrange to see the judgment when it is given. In libel and some other cases, either side can ask for trial by jury.

Family courts

Proceedings concerning families, children and marriage are heard in the High Court, county courts and magistrates courts. In magistrates courts, the media have long been able to cover family hearings, other than adoption. But reporting is restricted, essentially to a concise statement of accusations and defences (*see* McNae).

Family hearings in the High Court and county courts have been private but, in April 2009, Justice Secretary Jack Straw opened them to the media, subject to the normal rule that young people under 18 should not be identified. This followed a campaign by *Times* leader-writer Camilla Cavendish, who pointed out the power of social workers and expert witnesses in secret proceedings, and the injustice of some decisions to take children from their parents. She was joint winner in 2008 of the Paul Foot Award for investigative or campaigning journalism.

However, though Straw opened family hearings to the media, laws restricting or preventing coverage of the hearings remained in force. Section 12 of the Administration of Justice Act 1960 prevents reporting without the judge's special permission. The Family Proceedings Rules allow for the media to be excluded in the interests of a child. And judges could rule that evidence is private and not to be published.

The Children, Schools and Families Act 2010 allows family proceedings to be covered but no one involved except professional witnesses to be identified. However, if a court order names adults, that may be reportable.

Inquests

If Grandmama is such a pest
We'll send her to her last long rest
And fix it that there's no inquest.

(From a school pantomime song, 1939)

A new national coroner service is being set up to inquire into possibly suspicious deaths in England and Wales. Under the Coroners and Justice Act 2009, coroners will normally hold inquests without a jury unless someone died in custody or a police officer was involved. Coroners should tell the press when they are holding inquests. Only in the interests of national security can press and public be kept out.

Coroners may protect anonymity Police officers who shot Brazilian electrician Jean Charles de Menezes, mistaking him for a terrorist, were not named at his inquest. In the March 2008 inquest into the death of Manchester police chief Michael Todd, women with whom he had corresponded were not named.

Few inquest verdicts are so interesting you need to start your report with them. Claire Still wrote a clear, straightforward intro for the *Ilford Recorder* (1 03 07): *A blunder at King George's Hospital led to the death of a 41-year-old woman, which has left five young children facing a future without a mother.*

Do not leave your best line languishing in the middle of your report. This intro from the *Evening Gazette*, Middlesbrough (27 06 06), was short and to the point: *A grandmother died after her Christmas tree caught fire*. But it could have read, more informatively: *A smouldering Christmas tree, giving off an 'unbelievable' amount of thick smoke, killed grandmother Carol Churchill.*

Tribunals and inquiries

Much employment, health-service and other law is administered by tribunals, not the courts. Employment tribunals normally sit in public. They frequently hear newsworthy disputes over dismissal and discrimination, and mouth-watering claims for compensation. Employment tribunals can rouse strong feelings. So they need careful reporting, especially if there is an adjournment with only one side's case heard. If irrelevant things are said, reporting them may not be privileged.

If sexual misconduct, or discrimination against someone disabled, is alleged, a tribunal can specify people who must not be identified until the tribunal's decision is promulgated, which could be months later. The press has no right to challenge such a restricted reporting order, but the tribunal can allow it to do so. A woman who complains of, say, indecent assault cannot be identified. She is protected by the Sexual Offences (Amendment) Act of 1992.

If you are in doubt about the detail of a case, tribunal staff may help. They are instructed to give a reporter full addresses and also the tribunal's decision if this is reserved.

Under the Contempt of Court Act, tribunals exercising judicial powers – for example, mental health review tribunals – count as courts. It seems that the Act also covers employment tribunals.

Valuation courts are not courts, despite their name. Nor are professional disciplinary bodies.

Sharia courts

A junior justice minister, Bridget Prentice, announced (*Mail*, 25 10 08) that the decision of a sharia court in a family or divorce case can be recognized if the parties together submit the decision to an English court. Islamic justice favours mediation and reconciliation.

The police

The police outside London are organized in constabularies, some covering more than one county. These are headed by chief constables. Under Cameron government proposals, they and other crime agencies will be overseen by a locally elected commissioner. The Independent Police Complaints Commission www.ipcc.gov.uk oversees the handling of complaints in England and Wales. It has regional offices: see The White Book.

A constabulary usually has a press office which may put details of accidents and incidents on a recorded message. The press office will help you talk to an officer who knows what you want to know. If you feel you have been denied information, complain to the press office.

All forces now publish local maps showing patterns of crime. The West Yorkshire force's maps, for example, are at www.beatcrime.info. Those of the Metropolitan Police (http://maps.met.police.uk) will tell you about crime risks, for example, where you are at greatest risk of being robbed in the street.

For minor news, you will still need to call on a local police station. Make calls in person if possible, to let officers know who you are.

The Metropolitan Police cover the London boroughs – except the City – plus parts of Essex, Hertfordshire and Surrey. They are divided into areas, each of which has a press office in addition to the press bureau at New Scotland Yard.

Under the Freedom of Information Act, every constabulary must have a scheme putting its publications online. Also worth noting are both the (annual) *ACPO UK Police Directory* (PMH Publications, £39.99), which is full of contacts, including at ports, airports, prisons and overseas; and the website http://www.hmprisonservice.gov.uk.

Questions

1. In what circumstances can journalists be excluded from court hearings?
2. How do you ensure your reporting is fair?

10 Government and the media

Many contest, protest and suggest, but government decides on anything from your plan for a bungalow in the back garden to whether the nation goes to war. Elections, mainly contested by political parties, determine who governs the national government and the local council. The website www.direct.gov.uk gives information about government agencies. www.statistics.gov.uk presents the UK in numbers.

Political parties

Every parliamentary constituency is likely to have a Conservative Association, a Liberal Democrat Association, a Labour Party, possibly a Green and/or national party. Each party may have a prospective parliamentary candidate. Each candidate will have an agent to run their election campaign.

Media covering elections should give candidates equal treatment. This is difficult with 20 or more candidates, most of whom will get few votes. But no candidate should be ignored. Get to know your local party agents and MPs and how to get hold of them. To reach MPs by e-mail, put their first initial after their surname and add @parliament.uk: for example harperm@parliament.uk.

MPs take up many issues on behalf of local people. They may press their views also on national issues. *Vachers Quarterly* gives information about MPs and others engaged in UK or European politics. The website www.publicwhip.co.uk will tell you about MPs' voting record in the House of Commons, listing occasions when they voted against their party's line. www.parliament.uk/about_commons/register_of_members_interests.cfm lists MPs' financial interests.

www.parliament.uk/hansard offers you *Today in the Commons*, which reports debates three hours behind real time. *View by date* also gives parliamentary questions and answers, and ministers' statements. And you can *View by member.* The site similarly covers the Lords. Hansard is not a verbatim report – its reporters neaten up incoherence and can be fallible. The site www. TheyWorkForYou.com provides links to MPs' speeches in Hansard, and to written answers to their questions. You can seek information by subject or MP. www.writetothem.com enables people to communicate with MPs and councillors.

Single issues

Single-issue politics is often livelier than party politics. Whoever wins a council election, the council is mainly engaged in doing what the legislation and the government require. Single-issue politics is attractive to newspapers and the public for its simplicity and clarity of purpose and for its assiduous digging out of facts. It says 'Repair our local playground', 'Stop through-traffic', 'Keep the post office open', 'Eat local grown food'. If a single issue involves enough voters – like the campaign against extending Heathrow – it stirs up party politicians.

Single-issue campaigns often need public-relations help and may overstate their cases. Journalists, while welcoming the information provided, need to consider:

1. Will this campaign bring about real improvements? A campaign against supermarket packaging lost momentum in 2008 when it became plain that much unpackaged food gets damaged and wasted.

2. Does this campaign conflict with other objectives? A campaign says: 'Don't build houses here'. But many people need better homes.

3. Does the arithmetic justify the campaign? Air miles sound bad for global warming. But flowers grown in and flown from Kenya mean smaller carbon dioxide emissions than those grown in Dutch greenhouses.

4. Will the success of this campaign have costs?

Organizations involved in single-issue politics – Greenpeace, Friends of the Earth, Fairtrade – may well have local or regional spokespeople you can talk to. www.GroupsNearYou.com will put you in touch with community e-mail and online groups in your area.

Websites with useful information include:

• www.airquality.co.uk. You can find graphs showing particulates, nitric oxide and nitrogen peroxide in the air at local sampling sites. The graphs show when and on what days these pollutants reach their peaks.

• www.environment-agency.gov.uk. Gives flood warnings, tells you about pollution locally and what the agency plans to do about it, and records river pollution incidents. The Environment Agency controls pollution from major plants, local authorities from smaller ones.

- www.ofwat.gov.uk. Ofwat regulates the water companies. It collects data on leaks from water pipes.

- www.oft.gov.uk. The Office of Fair Trading's site, includes paragraphs about banned estate agents and refusals of consumer credit licences.

Local councils

Hundreds of elected and unelected authorities provide local services on behalf of the government, which – in England – makes its wishes known through the Government Office Network of regional offices: the Government Office for the South-East, the Government Office for the East Midlands, and so on (see *The White Book*, described in the Stormont, Holyrood, Cardiff, and Westminster section below).

The elected local authorities are the local councils and some mayors. The main unelected authority is the National Health Service. Which authority does what is constantly changing. Much work is contracted out to not-for-profit agencies such as Age UK, or commercial firms. Some councils work together in multi-area agreements.

The Local Government Act of 2000 requires councils to promote economic, social and environmental wellbeing within their boundaries. More prosaically, they fulfil the duties and exercise the powers imposed or granted by a plethora of Acts of Parliament. They care for children and their schools, elderly and disabled people, operate the planning laws, mend roads, provide help with housing and seek to promote local activities. Councils have officers called directors to administer these services. A council's chief officer is now normally styled chief executive (unless it has an elected mayor). On the Oneplace website (www.direct.gov.uk/oneplace) inspectors give councils green flags for successes and red for failings. In February 2010, Barking and Dagenham, for instance, had green for green industries and roof gardens, red for health.

In all of Scotland and much of England, a single council, or unitary authority, provides all the council services in its area. Unitary authorities may cover a city, a town and its rural hinterland, even a county. English villages have parish councils. These are called community councils in Scotland and Wales.

In some English counties, county councils still provide some services while district councils cover housing, refuse, leisure, environmental health and local planning.

The legislation gives councils a choice in how they operate. A town or city can have an executive mayor, chosen by the electors, provided the electorate agrees. The mayor must share decision-making with a cabinet or executive drawn from the elected councillors.

Mayor Martin Winter of Doncaster refurbished the racecourse but faced complaints of shortcomings in services (BBC Newsnight, 4 03 09). He resigned in March when children's minister, Ed Balls, ordered Doncaster to bring in new management for its children's department. At Stoke, the citizens voted in October 2008 not to have an executive mayor any more.

It is more common for a council's affairs to be run by its leader – the leader of the largest political party on the council – and a cabinet of councillors.

Redbridge, which covers Ilford, Woodford and neighbouring areas of North-East London, is run by leader and cabinet. The cabinet – whose ten members are appointed by the council – makes the decisions necessary to carry out the council's policy. Individual cabinet members make proposals for decisions in their field (portfolio) – adult services, children's services, leisure, highways. These proposals are set down in a forward plan – to allow time for comment. Then the cabinet decides. Redbridge cabinet decisions are subject to scrutiny by committees of back-bench councillors. These scrutiny committees can ask the cabinet to think again but cannot overrule it. Cabinet decisions can also be requisitioned for discussion by the full council. But, again, the council can ask only for reconsideration. It cannot overrule. Its main powers are to set the council's priorities and approve the budget based on them.

Cabinet dominance remains controversial. One reason for a revolt by Tory councillors in Birmingham in April 2009 was their desire for more say. In Glasgow, the full council got the task of deciding on major development schemes. It also made the final decision on a plan to close crumbling and/or underused primary schools (though, in fact, the decision had already been decided in a Labour group meeting).

Local government is overseen by local strategic partnerships. That for Redbridge brings together the council, the police, the health service, the fire service, local businesses and voluntary organizations. The partnership has drawn up a sustainable community strategy which aims to make Redbridge greener, safer, healthier and more community-minded and develop skills and the economy. To check on progress, the Redbridge partnership has negotiated with the Government Office for London a local area agreement. This is a somewhat bureaucratic document assessing progress by measurements such as number of households in temporary accommodation, number of obese children and numbers on benefit.

Protecting children

Since the outcry over the violent death of a child, Victoria Climbié, in 2004, English councils have been obliged to have a single department covering both children's welfare services and schools. According to Chris Woodhead, former chief schools inspector, these departments are behemoths with tasks beyond their abilities (*FT*, 19 11 08). At Redbridge, the Children's Trust manages children's welfare services on behalf of both the council and the health service.

England, Scotland and Wales all have a children's commissioner, to protect children's welfare and rights.

Redbridge council has a licensing committee – councils have taken over licensing from local magistrates. Planning decisions in Redbridge are taken by three regional planning committees and a regulatory committee (for the more important applications). Unsuccessful applicants can appeal to inspectors appointed by the government, who usually make decisions based on the paperwork but can hold hearings. Decisions on large schemes can be overturned by the Mayor of London. Planning applications are on file in the local studies section of the central library in Ilford.

Councils have to maintain public registers of child minders, residential homes, pollution data, fire precautions, food premises and sportsground safety notices.

Redbridge has area committees, each made up of councillors from two wards. They can make local decisions on traffic management and give small sums for local activities and needs. Their main function is to hear what members of the public have to say.

Redbridge has two arms-length management organizations (Almos): the Children's Trust (see above) and Redbridge Homes which manages council houses. (Redbridge Homes made a headline in the *Wanstead Guardian* (30 07 09) because of the cost of its temporary managers.)

The Learning Disability Trust provides services on behalf of Redbridge, neighbouring Waltham Forest and the health service. Redbridge Community Care provides services for disabled and elderly people and recovering hospital patients in their homes.

Other cabinet-governed councils have the same basic organisation as Redbridge but the detail may differ. Cumbria has local committees for towns and areas, comprising their local county councillors. It has also set up pilot community boards, in Barrow and elsewhere, to encourage more people to get involved.

People who think their local council has treated them unfairly can take an allegation of maladministration to a commissioner for local administration (ombudsman).

Councillors

The patterns of local government may have changed but many decisions are still made by groups of councillors behind the scenes. To know what is going on, you need to know councillors.

David Bell, who covered Birmingham's council for the *Birmingham Mail*, said in an interview that little happened at council meetings. 'I go and show my face. Then I go and stand in a different room and have a coffee and stories walk up to me.' Local government reporting, he said, is all about contacts. 'You have to get people to trust you, so that they know what they tell you off the record isn't going to have their name associated with it.'

A borough or district councillor represents a ward – a small portion of the council's area – and is elected for four years. A ward may have more than one councillor. Many councillors hold surgeries on, say, Saturday mornings, at which people can tell them their problems. These may draw attention to matters of public interest.

Party politics means party groups on the council – the Conservative group, the Labour group, the Liberal Democrats, the Greens. These usually have a leader and deputy leader. They meet to decide their view on different issues. These discussions are private but may leak into the press.

Until recently, a weakness of councils was that their members were unpaid, and the number of people able to give the time necessary for council work was limited. Councillors now receive allowances – cabinet members can receive £25,000–£30,000 a year plus expenses.

Councils must have codes of conduct. These require councillors to declare:

- Employment and business interests.
- Election expenses.
- Financial interests above £25,000.
- Land holdings.
- Membership of a company, charity, trade union, professional association or masonic lodge.

In addition, councils must maintain a register of councillors' interests. A councillor who has 'an interest' in a matter being discussed in a meeting must say so and refrain from voting. 'Interest' is often but not always financial. Four councillors withdrew from a discussion of parking, two because they knew people involved, another because she lived in an adjacent street and the fourth because his son attended a school near by.

People can communicate with councillors through www.writetothem.com. They can tell their council of problems through www.FixMyStreet.com.

Stories in the minutes

The breadth and detail of local government can be seen in the minutes and agendas published by councils in print and/or on the internet. Council website addresses follow the pattern www.redbridge.gov.uk.

Minutes set out what has been recommended by a council's committees and advisory groups. Agendas include reports which committees or an executive cabinet are to receive. Cabinet agendas and reports must be available five days before meetings.

Here are stories in minutes at Redbridge in early 2008. The higher birth rate (see 10) is typical for London boroughs

1. Nearly 400 people have signed a petition against building houses on the site of Chepstow, a large old house in Wanstead.

2. Councillors are trying to stop people paving front gardens in an Ilford bungalow estate.

3. The Transport Police have appointed a new inspector to cover Redbridge.

4. Gates are to be installed to block a back lane at Chadwell Heath, mis-used by drug-users and fly-tippers.

5. Residents are complaining about young people smoking pot on a railway bridge and overcrowding buses. They also complain about noise from a station tannoy.

6. People in a Wanstead street want a bus service. (Eighteen months later, the Leytonstone–Romford service was diverted down this street.)

7. A developer is being sought for an area near Ilford station.

8. Seven Kings station is to have a facelift.

9. There is a plan to open a new takeaway on Wanstead High Street.

10. A report argues for a bigger budget for children, the current budget being overspent by about £1 million. The birthrate has risen 40 per cent in five years. The borough is supporting 16 young people at university who used to be in care. Fostering children through an agency costs £44,000 a year, four times as much as with a foster family. With more premature babies surviving and more families arriving from neighbouring boroughs, Redbridge has more disabled children.

11. A hotel wants to take over the nursery next door and provide 13 more rooms.

12. There are to be three new centres for children, parents and families.

Redbridge agendas drew attention to forthcoming reports on lottery funding for play projects, on CCTV, on housing needs and on life expectancy. Armed with a report, a journalist can seek comment from councillors and write a story. Try to canvass councillors other than those who are quoted every time.

Minutes and agendas gave e-mail addresses for prominent councillors and phone numbers for officials who would answer further inquiries. If something is not clear to you, ask.

Watch out for the item which seems dull but raises an issue of explosive interest. It is worth spending time to disentangle the meaning from the jargon. An investigation by Andrew Gilligan of the *Evening Standard* into organizations receiving London Development Agency grants sprang from answers given to the London Assembly and published on its website (*see* p. 156).

The cabinet meets

Redbridge's cabinet meeting gave time to residents who had said in advance they had a point to raise. The cabinet heard from allotment holders opposed to the sale of allotment land to raise money. Cabinet members agreed on a plan to consult the public about new projects and how they might be paid for.

A woman told movingly how her mother had benefited from an elderly people's centre, which the cabinet proposed to convert into a centre for people with learning difficulties.

After an hour, the cabinet voted to exclude the press and public from the meeting. Cabinets need meet in public only when making 'key' decisions, involving 'significant' sums of money or 'significant' numbers of people. In general, council committees are open to press and public but they can exclude them if any of seven types of exempt information is to be considered:

1. Information relating to any individual.

2. Information which is likely to reveal the identity of an individual.

3. Information relating to the financial or business affairs of any particular person (including the authority holding that information). *This exemption keeps information about commercial contracts confidential.*

4. Information relating to any consultations or negotiations concerning any labour relations matter.

5. Information in respect of which a claim to legal professional privilege would be maintained in legal proceedings.

6. Information which reveals that the authority proposes to give under any enactment a notice imposing requirements on someone, or to make an order or direction under an enactment.

7. Information relating to any action taken or to be taken concerning the prevention, investigation or prosecution of crime.

The exemptions should be applied only when absolutely necessary. The body considering a report deemed exempt can vote to remove the exemption.

The exemptions are not subject to any requirement that matters of public interest be openly discussed. However, it is possible to make a Freedom of Information Act request for information which it is in the public interest to disclose. This includes personal information relating to public servants' work. It also includes information about contracts. Owen Amos, then a feature writer at *The Northern Echo*, used the Act to get several North-East councils to disclose what they paid in subsidies to bus companies.

The council meeting

Redbridge's council meeting began with prayers and the mayor's announcements, which pointed to future newspaper stories. Colonel Paul (who's he?) was to celebrate his golden wedding. Two high schools were putting on a show. Redbridge schools were to perform in the Albert Hall. The council gave councillors and members of the public a chance to put questions to cabinet members. Besides their printed question, they could ask a supplementary. A petition was presented against a phone mast. A motion urged the cabinet to spend some of the borough's higher-than-expected government grant on its needier areas. A journalist could have written about Seven Kings, a heavily populated area that councillors kept alluding to in the debate. Its character has changed with the inflow of migrants.

The council provided a seating plan, which helped identify the councillors who spoke. However, the plan gave only surnames. Some councillors might not be sitting in their allotted places. A break in the meeting made it possible to approach councillors and ask questions. It was a chance to ask one or two less audible councillors what points they were making.

An area committee

Members of the public, and councillors, raised several newsworthy topics at a meeting of the Wanstead and Snaresbrook area committee:

1. Parking problems on Wanstead High Street.
2. Access for cyclists to a country park.
3. Pavement repairs.
4. Problems in enforcing planning decisions.
5. Plans to collect garden rubbish and cardboard.
6. High school science laboratories – the worst in the borough.
7. £1000 grants for two musical performances.
8. Argument over blocking or not blocking a road to through traffic.
9. Call for removal of road humps.
10. A playground being refurbished.

Council officers

Councils generally employ a public relations staff but journalists also speak to senior officers. Contact the press office or the head of a department rather than a subordinate – unless the subordinate has been given as the contact on a particular subject. To learn about council policy or attitude, it is usually fairer to approach the leader of the council or the relevant cabinet member rather than an officer. Ask the press office for comment if the council is attacked by an organization or in a reader's letter. Reporting its answer will save you from presenting a one-sided version of the issue.

Table 10.1   Redbridge's proposed budget, 2008/9, in £000s

Adjusted base budget	177,284
Inflation and corporate items	7611
Adult social services	−897
Children's services	−228
Community safety	384
Highways and cleansing	462
Housing and health	−472
Leisure, culture, Olympics	259
Planning, regeneration and environment	170
Resources and communications	775
Increase in revenue budget	**8064**
Cost of new borrowing	—
Total budget requirement	**185,348**
Less grant (from government)	91,605
To be met from council tax	**93,743**

Council finance

Instead of listing the totals budgeted for each service, as you might expect, the proposed revenue budget started out from a base figure representing the previous pattern of spending (*see* Table 10.1). It then showed how much each service was expected to spend above or below its previous pattern. Against adult social services, the figure −897 meant that these services were expected to cost £897,000 less. Highways, in contrast, needed an extra £462,000. Later tables showed in detail where savings were being made and extra spending was planned.

In total, these adjustments, plus the likely rise of prices, meant that the budget was £8,064,000 above the original base figure, £185,348,000 in all. About half of this total would be met by government grants, half from council tax.

The Audit Commission, which audits councils' books, shows how patterns of spending vary from council to council. The Cameron government wants private auditors to do this from 2012. Under the Audit Commission Act, council tax payers can inspect the council's accounts during 20 working days each year. On those days you can see all the books, bills and contracts. There is no commercial-confidentiality bar.

Scotland has the Accounts Commission, which examines how councils manage their money. It is helped by Audit Scotland.

Figures for councils' spending are published by the Chartered Institute of Public Finance and Accountancy. Birmingham University has an Institute of Local Government Studies (0121 414 5008; www.inlogov.bham.ac.uk). It also has the Health Service Management Centre (0121 414 7050; www.hsmc.bham.ac.uk).

The local government bible is the Municipal Directory, which gives contact details for councillors and others. The nearest library will have a copy.

Capital spending

Apart from the revenue budget, councils also spend lump sums on one-off projects – anything from building a school or improving homes to acquiring recycling equipment. This is the capital programme.

At Redbridge it is divided into two parts. One, 'externally financed', uses money from the government (plus, in Redbridge, Transport for London and the Mayor of London). For the other, 'internal' programme Redbridge must find the cash itself.

Councils can borrow money for these internal projects. They are wary, however, of incurring payments on their borrowings, which must be made out of council tax in subsequent years. What they raise in council tax can be capped by the government.

In 2008, Redbridge asked residents to help decide on a possible £265 million programme. It included schools for the growing number of children, plus roads and homes. It also included a swimming pool, badminton hall and gym to replace an old swimming bath. The sale of council-owned land looked the only way – apart from borrowing – of raising anywhere near £265 million. But the property recession made land sales unattractive. After the consultation, a cross-party panel recommended spending just £37 million, on schools and roads.

The government has encouraged councils to undertake joint projects with private companies and other agencies. These, too, were hit by the 2008 property recession. In 2010, the government plans to let councils levy a supplementary rate on businesses. The money could be used to finance capital projects.

Hull City Council financed the £47 million KC football stadium and other projects largely by selling shares in the Hull telephone company, Kingston Communications.

London

In Greater London the Mayor is overlord for planning, runs Transport for London, appoints deputy mayors and the board of the London Development Agency; and can take what decisions he/she wishes. The London Assembly can only scrutinize. It can reject the Mayor's budget but only if it can muster an unlikely two-thirds majority to pass its own. There is no scrutiny of advice given by the Mayor's advisers.

In the United States, the city mayors and state governors on whom the London mayoralty was modelled do not have the same freedom of action. They must get their decisions endorsed by their local legislatures.

Primary Care Trusts

In England, local Primary Care Trusts (PCTs) use Health Service money to pay for hospitals, dentists and doctors for patients of medical practices in their areas. (In Scotland, 14 health boards both provide and pay for services. Their members include local council representatives and will also include people elected by the public. Board meetings, when exercising their executive functions, are open to media representatives.) In 2010 the government was planning to switch spending decisions from primary care trusts to groups of family doctors. In Cumbria this approach is already moving work from big hospitals to smaller centres and even into patient's homes.

PCTs pay by results. Replacing a hip, for example, attracts a set fee. They commission a hospital to replace, say, 500 hips in a year, enabling it to employ hip-replacement staff. However, it is patients and their family doctors who decide the hospital to which patients will go. So, over the year, there could be 700 hips replaced, or 300.

For almost every organization, disease, treatment and agreement there are, it seems, initial letters. People don't have heart disease. They have CVD (cardiovascular disease).

PCTs are run by executive and non-executive directors, with a non-executive chairman. They also have professional executive committees, which deal with clinical matters, and local medical committees, which represent doctors. PCT meetings are open to media and public, with an opportunity for members of the public to speak. Meetings can go into private session for exempt business.

NHS Redbridge is the PCT for Redbridge, spending £215 million a year. It sends the meeting papers to journalists in advance. The papers for one meeting, and three hours of discussion, provided many leads for stories:

1. Three local hospitals (Barking, Havering and Redbridge) struggled to treat accident and emergency patients within four hours. They had too few midwives to cope well with the higher birth rate. (*A newspaper would clearly want to cover also the next public meeting of the BHR hospital trust.*)

2. A row between the Secretary for Health and doctors' leaders over extending surgery hours had set off a local dispute.

3. NHS Redbridge had appointed a new medical director.

4. A screening service for bowel cancer was now running.

5. NHS Redbridge was setting up its first polyclinic (to offer X-ray, outpatients and other hospital services, health advice, a pharmacy, a cafe and access to doctors 12 hours a day including weekends).

6. The ambulance service had new targets for quickly reaching patients whose lives are in danger.

7. There were problems in getting patients to the right specialist. A child with a heart murmur ended up in an asthma clinic.

8. NHS Redbridge was engaged in 63 projects worth £15 million.

9. Simvastatin, the cheapest statin for reducing cholesterol in the blood, did not suit everyone. At one medical practice, 15 per cent of patients had to change to other statins.

10. A computer system for child health was not fit for purpose.

11. The local, privately run independent sector treatment centre – working alongside NHS hospitals – was getting less work than it was being paid for.

12. The vice-president of Diabetes UK wanted to run Canadian-style classes for diabetics at NHS Redbridge's office.

A hospital trust

Whipps Cross is a large, architecturally bizarre hospital serving the western part of Redbridge plus the adjacent borough of Waltham Forest. It is run by the Whipps Cross University Hospital Trust, one of many hospital trusts around the country. It has a board of executive and non-executive directors that holds public meetings. Representatives of staff sit with the board.

A meeting pointed to the following stories:

1. A staff representative spoke of nurses' heavy workload. The hospital had 98 per cent of beds occupied. The shortage of empty beds made it difficult to deal with accident and emergency patients in four hours.

2. Whipps Cross also found it hard to see patients within 18 weeks of their being referred by family doctors. It would suffer financially if it did not hit 18 weeks for the bulk of patients by the end of 2008. Sending some patients to the privately run independent sector treatment centre would help.

3. Whipps Cross had lost income because PCTs withdrew some work. It was bidding for other work to restore its finances.

4. BBC TV was making programmes about nursing at Whipps Cross.

5. Over the next few years, Whipps Cross plans to concentrate its work on a third of its present site. It will build a new six-storey block.

About 100 hospitals – not including Whipps Cross – are foundation hospitals. These have greater independence. They must pay their own way. If they make a profit, they can use it to improve their services. They have locally elected governors. They can borrow money.

Local involvement networks (Links)

Since April 2009, users of NHS and local council care services have had new champions called local involvement networks, or links, one for each English council. For instance, the Waltham Forest Link in London is hosted by Voluntary Action, an umbrella organization for voluntary agencies in

Waltham Forest. Members of the public are encouraged to join in. The Link's tasks include consulting the public, raising issues with NHS bodies and the council, and inspecting hospitals and other services. The Cameron government proposes a new service, Health Watch, to represent patients' interests nationally, regionally and locally.

It is worth consulting *Binley's Directory of NHS Management*. Also *The NHS Directory* and *The Institute of Healthcare Management Yearbook* (which includes independent hospitals). Ask for these directories in your local library.

Writing about local government

When reporting local government meetings, listen carefully so you know what's going on. Some accents can be difficult to grasp. Good shorthand is vital not only for accuracy but to capture fast, vivid exchanges without which your report may be drab. A reliable shorthand note is your defence if someone claims to have been misreported. Readers will particularly want to know how they may be affected by what a meeting has decided.

Bring back to the office the documents issued during a meeting. You may need these to quote from or to verify your notes. Always read them through. News of the poor state of a Wanstead school's laboratories was hidden deep in a Redbridge budget report.

Look out for possibilities for pictures. A story is more likely to be published prominently if a picture accompanies it.

If you work on a non-party publication, you need an impartial approach, giving a fair show to all sides.

Meetings usually produce more than one story. Ask your chief reporter or news editor how much you should write of each. You should also draw attention to any items which might be worth following up with interviews and phonecalls.

Translate the officialese

Local government reports are often hard to grasp because councillors and officials fail to speak or write plain English. A report in the *Evening Times*, Glasgow, about people abusing shop assistants (23 04 09), illustrates this. It quoted the national violence prevention manager of the Scottish Centre for Healthy Working Lives as saying: 'The consequences of work-related violence can have a negative impact on the physical or mental health of staff.' All this means is: Violence against staff can harm their physical or mental health. Similarly 'to put measures in place to deal with it' means no more than 'to deal with it'.

The Scottish divisional officer of USDAW, the shop workers union, was more direct. 'There is a small minority of shoppers who think it is acceptable to swear and threaten shop workers,' he said.

Journalists need to explain words and initials which their readers may never have come across. What do readers make, for instance, of oshl (out-of-school-hours learning), or multi-agency partnerships, or participation poverty or the signalization of the roundabout? (Signalization turned out to mean installing traffic lights.)

An article in the *Western Mail* (20 03 09) reported that grandparents spend more time caring for their grandchildren but it is not quality time. It did not define quality time or say why this does not include caring.

A *Guernsey Press* journalist (1 09 07) ran into wordy and defensive explanations when writing about 'desnagging and rectification works' at a new special-needs school. The basic questions were simple: what went wrong and how is it being put right?

And here is part of the official explanation of what happened to a missing Chinese girl, trafficked to Heathrow and, possibly, reclaimed by her trafficker: *Dalai was treated as an adult by UK Border Agency who sent her to a city in Wales where she was placed in initial Home Office accommodation. Soon after, Dalai was moved to another city in Wales and was put with adult females. A number of agencies and professionals became involved* (*Western Mail*, 18 03 09). Does this mean that Dalai was put in a detention centre and then moved to a women's prison? Perhaps not, because her accommodation – whatever it was – had a housing manager who *found a Chinese man hiding in her wardrobe. Dalai claimed he was her brother. Shortly afterwards, Dalai disappeared.* These were the liveliest lines in the story and would better have appeared near the start.

In contrast, Sally Williams cut loose from official explanations when she described in the same paper what happened when Powys County Council turned off two-thirds of its streetlights. She interviewed Blodwen Ockwell, aged 73, who tripped and suffered a black eye.

Stormont, Holyrood, Cardiff and Westminster

Devolved government made international headlines in August 2009 when Scottish justice minister Kenny MacAskill decided to release on compassionate grounds Abdelbasset al-Megrahi, a sick Libyan imprisoned for causing the Lockerbie air disaster of 1988.

The powers of national governments in the UK vary. The Scottish Parliament (Holyrood) and the Northern Ireland Assembly (Stormont) exercise all governmental powers in Scotland and Northern Ireland except those reserved to the UK government. The reservations include defence, foreign policy, immigration, employment, overall economic policy, drugs, broadcasting, telecommunications, post, aviation, genetics, nuclear energy, consumer protection, safety of medicines, oversight of medical professions, and gambling.

Stormont has some employment powers. Holyrood can vary some taxes. The difficulty with introducing 'tartan' taxation is deciding and listing those who would pay it.

After much wrangling, Northern Ireland politicians agreed in February 2010 on terms for devolving police and justice powers to Stormont.

The Welsh Assembly cannot vary taxes and has limited legislative powers. It runs the Welsh Development Agency, education, planning and the National Health Service in Wales and administers European structural funds. It has an annual budget of £15 billion. It has promoted Cardiff as a major city for sport and culture.

The BBC has summarized the powers of Stormont, Holyrood and Cardiff at www.bbc.co.uk/1/hi/uk_news/politics/546315.stm.

The UK government in Westminster is covered mainly, though not exclusively, by political correspondents. They are members of the lobby, 175 strong in 2008, of whom 25 represented regional papers. The lobby system began around 1870, to control the number of people pestering MPs.

Lobby correspondents can attend twice-daily Downing Street briefings. They can speak to MPs, ministers and sometimes civil servants, as can other journalists. The lobby is no longer the exclusive club it once was but lobby correspondents are well placed to get to know the people they talk to.

Press officers in government departments and both government and European agencies are listed in *The White Book*, issued twice a year. Journalists can buy copies from The White Book, PO Box 2004, Burgess Hill RH15 8WU (phone 01444 243691). In 2010 it cost £20 for a year. You can also download from www.coi.gov.uk/twb. You must input the user name *twb* and the password *establish* when prompted.

At Westminster, stories drop plentifully. This is not just because briefers pour poison into willing ears or because, in the first years of the century, the UK government information machine acted on the principle that the government itself would be chewed up, unless it fed the media monster. It is also because news is abundant.

No political correspondent, except a small Press Associartion team, spends much time in the House of Commons debating chamber. Reporters can rely on PA or TV monitor screens for alerts to unforeseen excitement. Government defeats entail trawls through voting lists, against the deadline clock, to identify high-profile rebels.

For non-lobby journalists, the Commons can be a confusing place to visit in these high-security days. For the simplest route, avoid the side exit to the Commons at Westminster Underground. Leave the station by the main exit into Bridge Street and cross the road to Parliament Square. Walk straight ahead along the railings to the St Stephen's entrance and join the queue for a photopass. Many MPs have offices in Portcullis House, next to Westminster Underground. Again, leave the station by the main exit, turn left and left again on to the Embankment.

Parliamentary questions

Regional reporters in the Westminster Lobby pay more quotidian attention to parliamentary questions (PQs) and debates. The daily agenda – the Order

Paper – lists these, for that day and days ahead. Correspondents can speak to MPs and write about questions before they are put to ministers, especially if they are about locally relevant topics. MPs sometimes see merit in raising issues which a newspaper in their area has alerted them to. Ministers' answers to questions may be useful or perfunctory.

MPs frequently put forward motions which publicize causes, from the weighty to the quirky. Other MPs can add their names, so the government may need to take heed. Or the motion might be of special local interest. Support by MPs from the area makes it a story. The device is called an Early Day Motion because it is put forward for debate at an unnamed early date, that is, never.

Speaking to MPs and ministers

The lobby job is not simply covering parliament and the Order Paper, and the Downing Street briefings which give largely stock responses to the big issues of the day.

Extra, franker briefings, or the foreshadowing of announcements, or words with ministers, may be by telephone. Regional reporters will talk to MPs on an unattributable basis if necessary but hope to quote them on political controversies. Newsdesks may ask for quotes from MPs on local topics. Regional correspondents will handle government announcements, usually seeking a regional slant.

Ministers may recognize links with their regional media, or at least try to keep their constituents on side. If a minister returns your call, it doesn't matter (much) if it's for patronizing reasons.

Government press officers have generally recognized a regional dimension to announcements, accommodating regional alongside national correspondents at, say, briefings to explain crime figures or hospital performance ratings.

Is it all too cosy?

To critics, the lobby seems too cosy. New-media adepts wonder whether internet cyber-revolutionaries may rekindle a public desire to know what is really going on. Blogger Guido Fawkes has had his scoops (*see* p. 97).

The internet has given political correspondents more work. David Hencke, chairman in 2009 of the Press Gallery, points out that, where they once wrote a single story, now they must write for the website as well as the paper and compose a blog and a podcast (*BJR*, September 2009). So correspondents have less time to ask questions and must rely more on spokesmen, who often have the upper hand.

At the same time, as John Lloyd writes (*FT*, 20 02 10), *the media have become crucial to the business of governing*. With ministers seeking to rally support through briefings and broadcasts, journalists probably knew more in 2010 about what went on in government than they ever had. John Simpson, world affairs editor of the BBC, points out in *Unreliable Sources* (Macmillan, 2010) that a century earlier, in 1914, it was different. Government decisions were reported through what ministers said in Parliament. As war approached, journalists had little information. *The Cabinet*, writes Simpson, *plunged the nation into the worst war in history after a decision-making process which had been entirely secret and extraordinarily fast.*

For further reading see Public Affairs for Journalists, by James Morrison (Oxford, 2009).

Questions

1. Attempt a translation into simpler English of the following: *The report encouraged the town to implement road pricing and said it should be possible by the use of resident exemptions or concessions, non-peak retail concessions and a focus on the times and links which cause maximum difficulty in the peak, to develop a scheme which encourages non-car journeys to work and encourages traffic with no business in the town to use alternatives* (from a report on congestion charging, reported in the *Reading Chronicle*, 25 09 08).

2. To give readers a clearer idea of what is being suggested above, what questions would you want to ask?

3. What stories can you find in the current minutes and agendas of your local council? How would you pursue them?

11 Reporting business

A world of stories

Business is full of intriguing stories. Here are two: *Redundant solicitor starts her own business as a pop-musicians' lawyer* (MEN, 17 03 09); *How an Australian became Central Europe's used car king* (FT, 17 12 07).

Business stories can have drama:

> *Shafiq, who imports garments from Pakistan, was horrified when he heard on the grapevine that his UK distributor was going under. All those unpaid-for leather jackets hanging in the warehouse in Blackburn. Hundreds of them. Worth thousands. The money would disappear into the maw of the company's collapse. It would wipe him out.*
>
> *So he phoned his brother. They took the van and went over. The loading door of the warehouse was open. They walked in. They were pushing the rails of jackets outside when the distributor ran through from his office, yelling. He grabbed the rail Shafiq was pushing. Shafiq punched him in the face. The distributor let go. The brothers finished loading and drove off. Shafiq shrugged when friends reproached him afterwards. What else could he do?* (Jonathan Guthrie, FT, 22 11 07).

Business enables people to make use of their talents, experience and discoveries to run a gym, raise ostriches, produce diesel from old tyres, help Ugandan farmers sell dried fruit, or organize adventure holidays in the Himalayas. Successful business people have often triumphed over difficulties.

Find out what the story of a business is. A *Western Mail* article about Carol Vorderman Overseas Homes (17 03 09) said that it *received a number of commissions to develop properties in a series of locations around the world*. Elsewhere, the article suggested that other developers did the developing. So what task did Carol Vorderman Overseas Homes actually perform?

Businesses often have stories about new products, new investments or big orders. Try to understand how the product is being made, how the new investment will help. What will the new machines do? In what way are they better than the old? Take opportunities to visit companies. Visits provide contacts and often produce documents with enlightening information.

Keep a record of businesses and the people you speak to. You may need to speak to them again. As well as good news about success, there could be bad news about closure or loss of jobs. If so, you need to find out what has gone wrong.

Journalists often decry business as profit-making but profit has practical advantages. It keeps an enterprise alive. It provides money to expand it. It offers reward for hard work. It encourages good service, through the hope of winning more business and making more profit.

If you are writing about a business, ask about its profit and turnover. If it is losing money and you did not realize that, you could be unpopular with people whose bills have not been paid.

Different types of business

Businesses can have a single owner. They can be partnerships, in which solicitors, say, or doctors share ownership. They can be companies. They can be associations – building societies, housing associations, clubs.

Companies can be profit-making, or non-profit companies limited by guarantee. They can be private companies, with a single owner or group of owners. They can be public limited companies, with shares owned by all and sundry and traded on the Stock Exchange. Companies not big enough for the Stock Exchange can raise money by selling shares through the AIM (the Alternative Investment Market).

Once sold, the shares of a public company cannot normally be sold back to the company. If you want to sell your shares, you must find a buyer. This means that the company can use for its trading, or for meeting its losses, the money which its initial shareholders provided.

Company managers like a high share price, particularly if they are shareholders themselves. When Robert Maxwell, former proprietor of the *Daily Mirror*, was struggling to save his key company, Maxwell Communications, he tried several stratagems – not all of them legal – to boost the price of its shares. In contrast, another tycoon, Tiny Rowland of Lonrho, tried to buy out minority shareholders in an African mine without their knowing how much their shares were worth.

Powerful shareholders such as insurance companies and pension funds press for higher dividends on their shares, so they can more easily meet their obligations to insured people and pensioners.

Company owners may resent sharing their dividend income with other shareholders. Some believed, before the credit crunch of 2008, that shareholders are expensive and that businesses can be run more profitably with borrowed money. This led to the fashion for private equity. In a private equity deal, a group of financiers or managers borrow money and offer to buy the shares of a public company. But the borrowing can be too expensive. Readers Digest Association was saddled with $2.2 billion in debt when it was bought in 2007. This was more than it could pay for when the credit crunch struck (*FT*, 19 08 09).

Understanding accounts

How well businesses are doing is shown in their accounts. Unfortunately, companies now often send newsrooms not full accounts but a handout containing a few figures. However, you may well find accounts on websites.

Companies must lodge information with Companies House including accounts, balance sheets, a list of shareholders, directors' reports, directors' names and addresses, and names of companies of which the directors are also directors. Directors' reports must contain a list of holders of more than 5 per cent of the shares. They must disclose directors' pay, shares and share options; also property revaluations and political and charitable gifts.

You can look at all this on the Companies House website for a fee. Small companies do not have to lodge profit-and-loss accounts or directors' reports. Sole traders and partnerships do not have to disclose any information.

The aim of the disclosure requirements is to stop people taking money out of companies without being noticed. The requirements are the price of limited liability, which limits to their shareholdings the liability of shareholders for their company's debts. (In fact, directors can sneak money out legally, if they have smart lawyers. The Phoenix Four, who took over MG Rover in 2000, charged it interest on money lent by former owner BMW (Inspectors' Report, Chapter 5, 11 09 09).)

Companies must keep up-to-date registers of shareholders and shareholdings and of share dealings by directors and their families. These registers are open to public inspection at companies' registered offices. If companies issue new shares, they must also issue a prospectus, which can be rich in information.

The *Stock Exchange Yearbook* shows companies listed on the Stock Exchange. *Kelly's Directory* lists a wider range of companies.

Tesco 2008/9

Company accounts can appear complicated and full of jargon and numbers. However, bear in mind that the accounts are there to tell the story of what has happened to a business during a given time period. Making this story understandable requires some form of comparison, usually with the previous year.

Here are accounts from supermarketeer Tesco's annual report and accounts for the year to 28 February 2009. Table 11.1 looks at the profit for the year, while Table 11.2 outlines what Tesco owns and owes.

Table 11.1   Tesco PLC group income statement for year ended 28 February 2009 (figures are in £million)

	2009	2008
Continuing operations		
Revenue (sales excluding VAT)	54,327	47,298
Cost of sales	(50,109)	(43,668)
Gross profit	4218	3630
Administrative expenses	(1248)	(1027)
Profit on property	236	188
Operating profit	3206	2791
Share of profit of joint ventures	110	75
Finance income	116	187
Finance costs	(478)	(250)
Profit before tax	2954	2803
Tax	(788)	(673)
Profit for the year	2166	2130

Table 11.1 shows how Tesco has made its profit. Figures in brackets are minus figures, to be deducted from those that have gone before. All of the figures are summaries. More detail is shown in the notes to the accounts.

The statement starts with *Revenue*, or what Tesco has received from its customers (excluding VAT, which it collects on behalf of the government). *Cost of sales* will include the costs of purchasing products for sale, running supermarkets, transporting goods and depreciating supermarket assets and equipment to reflect their loss of value over time. Deducting cost of sales from revenue gives Tesco's *Gross profit* from its sales. From this it deducts *Administrative expenses*, the cost of running the business, and adds on profit from property-related items to give the *Operating profit*.

Tesco then takes into account financing income and costs (mainly interest paid and received) and profit made as part of joint ventures (where it has a significant interest but no control). This gives *Profit before tax*. Deducting tax from this leaves the *Profit for the year*, part of which is paid out to shareholders as a dividend, the rest being reinvested in the business.

Table 11.2 is Tesco's balance sheet. *Net assets*, at the bottom, are equal to shareholders' funds, what the shareholders have invested in the business. This is Tesco's book value. A more realistic value is the market capitalization – the number of shares issued, multiplied by the share price.

Net assets have risen by £1,093 million since February 2008. The major element in this increase is profit reinvested in the business.

The balance sheet begins with *Non-current assets* (also commonly called fixed assets). These are assets which are intended to be used within the business, not traded. Broadly, they are made up of three elements – tangible assets, intangible assets and investments and financial instruments (which, for example, insure against losses in foreign currencies).

The *tangible assets* are those that can be touched – property, plant and equipment. Since February 2008 some have been purchased, some sold.

Table 11.2   Tesco PLC group balance sheet for year ended 28 February 2009 (figures in £million)

Non-current assets		
Goodwill and other intangible assets	4027	2336
Property, plant and equipment	23,152	19,787
Investment property	1539	1112
Investments in joint ventures	62	305
Other investments	259	4
Loans and advances to customers	1470	–
Derivative financial instruments	1478	216
Deferred tax assets	21	104
	32,008	**23,864**
Current assets		
Inventories	2669	2430
Trade and other receivables	1798	1311
Loans and advances to customers	1918	–
Loans to banks; other financial assets	2129	–
Derivative financial instruments	382	97
Current tax assets	9	6
Short-term investments	1233	360
Cash and cash equivalents	3509	1788
	13,647	**5992**
Non-current assets held for sale	398	308
	14,045	**6300**
Current liabilities		
Trade and other payables	(8522)	(7277)
Financial liabilities		
Borrowings	(4059)	(2084)
Derivative financial instruments	(525)	(443)
Customer deposits	(4538)	–
Deposits by banks	(24)	–
Current tax liabilities	(362)	(455)
Provisions	(10)	(4)
	(18,040)	**(10,263)**
Net current liabilities	**(3995)**	**(3963)**
Non-current liabilities		
Financial liabilities		
Borrowings	(12391)	(5972)
Derivative financial instruments	(302)	(322)
Post-employment benefit obligations	(1494)	(838)
Other non-current payables	(68)	(42)
Deferred tax liabilities	(696)	(802)
Provisions	(67)	(23)
	(15,018)	**(7999)**
Net assets	**12,995**	**11,902**

Others, excepting land, have been depreciated – that is, had their value written down – during the year. *Intangible assets* cannot be touched: in Tesco's case, they include goodwill, licences and software. Goodwill reflects the premium that Tesco paid when it purchased other companies. It is the amount by which the value Tesco places on the purchased companies exceeds the fair value of their assets. The value of goodwill is frequently overestimated in an acquisition, for example when Royal Bank of Scotland bought ABN Amro. (The *Financial Times* (27 01 09) described goodwill as an accounting wonder.)

Loans and advances to customers – listed among Tesco's non-current assets – reflect its move into banking and financial services in December 2008, with the buy-out of the half Tesco had not previously owned of a joint venture with RBS. This brought £1470 million of longer term (over one year) loans and advances to customers on to the balance sheet.

Typically, assets are shown at depreciated historical value. Some old assets may be valued at zero (being fully depreciated). Property valuations in the balance sheet do not necessarily reflect current values (unless the property has been revalued). Assets can never be shown at more than they are currently worth.

Current assets, the next section of the balance sheet, are those involved with trading. Typically they will be *cash,* or items like *inventory* – also known as stock – and *receivables* – also known as debtors, that is monies owed to the company by customers and others. Tesco's holding of cash has doubled over the year, improving its ability to pay bills as they turn up.

At Tesco, trade receivables have usually been low as Tesco is paid immediately by customers, in cash at the tills, or quickly by credit card companies. Customers who are unable to pay are bad debtors and these debts are written off (shown as a cost in the income statement).

Among current assets, Tesco's move into financial services is reflected in some £4047 million of short-term loans and advances – some to customers and some to other banks.

Tesco's current assets are exceeded by its *current liabilities* (amounts due to be paid within one year). *Net current liabilities* (£3995 million) show by how much. Among current liabilities, Tesco's *Trade and other payables* – monies owed, most commonly to suppliers – are greater than its inventory (listed among current assets). This implies that it is suppliers' credit that keeps Tesco's shelves stocked. Another way of expressing this is that, on average, Tesco does not pay suppliers until after the goods have been sold.

Borrowings due for repayment within a year and *Customer deposits* – reflecting the move into banking – have increased by around £6500 million at February 2009.

The *Non-current liabilities* – amounts due to be paid after more than one year – have also increased, the main element being an increase in *Borrowings. Provisions* reflect allowances for potential future costs. The largest provision is for *Post-employment benefit obligations* – estimated pension obligations exceed the fair value of the pension plan's assets.

Interpreting a company's accounts is a matter of tallying the figures with the story. If the figures don't seem to fit the story then either the story is wrong or the figures are. Don't be too hasty in interpreting a company's accounts. There can be several reasons for a drop in sales. Ask what the reason is. The drop could be temporary.

Remember that a company may be complex. Tesco operates in the USA, Europe and the Far East as well as in the UK. Also, it has a financial services business as well as non-food and grocery.

The ruby in the footnote

Footnotes to accounts help explain the figures in them. They can also contain news. A footnote to the accounts of restaurant firm Gordon Ramsay Holdings showed that it had breached covenants (agreements) with Royal Bank of Scotland. Later accounts showed that celebrity cook Ramsay and his father-in-law had put in £5 million to stave off administration (*FT*, 3 07 09).

Amy Bould, business editor of the *Shropshire Star*, was curious how a local civil engineering firm, Wrekin Construction, could have net assets above £6 million in its 2007 accounts. She found an astonishing footnote. This said Wrekin had used preference shares to buy from its leading shareholder, Tamar Group, a ruby called The Gem of Tanzania for £11 million, a price which would make it the most valuable ruby on earth. The FT's headline (14 03 09) read: *Treasure hunt begins for £11m ruby found on struggling builder's books.*

Mark Whittington, an accountancy lecturer at Aberdeen University, looked up Tamar's 2007 accounts on the Companies House website. He found that Tamar had the Gem of Tanzania revalued before selling it. It had previously been valued at £300,000.

Jonathan Guthrie reported in the *Financial Times* (1 10 09) that the gem was a big purple rock weighing over two kilogrammes. Administrators for Wrekin sold it for £8010 (*FT*, 17 02 10).

How a £114 million surplus can also be a £2730 million loss

ITV had net earnings of £114 million in 2008. Yet it declared a loss before tax of £2730 million even though it paid comparatively little interest on borrowed money. How could this be? The answer is that the assets of a broadcaster such as ITV are different in nature from those of a retailer such as Tesco. Tesco's main assets are tangible – buildings, vehicles, stock. ITV's main asset is intangible – its potential for earning from advertising. With advertising less buoyant, this asset was less valuable. ITV cut the value of its intangible assets by £2695 million and showed total net assets of only £534 million, a sixth of the 2007 figure.

The 2008 accounts of Aviva, which includes the Norwich Union, told a similar story in a different field, insurance. It showed an increased operating profit but a loss before tax of over £11 billion, largely because of losses on its holdings of stocks and shares. On a different accounting basis, its loss would have been much smaller – £1.3 billion. ITV and Aviva may have felt that, if they announced big losses in a bad year, their news could only get better.

Why businesses go bust

The reasons for company failure were succinctly summarized by Jennifer Hughes (*FT*, 8 11 08): She wrote: *There are two basic forms of insolvency. The first and more common is cashflow insolvency. This is when a company finds itself unable to pay its debts as they fall due. The second is balance-sheet insolvency in which liabilities outweigh assets.* The directors or a creditor can have a company voluntarily liquidated (wound up), or liquidation can be ordered by a court. Alternatively, the company can go into administration, which allows it to be sold as a going concern. It is fraud to trade if you can't pay your bills.

JJB Sports (*FT*, 7 07 09) became the first company to be saved from administration by a company voluntary agreement with creditors.

After a company has been wound up, the directors or staff members – provided they are not banned from directing – can trade again, with the company's debts written off. They can use a new company name or they can buy the company name back from a liquidator if he/she gets no better offer for it. The manager and staff of Woolworths in Dorchester relaunched it as Wellworths.

Businesses can fail even though they have extensive assets. The fall of the Northern Rock bank is a classic case. To finance new mortgages, it borrowed money from other lenders for short periods. But, suddenly, lenders wanted their money back. It could not repay because it had lent the money to homebuyers.

Assets can fall in value if they are in a falling currency. In the 1980s, the assets of Polly Peck, a fruit company based in North Cyprus, fell with the Turkish lire. Polly Peck collapsed.

Terms you may need to understand

- *Basis points* – Aficionados sometimes write about an interest rate rising 50 basis points. A basis point is a hundredth of one per cent. So 50 basis points is half of one per cent.

- *Bonds* – These are certificates of debt issued by the government, a local authority or a company to a lender.

- *Capex* – capital expenditure.

- *Carry trade* – The carry of an asset is the return from or cost of holding it. 'Carry trade' describes a tactic of borrowing a currency on which the interest rate is low and investing the borrowing in a higher-yielding one. The borrower then pockets the higher interest while paying only the lower interest on the borrowing.

- *Collateral* – Borrowers may give lenders a claim on some of their assets, which can be sold if they do not repay. These assets are known as collateral.

- *Credit default swap* – A type of insurance bought by lenders. The seller of the CDS pays up if the lender does not receive his due payments from the borrower.

- *Derivatives* – These include futures, options, swaps and other devices for reducing risk or making a profit. For example, a trader might strike a deal with a farmer to buy wheat at a given price in six months time. This is a future. Both trader and farmer reduce their risks. The trader knows he will get the grain. The farmer has a guaranteed price.

Buying options takes this a step further. A trader buys an option to purchase something at an agreed price on an agreed date. But he/she does not have to buy if, when the day comes, the market price is below the agreed price. Option-buying was made possible by the Black-Scholes model devised by American mathematicians in the 1970s. The model enables options to be priced.

Besides options to buy, there are options to sell, called 'put' options. Financier A buys shares with the option to sell them again at a given price on a given date.

- *Due diligence* – This indicates that people buying a company or placing an investment have carefully investigated what they are buying.

- *EBITDA* – Earnings before interest, taxes, depreciation and amortization. (Amortization is the depreciation of intangible assets such as patents and licences.)

- *Hedge funds* – Groupings of private investors which can take more risks than a public fund. They may 'hedge' their investment in company A by selling shares in company B. If share prices go down and they lose money on company A shares, they can probably buy company B shares at a lower price than they sold them. (See short selling below). Investors can withdraw money from a hedge fund more easily than from a private-equity deal.

- *Islamic finance* – The Qu'ran, like the Bible, forbids usury, that is, receiving interest on loans. However, receiving rent or a share of profits is OK. So Islamic finance, or sukuk, seeks to offer deals which reward Muslim lenders with rent or a profit-share, rather than interest. If Muslim lenders have lent to a company that cannot repay, they may not find it easy to claim assets pledged to them as collateral. *The Times* reported (12 11 09) that Islamic bonds have an 'obscure and untested legal structure'.

Islamic law forbids gambling and speculation. This means that an Islamic hedge fund can hedge against risks but cannot easily run them.

Standards of practice are issued by the Islamic Finance Service Board and the Accounting and Auditing Organization for Islamic Financial Institutions.

- *LIBOR* – The London Inter Bank Offered Rate is the interest rate at which one bank will lend money to another.

- *Mezzanine loans* – Loans are normally secured against the assets of the borrowing business. Mezzanine loans are secured only against the shareholders' capital. So, if the shareholders lose their shirts, the mezzanine lenders may do, too. Mezzanine loans therefore attract higher interest payments. But managers needing cash may prefer a mezzanine loan to selling shares and being forced to pay dividends to the new shareholders.

- *Preference shares* – Companies pay dividends on these before they pay ordinary shareholders. But preference shareholders do not normally have a vote at company meetings. The government bought many preference shares in banks in 2008/9.

- *Price/earnings ratio* – This measures the price of a share relative to the company's net income. It provides a way of assessing whether a share is cheap or expensive. Another yardstick for shares is EV/EBITDA – enterprise value relative to earnings before income, taxes, depreciation and amortization.

- *Rights issue* – A company seeks to increase its capital by selling more shares to its shareholders. This is a rights issue. It is likely to be underwritten by a bank: that is, the bank will take any unsold shares.

- *Scrip issue* – A company issues free shares to its shareholders.

- *Share options* give managers and employees an option to buy shares in their company at the current price at a later date. This gives them an incentive to work hard and boost the company's share price so that, when they buy their shares, they will show an immediate profit.

- *Short selling* – If speculators expect the price of a company's shares to fall, they may sell shares they do not own. They hope to buy shares more cheaply later. Short-sellers need to buy shares eventually. They were initially blamed for the share-price slump of 2008. But shareholders who sold shares because they needed the money proved more damaging.

- *Sovereign risk* – The risk that a foreign central bank will change its foreign exchange regulations.

- *Sovereign wealth funds* – Several countries including China, Singapore, Australia and Middle Eastern oil states earn more abroad than they spend there. As a result, they hold billions of dollars. They may invest them in enterprises abroad through a sovereign (state-owned) wealth fund. The largest of these is the Abu Dhabi Investment Council, which has holdings totalling nearly $9 billion. The leading Chinese fund, the China Investment Corporation, held $298 billion in 2008. The Government of Singapore Investment Corporation held $330 billion.

Other business organizations

Building societies and some insurers are in mutual ownership, that is, they are owned by their customers. Many building societies became banks but mutual societies also remain. The easiest way to obtain the accounts of a building society is to ask them for it or look at their website.

A private school may be a private business or it may be a charity. A gym or sports centre may be run by entrepreneurial managers, but its legal form may be that of a membership club. Then there are housing associations, which supply affordable homes. As landlords they are supervised by the Tenant Services Authority, as builders by the Homes and Communities Agency (mail@homesandcommunities.co.uk), which promotes regeneration. The TSA has offices nationwide reachable through 0845 230 7000.

Accounts and names of committee members for over 2000 housing associations can be inspected at the TSA, 149 Tottenham Court Road, London W1P 0BN (press 020 7393 2115; www.tenantservicesauthority.org).

Trade unions produce accounts for the Certification Office for Trade Unions and Employers Associations, 180 Borough High Street, London SE1 1LW (press 020 7210 3719/3651; www.certoffice.org).

Details and accounts of charities are filed with the Charity Commission, Harmsworth House, 13–15 Bouverie Street, London EC4Y 8DP (press: 020 7674 2366/2332/2528; www.charitycommission.gov.uk).

Alternatively, you may simply ask organizations for their accounts.

Trade unions

Trade union militancy was growing in 2008/9. A strike by Shell tanker drivers won a 14 per cent pay increase over two years. Supplies of petrol were interrupted earlier by a strike at the Grangemouth refinery in Scotland over pensions. The year 2009 saw strikes at construction sites, aimed at preserving jobs for British workers.

If you have to cover a strike, go behind what employers and unions say and find out what the strike is really about. Disputes are usually about money and jobs. Report both sides fairly and sympathetically. It is helpful if you have already met the trade union representatives, perhaps by attending the local trades council. They may also come to your local council's advisory committees.

Trade unions have gone through much amalgamation. The Shell strike made Unite national news. Formed in 2007, it is Britain's largest union, organizing workers in transport, construction and manufacturing. It includes both of the giants of old: the Transport and General Workers and the Amalgamated Engineers.

Another giant union, Unison, dominates local government and the health service. It was formed in 1993 from the National and Local Government Officers Association, the National Union of Public Employees and the Confederation of Health Service Employees.

The GMB (General and Municipal and Boilermakers) continues alongside these. So do the RMT (Rail and Maritime), UCATT (the building industry union), the National Union of Teachers, the NASUWT (National Association of Schoolmasters/Union of Women Teachers), the British Association of Social Workers, the British Medical Association (of doctors), the Royal College of Nursing and others.

Questions

1. What unusual companies would you like to write about?

2. Write a story from the accounts of a local company. If its sales are down, why has this happened? With what money does it finance its operations? Do the accounts mention salaries paid to directors and other high-earners? Do the accounts contain important footnotes?

3. Has a local company failed recently? Why did this happen?

12 Investigative reporting

Time and Haditha

Before *Time* magazine published its report 'One Morning in Haditha' (27 03 06), the media had frequently alleged that American soldiers, hit by bombs in Iraq, had fired indiscriminately, killing civilians. But most of these allegations left open the possibility that the shootings were accidental or in response to insurgent fire. Accounts of the Haditha incident, which took place on 19 November 2005, could have been similarly vague. According to a US Marine communiqué, a bomb went off, killing a marine and 15 civilians. Marines came under fire which they returned, killing eight insurgents.

However, *Time* went to Haditha and interviewed local people, including six whose relatives had died. One of the six was nine-year-old Eman Waleed who described how her relatives were shot. A doctor said that the bodies had bullet wounds, not bomb injuries. A local journalism student made a video which *Time* saw. It showed dead women and children still in their night-clothes. House walls had bulletholes on the inside.

Time's article, like the pictures of maltreated prisoners in Abu Ghraib (Baghdad), resulted in a trial of those accused of being responsible. It shows what investigative journalism is about.

It looks beyond confusing reports of allegation and reply and seeks to establish the truth. Those who do not wish to confront truths are obliged to. Some people may get sent to prison. Others, wrongly imprisoned, may be set free.

The effectiveness of investigative reporting varies. Exposing the truth brings no change unless someone takes action. Freelance Duncan Campbell has spent a lifetime exposing telephone-tapping by the American and British governments. They still tap.

Around 2000, some writers were bemoaning the death of investigative reporting, because of its cost to cash-strapped media. Websites, however, with their need for publicity and their desire to determine the news agenda, have given it a fillip.

Where's that public money gone?

In autumn 2007 and winter 2008, the *Evening Standard* brought to light weaknesses in government at London's City Hall. Columnist Andrew Gilligan established there seemed little to show for over £3 million granted to 13 businesses through the London Development Agency, the Mayor's business-and-jobs promoter.

How did Andrew Gilligan locate and pursue the story? He explained in *Press Gazette* (18 01 08) that he found on the London Assembly's website a reference to a grant of £287,000 for premises, to an organization called Brixton Base. Another reference said that Brixton Base occupied a Mayor-owned building rent-free.

He looked at the Companies House file on Brixton Base and found it had not accounted for the public money. He found, too, that its patron was Lee Jasper, an adviser to Mayor Livingstone, and its director a friend of Jasper's. He looked up other companies with the same address and found 11. They had been granted at least £2.5 million in public cash.

Calls to contacts garnered leaked e-mails and dozens of interviews, on and off the record. 'The more you know before you call someone,' Gilligan says, 'the likelier they are to help you.'

He knew Mayor Livingstone would denounce him as a racist. So he kept publishing more and more evidence, establishing that he was not just expressing prejudice – there was a case to answer.

Gilligan also comments. 'Anonymous sources, however accurate, are not enough. This story rests on signed statements, taped interviews, documents.' These enabled Gilligan to prove he had reason to suspect something was wrong. He might have to prove this if there was a libel case.

Investigations in the provinces

Provincial journalists have made some celebrated investigations. In the 1970s, Ray Fitzwalter – then deputy news editor at the *Telegraph and Argus*, Bradford – exposed the conspiracies of John Poulson, an architect who won construction contracts from public bodies by offering inducements to councillors and officers. Also in the 1970s, Bob Satchwell, then news editor at the *Lancashire Evening Post*, brought about the dismissal of Lancashire's chief constable, Stanley Parr. Rob Waugh of the *Yorkshire Post* was among those short-listed for the Paul Foot Award for investigative or campaigning journalism in 2009. Whereas others were listed for one investigation, he was listed for three: his exposure of cavalier spending at Leeds Metropolitan University, his expose discrediting the takeover of Sheffield Wednesday and his long-running investigation into Leeds City Credit mismanagement (*BJR*, December 2009).

Community newspapers have often been prominent in local investigations. Jim Oldfield, editor of *Rossington Community Newsletter* (South Yorkshire), was short-listed for the Paul Foot award in 2008.

Investigative success pleases the readers. Geoff Elliott, former editor of the *News*, Portsmouth, said in an interview: 'People like their newspaper to be the means by which what is really happening is exposed.' It follows that the most useful investigations for a newspaper are into matters affecting readers and their interests.

Doing it right

Investigative reporting has been described as afflicting the comfortable and comforting the afflicted. It has also been summed up, by *The Sunday Times*, as *We name the guilty men, The arrow points to the defective parts* or *Stop these evil practices now.*

It stands to be judged not just by its conclusions but by the manner in which it reached them. As *Digging Deeper* by Cribb et al. (Oxford, 2006) puts it, don't lie, don't steal, don't misrepresent yourself.

According to the *Neue Zuercher Zeitung* (6 06 08), the investigative methods used by the British media are notorious. The problem, said the NZZ, was the temptation: *The more interest in someone grows, the less that ethical rules, the law or the police can do about it.*

Magnus Linklater (*BJR*, September 2008) urged reporters to behave better. It is their responsibility, he wrote, to remember that 'the measure of an intrusive inquiry should not just be the depth of tomorrow's headline but the human being on the receiving end of it'.

If you damage someone's reputation, the life of your target may be changed. He/she may have to move house and start life again. He/she can also bring an action for libel – and how fairly you conducted your inquiries can bear on the outcome. The someone who sues may not be the target of your article. It can be someone you mentioned in passing.

Journalists and media can defeat a libel claim if they can show that what they wrote is true or is fair comment – more accurately, honest comment – or is privileged (you wrote a fair and accurate report of a public hearing or meeting). The fair comment defence requires that the facts underlying the comment are true and that the comment is clearly comment, not a statement of fact. McNae points out that, in the George Galloway case alluded to below, the *Daily Telegraph* argued that a headline referring to *damning new evidence* was fair comment. Mr Justice Eady disagreed. He saw 'damning' as an allegation of fact, that the evidence damned Galloway. (Eady similarly decided in 2009 that a *Guardian* article saying there was not a jot of evidence for some claims by chiropractors was asserting a fact, not making a comment. But this decision was overruled by the Court of Appeal.)

Fairness and the Reynolds defence

Fairness in reporting is not in itself a defence to a libel action. But it does help establish a Reynolds defence (see next paragraph). The evidence in a libel case can include the manner in which the reporters behaved. Were they fair and evenhanded in their inquiries? Did they give to the people they accused a fair and timely chance to reply?

The law lords introduced the Reynolds defence in a case brought by Albert Reynolds, a former Irish prime minister. It can give the protection of privilege to defamatory statements, even though they are not reports of what was said on privileged occasions. Stuart Patrick, night lawyer for national newspapers, commented in *The Journalists Handbook* (2001): 'It is becoming increasingly clear that all that stands between a successful defence of privilege and a six or seven-figure bill for damages and costs is the honesty and thoroughness of the journalist's inquiries.'

Patrick set out the considerations affecting a successful Reynolds defence. They include:

1. The seriousness of the allegation.

2. The nature of the information and whether it is of public concern.

3. The source of the information (no axe grinders or paid informants).

4. The steps taken to verify the story.

5. Whether comment was sought from the person criticized and whether the gist of what he/she said was given.

6. The tone of the article.

7. Whether it was urgent to publish the article (or it could have waited for further inquiries).

Before a libel action is heard, there is a process called discovery. An accused newspaper can ask to see relevant letters and documents held by its accuser. Similarly, the accuser can ask to see the notes and notebooks of the reporters. Notes taken should therefore simply be notes. Any rude or flippant remarks will create a bad impression in court.

Since October 2006 the public have been able to see documents filed in court proceedings, including statements of case (setting out claim and defence). The *Financial Times* (12 08 08) used documents from civil proceedings to investigate drugmakers' meetings, alleged to have cost the Department of Health £60 million.

Earlier, in February, the *Financial Times* secured a court ruling that the right to see includes documents relating to judicial reviews of the actions of the government and public authorities.

People can bring a libel action even if they are not named in your report. This means that generalized allegations which could refer to several people are dangerous. Any of them could sue.

The Police Federation brought a series of what were called 'garage' actions (because they yielded enough money to build a garage). It sued newspapers which had accused unnamed police officers of malpractice. It argued that fellow officers knew who they were, even if they were not named.

The law of libel is not the only law to trap investigative reporters. The law of confidence can, too. Under this law, employees have a duty to protect their employer's confidential information. Documents produced by an organization are the property of that organization. If someone has given you an incriminating document, don't spread the good news and don't keep the document longer than you need. The organization that produced the document can demand it back, which can mean trouble for the reporter and for whoever supplied it. In 1984, the *Guardian* was obliged to surrender a copy of a Ministry of Defence document. As a result, Sarah Tisdall was identified as the source and jailed for six months under the Official Secrets Act. However, the European Court of Human Rights in 2009 overturned a UK judgment that the media should hand over leaked documents concerning Interbrew, a Belgian brewer. The court held that the threat to Interbrew did not outweigh the public interest in the protection of journalists' sources (*FT*, 16 12 09).

In October 2009 a firm called Trafigura obtained a High Court injunction stopping the *Guardian* and other media reporting a Parliamentary question about a legal dispute concerning waste-dumping in the Ivory Coast. Reporting on US-based Twitter, however, defeated the injunction (*FT*, 14 10 09).

McNae points out that judges have extended the law of confidence to cover situations where confidentiality might be expected, even though there is no contract or relationship requiring it. In this context, confidentiality means much the same as privacy, to which people also have a claim under the Human Rights Act. In a case concerning the model Naomi Campbell's drug therapy in 2004, the law lords held that the unjustified publication of private information was actionable.

In July 2008, Mr Justice Eady followed this up. He said (*FT*, 25 07 08) that Max Mosley, head of Formula 1 motor racing, had a reasonable expectation of privacy for sexual activity between consenting adults. He awarded £60,000 damages against the *News of the World*, which had exposed a sadomasochistic session involving Mosley and five women. One of the women took a secret film. Mr Justice Eady said his decision would not inhibit investigative journalism in the public interest. So, to justify secret filming behind closed doors, you need to show a stronger public interest than there was in exposing Mosley's session.

The Press Complaints Commission Code gives these examples of what is in the public interest:

1. Detection or exposure of crime or serious impropriety.

2. Protection of public health and safety.

3. Prevention of the public from being misled.

4. Upholding freedom of expression.

In 2007/8, police unearthed from the common law a new weapon against inquiring journalists, and those who give them tips – the offence of aiding and abetting misconduct in a public office. This was the allegation against Tory MP, Damian Green, in November 2008. In May the previous year it was alleged against Sally Murrer, a reporter for the Milton Keynes Citizen, and Derek Webb, a private detective working for national newspapers.

Sally had been pursuing stories about a young offender, a footballer and a murder victim. Police put a bug in the car of her contact, a detective sergeant. In November 2008 her barrister at Kingston Crown Court argued that the bugging breached the

European Convention of Human Rights. The judge ruled that the police had failed to establish an overriding public interest in identifying Sally Murrer's source by covert means. She, Webb and the sergeant were cleared (Press Gazette, 29 11 08).

Most stories to investigate come from people

Stories to investigate may come from the web, such as Andrew Gilligan's London Development Agency inquiry and a *Guardian* story about corruption in Kenya which came from the Wikileaks website (31 08 07) (http://wikileaks. org) which publishes anonymous leaks of sensitive documents.

But most ideas for investigative stories come from people, who may have their own reasons for giving them to you. They may have a strong sense that something is wrong. They may have a score to settle. You want from them documents which support their allegations. Jimmy Burns, social affairs correspondent at the *FT*, remarked in an interview: 'Editors crave documents. They trust documents more than people, who will lead you up the garden path.' Freelance Mark Hollingsworth said: 'People's memories aren't reliable whereas, if what they say is documented, it's more reliable.'

Bob Satchwell's case against Chief Constable Parr was based on his success in obtaining a secret report by another chief constable on what Parr had done.

Documents can be hoaxes, so you need to satisfy yourself that they are genuine. Is the handwriting that of the person who supposedly wrote the letter? The websites of Companies House and the Charity Commission can provide written evidence. The Charity Commission site provided basic facts for Sue Reid's report on Sentebale *(Mail, 25 10 08)*, a charity sponsored by Prince Harry, which helps children in Lesotho. Leaders of two children's projects complained they were struggling because Sentebale had given them less money than it promised. Sentebale replied that it could not give money until it was sure this would be accounted for.

By going to Sentebale on the Charity Commission website and clicking *View accounts* on the left-hand side of the opening page, inquirers could discover that, in its first 16 months to August 2007, Sentebale:

1. Had an income of over £1 million.
2. Made grants totalling £84,000 to Lesotho children's organizations.
3. Paid one employee £90,000 to £100,000.
4. Spent £49,000 on motor vehicles.

It seems churlish to criticize a charity, particularly one sponsored by a popular prince. However, as *Digging Deeper* points out, people running a charity are running a service. How well they plan and run it and what they spend its money on are important to the consumers – both the people who give money and those who hope to benefit.

A guide for investigative reporters

- Read all the written material you can find.

- Be patient in reading reports and accounts carefully.

- Speak to everyone relevant and go to everywhere relevant. Hearing of the My Lai (Vietnam) massacre a year after it happened, American investigative journalist Seymour Hersh traced 60 members of the company involved (Simon Kuper, *FT*, 2 08 08).

- Be persistent. John Ware of Panorama worked for years on the Omagh bombing in Northern Ireland which killed 29 people. One reporter said: 'You have to have a feeling of outrage about wrongdoing.'

- Ring up every day till you catch the people you need to speak to. Missing one could leave you with less than the full story or even with a libel action.

- Be fair and even-handed in inquiries. Give opportunities for reply.

- Don't take everything and everyone at their face value. Ask: Why have I been given this story?

- Tape what you can, including what you say yourself. Keep good, dated notes of what you can't tape. Get people to sign statements.

- Don't cause trouble for people who help you. No one's livelihood is worth a two-page exclusive in your paper.

- Be nice to people. You want them to talk to you. Explain why, and how you propose to use the information they give.

- Dig out your own facts, if possible, rather than simply relying on other people's allegations. (Peter Watson and a Channel 4 team who exposed art and antiquities smuggling did not rely simply on documents that Watson had been given. They showed that what the documents alleged actually happened (*Sothebys: Inside Story*, Bloomsbury, 1997).)

- Find additional evidence to put in if your evidence is challenged. After your article is published, valuable new witnesses may ring up. If your article is published online, it may attract useful comments.

- Get original documents. Photocopies are hard to use as evidence.

- Don't devalue a good investigative story by including details that turn out to be inaccurate. BBC presenter Andrew Marr's best seller, *A History of Modern Britain*, was withdrawn from sale because of a reference to Erin Pizzey, pioneer of women's refuges (*Mail on Sunday*, 8 03 09). She got an apology and undisclosed damages from Macmillan, Marr's publisher (BBC, 1 04 09).

Investigative reporting requires the backing of editors and managements, because of both the time it takes and of the risks of a libel case. Andrew

Gilligan, then of the *Evening Standard*, wrote in *Press Gazette* (18 01 08): 'I work with one of the very few editors prepared to persist, to give serious investigations the time and space they depend on.'

How *Time* wrote the Haditha story

Good investigative journalism does not sensationalize and does not pass on rumours. It avoids exaggerated allegations. It makes clear what is fact, what is allegation and where the allegation comes from. It often presents its findings in a narrative, the simplest way to tell a complicated story.

Time magazine's account of the Haditha killings in Iraq in November 2005 starts with a deadpan introduction: *The incident seemed like so many others from this war*. The emotional charge of the opening page lies in the wistful picture of Eman Waleed, the nine-year-old survivor. The caption reads unemotionally: *Eman, 9, says she saw US troops kill seven family members*.

After the intro, reporter Tim McGurk outlines the facts chronologically, with detail that makes them authentic. We learn what company of marines was involved. We learn that the marine killed by a bomb before the shootings was Lance Corporal Miguel (T.J.) Terrazas, 20, from El Paso.

McGurk then quotes from the initial Marine communiqué on the incident, leaving the reader to conclude that the communiqué was misleading. He ends the opening paragraph with the memorial service, at which marines wrote such messages as 'T.J., you were a great friend.' In this way, McGurk makes the point that he is sympathetic rather than hostile to the marines.

In his second paragraph, McGurk outlines a different story from that of the marine communiqué. He then says that *Time* submitted this account to military officials who interviewed 28 people and concluded that 15 civilians were killed by the marines and not, as the communiqué had said, in the blast that killed Terrazas.

In this way, McGurk shows he is not simply making allegations. He is reporting a military investigation. *The military's own reconstruction of events and the accounts of town residents paint a picture of a devastatingly violent response by a group of US troops who had lost one of their number to a deadly insurgent attack and believed they were under fire.*

Having made his story as fireproof as possible, McGurk tells it in greater detail, quoting Eman Waleed and American military officials. His final, measured conclusion is: *The available evidence does not provide conclusive proof that the Marines deliberately killed innocents in Haditha. But the accounts of human rights groups and survivors and local officials do raise questions about whether the extent of force used by the Marines was justified.* (*Time* is not asserting that something bad definitely happened. It is taking the more easily defensible position that it has reasonable grounds for suspecting that something bad happened.)

The report ends touchingly with Eman Waleed taking a handful of sweets. *'It's for my little brother,'* she says. *'I have to take care of my brother. Nobody else is left.'*

When newspapers have lost

Here are cases where newspaper investigations have been successfully challenged.

- *2006*: The *Financial Times* settled a case brought by a moneybroker, over four articles based on allegations by a former employee. It paid £300,000 damages plus the broker's £2.2 million costs (*Independent*, 18 01 06).

- *December 2004*: Anti-Iraq-war-campaigner George Galloway MP won £150,000 libel damages from the *Daily Telegraph* over claims that he was receiving £375,000 a year from Saddam Hussein. Mr Justice Eady held that the *Telegraph* had not given Galloway enough opportunity to respond. He also said that the *Telegraph* had reported the allegations with relish, rather than in a neutral tone (*Independent*, 3 12 04).

- *2001*: *The Times* accused Grigori Loutchansky, a Latvian businessman, of money-laundering. A judge found that the report was of allegations, not *The Times*'s own investigations. He also said that efforts to get a reply from Loutchansky were inadequate and that *The Times* should have taken account of witnesses who did not support its story.

- *2000*: The *Sunday Mirror* (*Media Lawyer*, May 2000) accused James Gilbert Ltd of not inquiring as promised into an allegation that its Indian-made rugby balls were made by children. Mr Justice Eady found that the *Sunday Mirror* had not done enough to verify what it said and had not given the firm an adequate chance to comment. Mirror Group agreed to pay £10,000 damages under a new procedure for summary disposal of libel cases. (Gilberts had in fact sent an inquiry team to India. One lesson from this and other cases is that it is hard to establish that something did not happen.)

- *1989*: Damages of £470,000 were awarded against the *Mail on Sunday*. Sainsburys argued that an article had inferred it knowingly repackaged and sold food past its sell-by date. The article did not directly accuse Sainsburys. It said that canned spaghetti destined for Sainsburys was somewhere relabelled. But this appeared in a page headed: *The scandal of sell-by food*. (The story is told in McNae.)

Giving an opinion on a *Leeds Weekly News* report warning against a karate club run by GKR Karate Ltd, a judge found that a message to a pager was not a sufficient opportunity for the club to reply. The report should not have presented as fact an assertion that the club was ripping people off and it should have mentioned that Leeds Trading Standards had received no complaints. However, the judge acknowledged there was a duty to draw the club to public attention and that a reliable reporter, Sheila Holmes, had adequately investigated the allegations. The *Weekly News* escaped liability.

Investigative reporters who have been murdered

1. *Anna Politkovskaya* investigated atrocities in the Chechnya conflict. A Russian colonel there subjected her to a mock execution. She was shot dead in 2006, in the lift to her Moscow flat.

2. *Carlos Cardoso,* Mozambique's most prominent journalist, was shot in November 2000 while investigating corruption in two privatized banks.

3. *Veronica Guerin,* Ireland. Shot by a motorcyclist in 1996. She rattled Dublin criminals by confronting them in their homes.

4. *Tim Lopez,* TV Globo, Brazil, investigated claims of sexual exploitation at drug pushers' parties. Tortured to death in 2002.

An assailant ran down TV investigator Roger Cook with a car, fracturing his skull. Garry Lloyd and Julian Mounter of *The Times* were grilled for three weeks by police after they exposed corrupt detectives. They received menacing phonecalls at night.

Those who help with media investigations can lose their jobs. Margaret Haywood, a nurse who filmed secretly for BBC Panorama to expose dreadful conditions for elderly patients in the Royal Sussex Hospital in 2005, was struck off by the Nursing and Midwifery Council for breaching patients' confidentiality (*Mail*, 17 04 09). As the proverb says, no good deed goes unpunished.

For further reading see *Digging Deeper*, by Robert Cribb, Dean Jobb, David McKie and Fred Vallance-Jones (Oxford, 2006). This is a Canadian book but useful to non-Canadians. Among many other things, it explains in detail how to use Microsoft Excel spreadsheets to do calculations, and the Microsoft Access database manager to analyse data.

Questions

1. What legal dangers face investigative reporting?
2. How can they best be avoided?

Features: illuminating the world

Newsweek magazine said it wanted colour, quotes and anecdotes, when it offered a job to broadcaster and foreign correspondent Robin Lustig (*BJR*, September 2008). That is not a bad formula for features.

Anything in a newspaper which is not a news story or an advertisement is a feature. Features include the crossword, the horoscope, the TV programmes. However, this chapter uses a narrower definition. A feature here is what most readers would call an article. Features in this sense illuminate the world – the world of news, the world of people, the world as people experience it. They must therefore be well researched – see Chapters 2 and 3 – so that they tell readers something new.

Features can be topical, explaining the background to the news or the people in the news. They can even anticipate what will be news. Or they can be entertaining and informative, about holidays, cars, science, history, anniversaries, discoveries, nature, fashion, chess, art, homes, cookery.

Here is how a feature could come about. Buried in a sentence in the *Big Issue* (2 02 09) is the statement: *One in four of us is now teetotal*. If true, this is remarkable, given that being teetotal has been unpopular for a century. So is it true? Is it true in your town? If so, why? Have people given up alcohol for better health? Can they not afford it? Is it in part that many Britons are teetotal Muslims? Is it now more acceptable socially to drink coffee or orange juice when others are drinking wine or beer?

Choose your subject carefully

The infinite possibilities for feature-writing are a snare, particularly for free-lances. It is not enough that you are fascinated by the person you are interviewing or the subject you are investigating. You have to make a features editor think: 'I should have asked for a feature about that'. Or 'This is just the background piece I need to explain today's news'. Or, best of all, 'The readers will love this.'

Editors vary. Some play safe and rely on trusted writers and friends. Others are prepared to try someone new. Some are imaginative, others not. All should have in mind the question: will our readers read this?

Here are a few ideas and situations which made or might have made published features:

- City dwellers are greener than country dwellers. They throw away less rubbish, live in smaller homes, emit less carbon dioxide.

- A footballer rescues African boys abandoned in Europe by football agents.

- An old-style village library, and its customers, still go strong.

- How are people going to vote in the by-election?

- Are parking charges killing the town?

For Mothers Day 2009, the *Western Mail* interviewed a teenage mother, a surrogate mother, a celebrity mother, a foster mother, a mother of quads, a housemother at a boarding school and a grandmother caring for three grandchildren.

Preferably, before you start writing, you want the features editor's promise to use your piece, and a suggestion of length. A good picture to accompany it will help. Your feature must fall within the field of the editor you are approaching. Editors able to accept features on a wide range of subjects may be over-supplied. You may do better to offer a homes feature for the property page or a travel feature for the travel pages or a business feature for the business page.

Watch out for feature series – about outstanding people or small companies or unusual experiences, perhaps – which do not have a single author. The editors could be looking for contributions to keep them going. For the small-company series, for example, try to find the people who are doing something different – the man whose hawk chases pigeons off the cathedral. Don't be content with those making arty pots in a picturesque village.

Rather than acquire and unload a stack of information on a wide subject, concentrate on one aspect. You should end up with an easy-to-read article of manageable length. However, it helps the readers' understanding if you can put your subject in a wider context. Professor Brian Cox (Horizon, BBC2, 17 02 09) put his exploration of the power-generating potential of nuclear fusion in the context of the vast amount of electricity we will need if everyone in the world is to have a modestly decent standard of living.

A review of features, written over 20 years, suggests that the most attractive are about people with engaging things to say about themselves and their work. Descriptions of places in the news and possibly humorous accounts of incidents can also be attractive. It helps to have been to see what you are writing about. But workaday features, explaining a subject or the news background, are also important.

Don't sit on the fence

A good feature has an intriguing beginning, an illuminating middle – through which flows an unbroken thread of argument or narrative – and a conclusion answering the question you raised. Who is going to win the election? Is this person praiseworthy or not? If your feature is not particularly serious, its conclusion could be humorous.

If you don't want to put your own conclusion on a feature, you can use a telling quote from one of your informants. Mure Dickie ended a feature (*FT*, 22 11 07) about free speech and the rise of China with a quote from a Chinese professor: 'If people do not have the right of expression, there can be no rise to speak of.'

Ideally a feature should exactly fit the space allocated to it, because a cut from the end would deprive it of its conclusion. Even so, the end of your feature may get lost. So don't leave the meat of the feature till the last few paragraphs.

Ways to begin

A feature can start in much the same way as a news story: *Jerome Kerviel, the man who lost £3 billion and brought one of the world's major banks to its knees, was heading for cult status today* (*Evening Standard*, 29 01 08). This intro tells the editor at a glance what it is about. The editor can quickly decide whether to use it. To ensure that editor and reader know what you are offering, write an explanatory blurb paragraph (standfirst) and put it at the top of your piece. For the Kerviel story, you might have written: **What sort of man was Jerome Kerviel who cost Paris-based bank Societe Generale £3 billion? This article explains.**

Many features start with a story: *Emily was 19 when she was raped. One of the men present during her ordeal was a male 'friend'. She did not go to the police. She did not tell anyone. Instead, she buried the experience and lurched through her twenties* (Helena Drakakis, the *Big Issue*, 21 01 08). This feature returned in its last paragraphs to Emily and closed with a comment by her. Writers often round off their articles in this way.

Avoid starting your narrative with a 'when' clause. Many features start with 'when'. You can usually turn the sentence round, so the when clause comes second.

It used to be said that you should not start with a quote. But you can if it is striking like this one from Isaac Slade of The Fray, used by celebrity interviewer Jacqui Swift in the *Sun* (6 02 09): *'I dreamt I ran into God on a street corner. He looked like Bruce Springsteen and he was smoking a cigarette.'*

Martin Wolf, associate editor of the *Financial Times*, found an image to start a feature about the nationalized banks: *The government looks increasingly like a python which has swallowed a hippopotamus* (6 03 09).

Writer Anne Dunlop used a conversational approach in the *Belfast Telegraph* (6 05 09): *Maud was eight and she was off-colour. 'I feel tired,' said Maud. I wasn't very sympathetic. 'Stop waking up so early in the morning,' I said. Since she was born, Maud has woken at six and has woken her brother and sister at six and has woken me at six and our entire household is up at six every morning when eight o'clock would be perfectly fine.*

Here is another, rougher conversational approach: *John Cusack refuses to just shut up and act. 'I don't care what these people think,' he says of Right-wingers who believe that actors should be seen on the screen and not heard on the soapbox* (*London Lite*, 23 03 09).

In contrast, your feature could start like a chapter in a novel. *Oleg Deripaska had reason to be in ebullient form as the late August sun washed the grey steel hull and white superstructure of his yacht, the 72-metre Queen K, moored off the coast of Corfu* (*FT*, 25 10 08).

Many feature writers display their descriptive powers, whether lush – *The blooms come pushing through the clenched teeth of late winter, vivid with the colours of a concubine's wardrobe* (*FT*, 28 10 06) – or gritty – *Today, a large black crow sits guard on top of William Hunter's house, squawking at anyone who dares to look up. The long grass in the garden below is beginning to creep up the pebbledashed walls* (*Big Issue*, 14 04 08).

You can learn from communicators who are not journalists. Here are the engaging opening paragraphs of a short article about soil by Malcolm Bolton, Professor of Soil Mechanics at Cambridge (*Cambridge Alumni Magazine*, Michaelmas 2008). He handles long sentences, and adjectives, deftly. Features use more adjectives than news stories.

> *Soil is a natural material, freely available and, although it won't do everything perfectly – in fact it won't do many things perfectly – it is very cheap, pliable, long-lasting and almost indestructible. It is also sustainable and recyclable because, when you're fed up with your road embankment in one place, you can dig it up and it's just as good if you compact it and place it somewhere else.*
>
> *So soil is a very neat building material and economical, but it is also weak and very deformable. If you are careless with it, your building foundations will crack up or your railway embankment will creep and you will have to endlessly reset the rails. All these problems can and do occur, and it's our job to try and clarify the mechanisms of these aspects of behaviour in a way that graduate engineers will be able to grasp and apply in practice.*

Feature construction

Features should do what they promise. A feature headed *The man who risked his life to save mine* (*Evening Standard*, 29 01 08) would seem to promise considerable information about the saviour. However, it concentrated on Chris Corbin, the saved, a restaurateur who needed a marrow transplant. Of the donor we learn only that he is a Leicestershire businessman with two children, gets on well with Corbin and is very different from him. But in what way?

Tease out of your notes the most important and interesting material and put that high in your feature. Don't simply reproduce interviews in the possibly rambling order in which your informants spoke.

A David Attenborough TV programme about Charles Darwin (BBC1, 1 02 09) showed how to construct an explanation for a lay audience. He began with a short account of how Darwin developed his theory of evolution. Then he dealt with the questions Darwin's critics raised. What simpler life forms came before the complex fossils which were the earliest then known? Where were the missing links between reptiles and birds and mammals? Was the earth old enough for its diverse creatures to have evolved? What genetic mechanism underlay evolution? If frogs evolved in Africa, how did they get to America when they could not swim there?

An attractive way to construct a feature is to alternate quotes and narrative. This passage is from an article in *The Northern Echo* by Lindsay Jennings (30 06 06).

> *Not many people in Britain know the name Michael Stadther. A queue of excited children are waiting for him to sign their bookmarks. Michael, 54, has finished reading an extract from his book* A Treasure Trove, *an illustrated fairytale with a golden twist. They all loved it.*
>
> *'You're cool,' said a red-haired kid with freckles at the front of the queue. 'Thanks,' replies Michael. 'You're cool,' he says again, mesmerized.*
>
> *Michael grew up dirt-poor in Birmingham, Alabama, where he used to love digging for treasures – old bottle tops, anything – in his grandmother's backyard. He also loved the book* Masquerade *by British author Kit Williams – where people followed clues in the story to hunt for real buried treasure. He pledged to create a similar book one day. After he sold two banking software companies, he knew his time had come.*
>
> *'Before that I used to be in business meetings and, when nothing was going on, I would be thinking of how to put clues in a book.'*

Mummy's boy to businessman: a feature analysed

Here is an annotated feature from the *Financial Times*'s Mind Your Own Business series (19 03 94). Being about a young man from an immigrant community, it widened the scope of the series. It helps that he was a clear and engaging talker. The numbers in the text refer to the notes that follow.

> *People called him boring, a workaholic, a mummy's boy. But, at the age of 25, Ranu Miah is employing 18 people in a successful London business (1).*
>
> *His company, R and R Fashions, makes leather coats, jackets, trousers and skirts for ten shops in London, south-east England, Ireland and Manchester. The shops pay on delivery because they know they can quickly sell what he supplies (2).*

'A lot of businesses go down because they give a lot of credit. And I don't want to be a finance company,' he says (3).

Ranu is succeeding in a trade which, to most Bangladeshi leather workers around Brick Lane in East London, has offered only a poor living. Many have lost even this living because wholesalers buy garments from Pakistan or India (4).

Ranu, however, has a sharp fashion sense. 'Because I am young,' he says, 'I know what will sell. I read the fashion magazines. On Mondays I get feedback from the shops' (5).

'Other people are now doing the styles we had two years ago. When they copy something, we get rid of it.'

Ranu was born in Bangladesh where leatherwork is not regarded as a good job. But Bangladeshis settling in East London found work with Jewish leather businesses (6).

He was brought to Britain by his father, the first Bangladeshi to run a restaurant in Brick Lane. The restaurant became a haven for new arrivals. 'He was like the Salvation Army,' says Ranu.

'My father wanted me to study and I got a job in a bank. My supervisor said I didn't do the work right. So I left' (7).

He had been out of work six months when a relative offered to teach him the leather trade (8). He learned quickly. To widen his experience, he began working for Gap.

Then, aged 19, he used his savings to take a room and start his own business. His sewing machines came from a partner in a firm that was splitting up. 'I knew he was looking for a job, so I said: "I will give you a job in our place and we will slowly pay you what we owe (for the machines)"' (9).

Ranu's old boss at Gap promised some business. But, first, he needed an alarm to protect his stock of leather. With advice from the East London Small Business Centre, he received a Home Office grant of £750, three-quarters of the cost. The centre also made him a £3000 loan (9).

For the first 18 months, Ranu did not pay himself any wages. 'My parents couldn't give me any money for the business but they looked after me.'

He found work with wholesalers but decided to do his own wholesaling. Armed with a reference from a customer, he arranged to buy his own leather, from an Irish merchant (10).

He realized he could meet almost any request from customers. A competing wholesaler could have 100 customers but might not be able to supply required sizes and colours instantly (11).

He hired larger premises, with an office, from a Bangladeshi millionaire. 'Customers like to talk to you and have a cup of tea,' he says.

And he switched his bank account to a branch in Liverpool Street. His old bank 'didn't like the leather business. They thought we were going to go bust.'

The Liverpool Street branch understood the problems caused if the cheques he wrote for leather were cleared more quickly than those he received from shops.

In the year to last August he recorded turnover of £113,000 with a profit of £10,000. In the current year he reached £113,000 turnover in four months (12).

Young Bangladeshis, he says, are no longer going into the leather trade. 'My younger brother, who is 20, isn't talking of working. He's talking of studying. But this is my hobby as well as my work' (13).

Commentary

(1) The feature starts with two short, contrasting sentences, which provide the ideas for the headline.

(2) The second paragraph swiftly establishes what Ranu makes, where he sells it and why his offers are attractive.

(3) Two short, quoted sentences round off this opening section.

(4) The fourth paragraph gives some background.

(5) This paragraph establishes Ranu as stylish and self-confident, at home in a wider community. The feature alternates quotes with indirect speech. Both quotes and indirect speech use short sentences. One paragraph leads on to another, without the help of linking phrases and without jarring breaks in the chain of thought.

(6) This begins a chronological account of where Ranu has come from and how his career has developed. It is interesting that leatherwork is looked down on in Bangladesh. It suggests the influence of the Indian caste system.

(7) More of Ranu's laconic remarks.

(8) This sentence starts a brief account of how Ranu got his business going.

(9) New businesses need cash and equipment. These paragraphs show how Ranu got them.

(10) To make much money, he needs to buy his own leather and sell his own products, rather than simply cut and stitch jackets for a wholesaler.

(11) This further explains Ranu's competitive edge.

(12) Turnover figures show Ranu has a substantial and growing business.

(13) The last paragraph looks again at a wider picture. Ranu explains why he is still in leather, even though it's no longer fashionable for young Bangladeshis. The ending is a short, ten-word sentence. (The article would have been improved by including a sentence or two about Ranu away from work. Where did he live? What were his interests?)

Profiles

Profile articles, like the one above, tell readers about people in the news or people who are in some way fascinating. Usually, they are based on an interview with the person profiled. Sometimes, this is not possible. A quick profile was needed of Reginald Maudling, a minister in Edward Heath's government. The writer found a book, *Heath and the Heathmen*, which said a lot about Maudling.

Profiles can gain from the comments of friends, acquaintances and even critics who have known your subjects far longer than you have. People are not necessarily who they appear to be or present themselves as being.

What you want from profile interviews is an impression of your subjects and what inspires them, so you can paint them in words. What are they like in their surroundings? You want to know how they got involved in whatever it is they are doing now. What set their lives on new courses?

You also want to know about their other interests. But you don't want to bog down your feature in biographical details.

Dan Smith, the political boss of Newcastle in the 1960s, was tall and looked pallid as if he worked years down a pit. In fact, he didn't. He was an interior decorator. He was also a pianist, and keen to promote the arts.

Jimmy Cayne, chairman of the doomed investment bank Bear Stearns, owed his job to his skill at bridge. He was away playing bridge when Bear started to founder in 2008 (*FT*, 14 03 09).

Above all, you need telling and engaging quotes. A profile of the comedian Lenny Henry consisted almost entirely of the things he said and the way he said them.

Here is Miley Cyrus, Disney's Hannah Montana, talking to Shereen Low (*BT*, 4 05 09): *I don't necessarily feel like Mother Teresa so I don't know why people want to hear what I have to say. It's very strange going into a store and seeing people buy your face.*

So you need questions to get people talking. Childhood can be a good bet. Perhaps you will stumble on something that moves them, so you see the human being behind the public face. Here are the straightforward, easy-to-read opening pars of a profile of actress Kierston Wareing, by Kate Whiting (*MEN*, 19 03 09):

> *Kierston Wareing reckons she's an actress today only thanks to a chance meeting on a train with British film director Ken Loach.*
>
> *She had been a struggling actress for ten years before deciding to jack it all in and train to become a legal secretary. Just months before her course ended, she was put up for a role in Ken Loach's 2007 TV film It's a Free World, and endured a long and rigorous audition process.*
>
> *Then, on the day she found out she had made it into the final two, she took a tube train home from her part-time job at the High Court, and Ken Loach happened to get into her carriage.*

Question-and-answer

Some features appear in question-and-answer form. It can work well with a technical subject – all you need to know about a rise in the bank rate. But few people speak their thoughts as sparingly and logically as they might write them. So question-and-answer interviews can run to tedious length.

For an enlightening question-and-answer, you need questions which will elicit short, pithy and, if possible, unexpected answers. Here are a few from an interview with a writer (*FT*, 1 11 08): What is the last thing you read that made you laugh out loud? What books are on your bedside table? How do you relax? What book do you wish you had written? What do you wear while writing? (Answer: A frown.)

Diaries and gossip

These are hard to get right. But, if right, they are more fun than the preachy comment surrounding them. Essentially they need personality, in both their subjects and their writers who should cast a subversive light on the weaknesses and passions of the well-known. They have shown bloggers how to blog.

In the diary, we learn about the council leader's obsession with golf or the government spokesman's past work for a risqué magazine. Jonathan Guthrie (*FT*, 12 09 08) mused that Prime Minister Gordon Brown's gestures when he was speaking suggested a subconscious desire to be a loft insulation installer.

If profiles tell readers how successful people got successful, diaries reveal their uncertainties, oddness or generosity. Sarah Sands, deputy editor of the *Evening Standard,* for example, disclosed that Jenny Scott, when co-presenter of the BBC's Daily Politics, used to bake cakes each week. She gave half to the TV crew and half to Westminster homeless (*FT*, 14 06 08).

Diarists benefit from good inside information, a good eye for the revealing moment at public events, a good ear for bizarre snippets of news, for the funny remark or the illuminating funny story. If business leaders were playing golf when they should have been minding the shop, that is fuel for the diary.

Diarists may also view events in a different but illuminating way, exploring the role of class, for instance, in popular television shows such as tycoon Alan Sugar's The Apprentice and the talent contests featuring the Lord (Lloyd Webber). They can be a tad disrespectful. Jonathan Guthrie remarked that the National Trust is best known for *stinging suburbanites £9 a head to mooch round the gaffs of impecunious toffs* (*FT*, 19 02 10).

Comment: The Daimler of Destiny

Comment is growing in importance because it is popular with web readers. It is also relatively cheap. According to a saying, comment is free but facts are expensive. The *Electric New Paper* (Singapore) advertises as many comment columns as news stories.

Comment and column writers – like diarists and some critics – appear in print regularly, which creates a relationship with readers. So this is as near as newspaper writing gets to broadcasting. Broadcasters and columnists are engaged in a conversation, albeit one-sided, with listeners, readers and viewers. They must present themselves, therefore, as engaging people with a touch of originality. In *Thelondonpaper* (11 11 08) a 35-year-old banker from Greenwich wrote an engaging column on knee-high boots.

Many comment pieces and leading articles on serious subjects are dull because they say the same thing as one another. The memorable comment says something different.

Most of the *Financial Times* (6 11 08) enthused for Barack Obama after his election victory in 2008. Diarist Robert Shrimsley, however, satirized what he saw as empty rhetoric, both Obama's and that of another change-seeking politician, David Cameron, whom he imagined declaiming in an Obama-style victory speech: 'We have touched the arc of history. We have driven the Daimler of destiny.' A cartoon made the point that beggars ask for change, too.

Try for a more considered, better informed, less predictable view than your contemporaries' if you want to take pride in the comment you have written. If possible, you need new facts or observations which have eluded other reporters and commentators. Commenting on the 'dumbing down' of examinations, Sue Cameron (*FT*, 29 10 08) found sample questions, for a mock GCSE, that required common sense, not scientific knowledge, to answer. One was: Which of these is not an important safety feature on a car? A) Crumple zone B) Large wheels C) Seat belts D) Air bag.

New facts are often not hard to find, for press comment is frequently superficial, based on perceptions of what happened or was said. Before writing your comment, go back to what actually happened or was said. Overlooked facts can change your view of a situation and make less predictable comment possible.

The tone of comment is important. You do not want to appear to look down on people. Starting with a general statement can give a column a pompous tone. One in the *Western Morning News* (29 09 08) began: *It is the constant complaint of those accused of misdemeanours that the allegations are given banner headlines in the press and yet, when and if those same individuals are cleared months later, their innocence is lucky to merit a small paragraph.* Quite so. But, if this sentence had been struck out, the column would have started more cogently: *Fairness dictates that we should give some prominence to the fact that Westcountry Conservative MEP Giles Chichester did not play fast and loose with his expenses. He hasn't profited by a single euro.*

For the same reason, do not end with a general statement. A joke is better, as in this book review: Millennium *has required great feats of stamina from its author. A pity, then, that it should also test the readers'* (*FT*, 11 10 08).

Leaders

One form of comment – the leading article – affirms a newspaper's views and values. Most journalists need be right only today. A leader writer hopes to be still right next month.

A leader must say something, not simply rehearse the pros and cons. Saying something may simply require common sense, sound judgment and an ability to see through cant. Often it ideally requires a wide and deep grasp of whatever subject the news suggests for comment.

If you are asked to write leaders regularly, try to get to know the decision makers at the council, in the NHS, in government, in the football club on whose decisions you will be commenting. You need to understand what they are trying to do, while retaining your independence from them.

The following advice for leader writers came from Nigerian editor and teacher Dayo Duyile in his *Manual for African Journalists* (1990):

> Be exhaustive in finding and checking the facts, but be brief in setting down background information – don't tell the whole story over again. Go straight to the point and don't leave people in doubt where your paper stands.
>
> Be upright in your views and forceful in their expression. Be consistent with what your paper has said before. Watch out for flaws in your argument. Write with dignity.
>
> Don't be wordy. Say what you want to say and then withdraw.

And don't give even a hint of pompous condescension.

Obituaries

At the *Daily Telegraph* in 1986 the staff appeared as venerable and timeworn as the readers. But, in a fusty cranny of the office, Hugh Massingberd breathed new life into the reverential world of obituaries. And, where the *Telegraph* led, other papers followed.

Massingberd realized that it was not just the great and the good who led interesting lives. The not-so-great and not-so-good led them, too: Marie-la-Jolie, for instance, of Marseilles, *a celebrated brothel-keeper in that city's criminal heyday* who published her memoirs, a hair-raising account of smuggling, corruption, prison, vendettas and champagne (*The Daily Telegraph Fourth Book of Obituaries*, 1999).

And you did not have to be as not-so-good as Marie to be worth writing about. The Squire of Faringdon in 1974 punched photographer Cecil Beaton, sending him reeling into Cheyne Row. 'Known as the Mad Boy, he [the Squire] had a brief but hectic career in the Cavalry, acted as an extra in Hollywood, worked in a Lyons corner house (until spilling soup over a customer) and helped run a nightclub.'

Humour in obituaries needs care. The editor of the *British Medical Journal* offered to publish an apology to the family of a doctor obituarized as *the greatest snake-oil salesman of his age* (PCC report 63).

But Massingberd showed that obituaries can turn up unexpected stories. *The Times* (3 03 08) wrote about Sheldon Brown, a bespectacled American mechanic with a ginger beard and a phoenix-crowned helmet, whose internet advice on bicycles scored half a million hits a month. The *Financial Times* (11 07 09) rediscovered in an old soldier, Godfrey Rampling, the forgotten hero of the 1936 Olympics and father of film-star Charlotte.

The *Big Issue* (14 04 08) published a two-page obituary by Adam Forrest of William Hunter, whose body lay undiscovered in his bungalow in Northern Scotland for more than a year. Forrest manages a Massingberd touch: *An oddly flamboyant figure known to everyone in the village, he was tall, silver-haired, wore colourful silk shirts and well-cut suits and would carry a pet parrot to the local shop on his shoulder. Some knew Hunter as Golfing Bill, since he took a bus the five miles to Invergordon before 7am every morning to play a round.*

Obituaries are an opportunity for local and regional papers. The dinner lady who works evenings as a disc jockey lives only four streets away. So does the lecturer from Germany who wears a beret, writes poetry and has a passion for France. And there's the old seadog with the elbow crutch whom everyone sees outside the pavement cafes, sipping his coffee alone. Such obituaries need not be published immediately after death. You have a little time.

A death may also recall another story. The death of Bobby Fischer, the American who beat the Russian Boris Spassky to become world champion at chess, led the *Ilford Recorder* (24 01 08) to recall Bob Wade, a local man who helped Fischer win.

Reviewing

If you review a play, a concert or a television programme, say what you think. Not what you think you ought to think. Not what you think someone more knowledgeable would think. Your honesty is the more important if the performance is being repeated. You are helping people decide whether to spend their money on tickets.

Your review should say who took part and what they sang or played – if it was music – or what, in a nutshell, the plot was – if it was a play or film. You need to consider, if relevant:

1. The aims of the playwright/composer/artist.
2. To what extent the performance fulfils them.
3. The skill of the performers and the quality of their performance.
4. The effect on the audience.

Be generous and courteous, especially with amateurs. They have done their best. You do not want to demean them in their local paper. In mentioning them you may have to find ways of offering helpful criticism, without being unkind. Perhaps actor A would have been easier to hear if he had not let his voice fall at the end of sentences. Perhaps the production could have had more pace.

Here was a generous paragraph with a touch of humour from a *Financial Times* review (22 07 08), by the aptly named Richard Fairman. It concerns the opera Hansel and Gretel at Glyndebourne.

> *Adriana Kucerova, who sings with a soprano bright as a diamond, is a livewire Gretel who looks barely 11 years old, and Jennifer Holloway complements her as an older, more dogged Hansel. The pair of them are a whirlwind of hyper-active energy (how do they find the breath to sing?). So no more foods with E-numbers for them.*

While being generous, Fairman is also critical. He does not think Glyndebourne's presentation of Hansel and Gretel as an eco-fairytale comes off.

Here is an unpublished review of a television programme:

> *The producers of BBC1's Last Choir Standing seemed in two minds about their purpose. Was it to hold a singing competition? Or was it to tell stories of triumph over disadvantage? Lovers of choral music will have been disappointed that the story-telling got about as much time as the singing in the early programmes and some choirs were scarcely heard.*
>
> *When, in the third programme, five choirs competed for two places in the final, the least politically correct – Alleycats, a group of posh kids from St Andrews University – fell by the wayside, though in this listener's opinion they were the liveliest in the final sing-in.*
>
> *On the story-telling, the Brighton Gay Men's Choir had looked well in front along with Dreemz, a black group from the wrong side of the tracks in Birmingham. However, the judges – tenor Russell Watson, Holby City star Sharon D.Clarke and experienced choral judge Suzi Digby – were judging the singing not the talk and they plumped for two other choirs – Sense of Sound, a multicultural group from Liverpool, and Ysgol Glanaethwy, a monocultural community choir from unglamorous Bangor, North Wales.*

The review above tells the reader what the programme was, what happened, who the judges were, who took part and who were selected. It comments on the volume of talk in a singing contest. It also mentions that the reviewer would not have made the same choice as the judges.

Remember that what is shown on TV is local news and can be big local news. There will be a local reaction if something on screen produces a public reaction – as when the public kept voting to keep ex-Westminster journalist John Sergeant dancing in BBC TV's Strictly Come Dancing in 2008.

Write sparely

Reviews need to be sparely written. Too many words and you give an impression of pomposity as in this sentence: *It was a mark of their maturity that they were able to adjust to provide an appropriate and sensitive accompaniment for the young soloists when required (Lancaster Guardian, 4 07 08)*. This is a long-winded way of saying: *They accompanied the young soloists sensitively.*

On the other hand, you might be able to capture your opinion in a memorable phrase. Ludovic Hunter-Tilney (*FT*, 27 04 09) describes the *groaning, rasping* voice of ageing folksinger Bob Dylan as *a magnificent wreck, like crumbling masonry falling from a decrepit world heritage site.*

Below is part of a lively review by Tim Padfield in the *Lancaster Guardian* (4 07 08), of a performance by a young Spanish clarinetist:

> *You didn't have to be a football fan to see a winning performance from Spain this weekend.*
>
> *The day before Torres, Fabregas and friends were crowned kings of Europe in Vienna, there was another truly majestic Spanish display.*
>
> *Young clarinetist Maximiliano Martin stole the show at the Haffner Orchestra's latest performance in Lancaster's Ashton Hall.*

How to begin

Some reviews beat about the bush for several over-written paragraphs. You need to be a consummate stylist to get away with this. Far better to get to grips with the show.

A music review in the *Darlington & Stockton Times* (23 06 06) might have begun: *From the solid oak lectern carved by Mousey Thompson, Jonathan Storer launched con brio into Beethoven's Violin Sonata No 8 in East Layton's tiny church.* Actually it began with a drab generality: *Concerts in churches can be disappointing in terms of performers and acoustics. There might be draughts and the event often involves sitting in a cavernous space among a sparse sprinkling of fellow sufferers.*

Save a lively comment or quote for the end. This was the terse, ruthless conclusion of a review of BBC1's The Apprentice, by Shane Donaghey (*BT*, 2 05 09): *Mentor Nick moved in for the kill, using his words like bullets. 'Tell me about Pantsman,' he said, and Phil's chances to be Sir Alan's apprentice fell in the pouring rain into the gutter, twitched, then lay still.*

Tightly written film reviews by Edward Lawrenson in the *Big Issue* make every word count. Here is a Lawrenson review complete in a paragraph. It ends neatly with a short, sharp sentence:

> *El Cantante is a biopic of Hector Lavoe, a Puerto Rican salsa singer who became a huge star in the US in the 1970s, succumbed to drug addiction at the height of his fame and died of Aids, aged 49, in 1993. Singer Marc Anthony plays Lavoe with a wiry, fidgety charisma. But he's slightly outshone by his real-life wife Jennifer Lopez as the singer's lover Pucci, a poignant mix of infatuation with,*

and despair over, the self-destructive Lavoe. A pity, then, that this glossy movie is too clichéd and superficial to match the fine performances of its two leads. The music's good, though. (1 09 08).

Don't write pretentious rubbish: *Today's vacuum, Campos argues, can be a nasty blend of lawless voyeurism and authoritarian overreach* (FT, 20 08 09). How can a vacuum be a blend of anything?

The news and feature angle

Drama, concerts and even art shows can be news. A fight between two elderly women stopped a concert by Katie Melua in Los Angeles (BT, 7 05 09).

Art shows can inspire fascinating features. Jenny White (*Western Mail*, 16 03 09) got simple and attractive quotes from two Welsh artists: *I like early evening when you're just starting to get streetlights and window lights coming on; You can have a sunny day when it* [the sea] *starts off incredibly blue, then goes white and then, as the sun goes down, turns to fascinating reds and purples.*

It is worth talking to a play's producer to see if there is some story behind the performance, about how he/she found just the actor for a particular role, or about this being the 50th production in which John S has taken part, or about the number of different jobs which the cast do in ordinary life.

Books

Newspapers write about books for two reasons. One is to use the facts and stories in a book to cast light on a fascinating person or subject or the paper's local area. The other is to tell readers what the reviewer thinks of it.

A book about Trebitsch Lincoln, a brilliant speaker from Hungary who became a notorious MP, provided an opportunity to describe the first 1910 general election, an exciting moment in Darlington's history.

Look out for lively stories in the book you are reviewing. Then retell them, mentioning the book's title, author, publisher, price and possibly ISBN number. During the reading, you will have found out if the book is easy to read and cogently argued; or dull. You can add your comments. Some workaday factual narratives suddenly take off, into what reads like literature.

Make the most of your material. If the book focuses on a brilliant political writer, quote stories from the book to let readers see how brilliant he/she is.

It is different if you are assessing the book as a book to read. If it is fiction, you will need to outline the plot. Did the writer give you a new insight into other people's lives and thereby, perhaps, into your own? Were the characters true to life or simply saying things the writer wanted to say?

Was any character or turn of the plot specially memorable? Did the book have pace, tension and atmosphere? Did you find the book hard to put down or, once you had put it down, did it require willpower to pick it up again?

Who is the writer – a literary veteran, a local author or a young newcomer? What outlook or message did the book express?

Questions

1. Draw up a list of features you could write. Why should an editor use them?

2. Write a diary story.

3. Write a comment or column, on a light, humorous subject and on a current-affairs issue.

4. About what unusual people might you write a profile or an obituary?

14. Religion and diversity

Conflict makes God news

God was not big in the media when this book was first written in the 1960s. Local papers, reflecting community life, chronicled the sales of work of church congregations. But only a few religious stories commanded the fitful attention of national news editors. One was Pope John's Vatican Council, which sought to make Catholicism broader-minded. Another was Bishop John Robinson's shocking-at-the-time introduction to twentieth century theology, *Honest to God*.

Forty years later, God makes international headlines. This is because doctrines he is believed to inspire have led to conflict – in Ireland, Bosnia, Israel/Palestine, the Muslim world, India, Britain and even within the normally unemotional Anglican Communion.

As interpreted by Pope Benedict XVI, God rejects religious pluralism, moral relativism, economic liberalism, contraception, divorce, women priests and same-sex civil unions (*FT*, 7 02 09). Which brings the Pope into conflict with more liberal interpreters.

God in one Islamic manifestation – which horrifies most Muslims in Britain – uses modern telecommunications to promote a hardline interpretation of the Qu'ran. The Pakistani newspaper *Dawn* reported (27 01 09) that a Taliban broadcaster in the Swat valley told people most evenings what activities are 'un-Islamic' – selling DVDs, watching cable TV, singing and dancing, shaving beards and allowing girls to attend school.

Hardline Islam has two sources. One is the austere religion of Saudi Arabia and Iran. The other is the madrassa schools movement which sought to reinvigorate Indian Islam after the crushing of the so-called Mutiny erased the last traces of Muslim rule in India outside the princely states. In Pakistan and Bangladesh, madrassas now offer alternative education for the poor, largely devoted to religious teaching and a puritan view of the world.

The Islamic faith draws precepts from the Qu'ran and the Hadith (later interpretations of what the Prophet Mohammed said). These rules cover not only worship and how people treat one another but what they eat, drink and wear, how they invest money and how they are to be forgiven, or punished, for their transgressions.

Interpretation is not set in stone. For example, the Qu'ran says that women should cover themselves 'apart from their natural adornments'. Does this mean apart from face and hands? Does it also allow them to show their hair? Or should even faces be covered? Before the 1970s, Muslim women in Egypt did not cover their hair. Now, most do. Strict religious observance has become more important to identity and self-worth as other hopes have faded.

Narrow, authoritarian certainties are popular in an uncertain world. The saving grace of religion is that broader-minded attitudes keep breaking through.

Sheik Abdul-Rahman al-Marwany told the *FT Magazine* (28 03 09) about a visit to a hardline area in the Yemen.

❝ Gathering around were youngsters with long beards. I listened to their discussions. I asked them what they thought about tolerance and respect for human rights. I knew I had to be careful. If you contradict their thoughts, they think you are contradicting God and then things can turn nasty … We had to spend a lot of time discussing why I had shaved my beard. I told them there are plenty of men with big beards and long robes who are actually killers escaping justice … Sometimes I use humour. I tell them, if they kill all the Christians, there will be no one to make Mercedes-Benz cars. ❞

Don't call the vicar the Rev. Smith

Call me Parson, Brother, Friend
But do not call me Reverend.

So said an old rhyme. But even churchgoers refer to their priest or minister these days as the Rev. Smith. They are wrong. He is the Rev. John Smith – if John is his first name – or the Rev. John. He is not the Rev. Smith. The traditional name to give him is Mr Smith, after first using his full style, the Rev. John Smith. The abbreviation Mr stands for master of arts – all clergy were traditionally university graduates. If the Rev. John Smith is Anglo-Catholic, he may prefer Father John or Father Smith.

Archbishop Smith, Dean Smith, Canon Smith, Father Smith, Monsignor Smith, Dr Smith, Pastor Smith, Mr Smith are all fine. Though diarist Emma Jacobs did go a little far in referring to the Archbishop of Canterbury as Mr Williams (*FT*, 19 12 08).

But what do you call the Rev Deborah Parsons, after first giving her her full style? The *Torbay Herald Express* (27 09 08) simply called her Debbie. It called her vicar the Rev. Maude, a style some women ministers prefer even if incorrect. Alternatively the *Herald Express* could have repeated her full style, the

Rev Gillian Maude, or called her Mrs Maude or, if she was unmarried, Miss Maude. When writing about a woman minister, use the style she prefers.

Growing numbers of priests and ministers now style themselves the Rev'd, rather than the Rev.

A bishop called John Smith is styled the Right Rev. Thereafter, if he has a doctorate, he is Dr Smith. Otherwise, Bishop Smith. Do not be dazzled by the multititled. In a newspaper, the Lord Bishop of London is the Bishop of London. The Rev Professor Kenneth Newport is Professor Kenneth Newport. The Rev Lord Dr Leslie Griffiths is Lord Griffiths.

The Roman Catholic Church

This is the church of most Christians worldwide. At the Council of Trent in the sixteenth century, it decided to stand by its traditional doctrine and practice and make no concessions to the Protestant Reformation. This is still its basic position but it has changed in two important ways. It conducts its services in local languages, and it has largely abandoned its old alliances with aristocrats, supporting democracy and welfarism instead. It is organized in parishes headed by unmarried male priests responsible to the bishop of the diocese. The Pope appoints senior officeholders.

Besides this basic structure, the Church has many semi-independent orders and organizations, both ordained and lay, which may be represented in your area.

The Church of England

The key unit in the Church of England is the parish, headed by a vicar or rector, who cannot easily be removed from office. (The Rev. John Smith is vicar of St James's (the parish), not St James's Church.)

The independence of vicars – called the parson's freehold – enables a wide variety of views and practice. The Church can hardly ever speak with a single voice; but differences of opinion are honestly and vigorously debated.

However, two parts of the Church with clearcut views have grown in strength. One, the Anglo-Catholics, seeks to recover the spirit and practice of the Church before the Reformation. The other, the conservative evangelicals, stresses the Bible's authority. The Church of England, the Scottish Episcopal Church, the Church of Ireland and the Church in Wales belong to the worldwide Anglican Community.

The Church of Scotland and the Free Churches

These churches have different histories but are similar in basic organization. Except for the Quakers or Society of Friends, they have ministers – the

Rev. John Smith, the Rev. Mary Smith – who work with groups of unpaid leaders, usually lay but, in the Church of Scotland, the Presbyterian Church in Ireland and the United Reformed Church, ordained elders. The Church of Scotland has a parish system. Others have church-based congregations.

The Baptists baptize adults rather than infants. The United Reformed Church unites former Presbyterian and Congregational churches. The Methodist Church groups its churches in circuits, headed by superintendent ministers, covering a geographical area which can be as large as a county. Its website includes a searchable directory of around 4000 e-mail addresses.

In England, the Pentecostal churches – invigorated by enthusiastic African Christianity – form the largest Free Church movement. Once derided as a culturally insensitive American export, Pentecostalism with its celebration of the Holy Spirit has struck a chord especially in Africa and Latin America. According to Kwame Kwei-Armah (C4, 15 02 09), one Christian in four is now Pentecostal. Some congregations see godliness as a path to prosperity. Others provide a sense of community in Brazil's favelas or London's suburbs. Doctrinally, Pentecostalists are close to the conservative evangelicals of the Church of England. They and the Baptists often call their minister Pastor.

Judaism

The Jewish faith has four main forms – Orthodox, Reform, Liberal and Masorti – all of which have websites. The last three form the Progressive sector. Of the 270,000 people in the United Kingdom who identified themselves as Jewish in the 2001 census, two thirds were Orthodox. Most Orthodox synagogues in Greater London are members of the United Synagogue and use the description United. Outside London, synagogues are likely to be Orthodox unless they describe themselves differently.

If you are a man or married woman and attend an Orthodox Jewish service, take a hat. If the service is not Orthodox, only men need hats. Photography at a synagogue requires special permission and pictures cannot be taken during a service.

A Jewish minister might be the Rev. Peter Bloom or, if he is a rabbi, Rabbi or Rav Peter Bloom. After that he is Rabbi Bloom or, if he is not a rabbi, Mr Bloom. If he has a PhD he will be Rabbi Dr Peter Bloom.

Synagogues usually have several organizations attached to them, including groups for women and young people and for study and charitable work.

The Board of Deputies was founded in 1760. Its 300 representatives are together the chief voice of British Jewry.

Hinduism

Hinduism, noted for its colourful festivals, is one of the world's oldest religions, older than the word Hindu which is a Persian corruption of Sindhu.

Sapt Sindhu was the ancient Aryan name for the Punjab. Persian-speakers could not manage the initial S.

Because Hinduism began before recorded history, it looks back to no founder and has no orthodoxy based on a single holy book. Hindu 'gods' are visions of the same God. Hindus believe that God is one but accept that different people and different religions will see him in different ways. So pictures of Jesus may appear beside pictures of Hindu gods on an Indian bookstall. For Hindus, there is no single right way.

Reporters may have difficulty finding representative Hindus to speak to. Hindu temples in Britain tend to belong to language groups, Gujerati, Punjabi and so on, and to have priests from India speaking these languages. English-speaking Hindus may not go to temples often, though they retain kinship with other Hindus. Many look forward to returning to an increasingly prosperous India where Hinduism is part of the fabric of society.

Temples have boards of trustees and a trustee may be a useful contact. Other prominent Hindus serve on the inter-faith forums sponsored by local councils. Many Hindus object to being classed as 'Asian', alongside people of Pakistani and Bangladeshi origin. In fact, people with origins in the Indian sub-continent are likely nowadays to describe themselves as Hindus, Muslims or Sikhs or by their language group, rather than Asians.

Islam

Most Muslims – and the vast majority of British Muslims – are Sunni. Sunni mosques are self-governing. They have chairmen – usually lay – and committees, who are useful contacts for journalists. Mosques may use different languages. They may belong to associations, such as the Muslim Council of Britain. Sunnis have no decision-making hierarchy. Imams are prayer or community leaders.

British Muslims fall into two main groups, the brehelvi who are more spiritual and the deobandi who put greater emphasis on law. Deoband is the Indian town where the madrassa movement began.

Most Muslims want to prosper in British society. They are in Britain because it is economically good for them. Only a small minority are insular in spirit, wishing to keep themselves apart from other British groups.

In 2008 some moderates were concerned about the possible effects of the social isolation of Muslim communities in such places as Oldham. They would also have liked British authorities to stop parents sending girls to school in not-very-practical religious dress. When some parents do this, it puts other parents under pressure to do the same.

Many Muslim names have a religious meaning. They commonly have two main parts joined by ud, ul, ur, or uz (depending on what follows). Thus Alim-ud-Din (or Alimuddin), Ghaziul Hassan, Faroquzzaman, Serajur

Rahman. Din means religion. Abdullah, Abdurrahman and Abdul Razzaq all mean Servant of God. Strictly speaking, there is no such name as Abdul (servant of). In practice, Abdul does get used as a first name. Syed (Sayeed) is a title, not a name. So is Alhaji, used by people who have made a pilgrimage to Mecca. Maulana (our master) is a title used by Muslim religious scholars in Asia.

Sikhism

A retired teacher, Swarn Singh Kandola, is the elected president of over 24,000 Sikhs in North-East London. He works full-time and unpaid. His community has two gurdwaras (places of worship), in Barking and Seven Kings (Ilford). It has three priests and ten employees.

Seven Kings has a library for older people and a gymnasium for the young, providing activities for boys on Mondays, Wednesdays and Fridays, and for girls on Tuesdays and Thursdays. Every day volunteers serve breakfast from 6 am till nine, to anyone who comes. For Sikhs, eating together is an important sign of unity.

This East London community with an elected government is characteristic of the Singh Sabha movement dating from the 1920s. Down the road from Seven Kings is a different form of Sikh congregation headed by a sant (holy man). Another gurdwara, west of Ilford, belongs to a Sikh sub-group, the Ravidasi.

The Sikh homeland is the Punjab in North-West India. Like many other Sikhs, Mr Kandola moved from there to Britain in the 1960s when the government advertised for teachers.

Guru Nanak, a reformer and travelling preacher, founded Sikhism in the early sixteenth century at the time of the Mogul invasion of India. Believing in human equality, he was unhappy with Hindu imagery and the caste system. He championed the common people as children of God against both Muslim rulers and Hindu priests.

Reporting a diverse society

Journalists need to be fair, kind, accurate and sensitive in writing about people of different culture or different sexual orientation. Even more desperately than other informants, minority people need to speak, to be heard and to be understood. There are so many misunderstandings around, and the context in which people are heard is often unhelpful.

Refugees and asylum seekers, for instance, exist in a context in which asylum seeking is not encouraged. The government welcomes refugees reluctantly. Refugees have stories to tell but limited chances to tell them. Bernhard Gross from Cardiff University told a London conference organized by the Clemens Nathan Research Centre (7 04 09) about his study of the few opportunities afforded to refugees and asylum seekers to put their point of view on television in 2006.

One of these opportunities fell to Afghans who hijacked a plane to Britain in 2000 to escape the Taliban government (C4, 13 05 06). But what they had to say was shown in the context of an item about politicians' complaints against the Human Rights Act – the act which gave the hijackers asylum in Britain. Gross argued that, in this unfriendly context, viewers would see what the Afghans had to say as special pleading.

In *Reporting Diversity*, published by the Society of Editors in 2006, Geoff Elliott, former editor of *The News*, Portsmouth, urges journalists to interview and feature people from minority communities and to report and celebrate the good things happening in these communities. He also calls for careful use of language, including the word ethnic – we are all members of an ethnic group. The British-born children of Pakistani parents are British, not Pakistani. (The Press Complaints Commission Code asks journalists not to detail someone's race, colour or religion unless it is genuinely relevant to the story. Apart from this, stirring up religious or racial hatred is a crime. Journalists reporting election candidates and other public speakers may need to tone down the language they report. Reports can be outspoken but must not be threatening, insulting or abusive.)

The sub-title of Elliott's book is 'How journalists can contribute to community cohesion', which has become a more complex task since he wrote it. The multiculturism advocated by politicians has a downside. As the *Financial Times* pointed out (9 02 08), it may push minority members into the shell of separate religious identity.

Minorities have been defined as non-dominant groups, with different characteristics from the majority and sticking together to preserve their culture. This definition separates minorities from other people. Yet they need also to be parts of a larger whole.

Research for this book suggests that the communities in Britain, however obvious their differences, do have common ground. People from all communities want to make their way in the world and to behave kindly towards people they meet. A nurse in a veil is, first and foremost, a nurse.

An important part of the common ground in British society is civil liberty – the freedom to do things, say things and write things, which is particularly important to journalists. Encroachments on this liberty, whether by a government concerned about public safety or by believers eager to stifle discussion and criticism, need to be resisted. Freedom of expression includes the freedom to discuss beliefs and to sing a discordant song, even though the authorities may wish that troublesome song went unsung.

But, if you want people to be liberal and enlightened, you have to understand their problems and points of view. Government policies and social realities can affect different communities differently. Police stopping, searching and collecting DNA samples stir black resentment. Anti-terrorism policy bears on the Muslim community and fosters anti-Muslim feeling. People from different communities compete for homes, and the less strong competitors can be boxed into limited areas of poor housing.

Journalists need to foster a just society in which everyone is sympathetically heard.

The media's three blind spots

If British media have felt constrained to treat minorities sympathetically, some have continued to reflect popular dislike of gypsies, terrorism suspects and illegal workers.

A page of the *Westmorland Gazette* (4 07 08) carried side by side two stories expressing contrasting attitudes towards a minority. One defended Muslims against leaflets blaming them for the heroin trade. The other, about 13 illegal workers found in Indian restaurants, showed little concern for the 13.

BBC London (7 01 09) reported that Romanians posing as Portuguese were cleaning in a Kensington hotel. But the reporter admitted that not many British workers wanted to clean hotels. Romanian cleaners – and Bangladeshi cooks and waiters – are not public enemies. They render valued services.

There is no obvious way to prevent poorer people trying to move to a wealthier country. The constant arrival of immigrants has changed the character of some British urban areas. But Panorama (BBC1, 9 03 09) illustrated the cost and cruelty of trying to send all illegals home. A study by the London School of Economics put their number at 725,000. London Mayor Boris Johnson suggested an amnesty for them.

Government and Conservative spokesmen replied that an amnesty would encourage more to come (*Mail*, 10 03 09). Meanwhile, the government was seeking to discourage illegals by driving them out of work, presumably into penury.

Terrorism and journalism

Freelance journalist Shiv Malik has pointed out (*New Statesman*, 5 07 07) that it is hard to become an effective terrorist in Britain, since there are no training grounds for practice. Nevertheless, British law enforcers are taking no chances.

In the IRA days, they sought to find who committed terrorist crimes. Now they seek to prevent them. Therefore they shadow and sometimes arrest suspects who might get involved in terrorism. Anyone can be a suspect, especially if from Pakistan. Any group of friends might be plotters. Any conversation about girlfriends or the weather can contain a message in code.

Whatever the propaganda when arrests are made, journalists should wait for the court case before deciding that suspects are guilty. Intelligence about people is not the same as evidence. Twelve suspects, mainly students from Pakistan, arrested with much fanfare in April 2009, were not charged.

The campaign against terrorism has created new, ill-defined restrictions and hazards for journalists and their sources. Peter Noorlander, legal director of the Media Legal Defence Initiative, which defends journalists world wide, discussed this at the Clemens Nathan conference in April 2009 referred to above. He pointed out that what can be published about terrorism is restricted. Terrorism must not be incited or encouraged. Could strong criticism of the authorities be construed as encouragement?

Anti-terrorism law restricts the possession of 'terrorist material'. It could restrict taking pictures of law enforcers, if the pictures would be useful to terrorists. (Scotland Yard guidance (*Press Gazette*, 5 08 09) makes it clear that media photographers are free to photograph public events and police officers. It also advises caution in stopping and searching photographers under the Terrorism Act with a view to seeing their pictures. Police may require a court order to see such journalistic material. But police continued hassling photographers in sensitive parts of London.)

Noorlander mentioned TV producer Neil Garrett who disclosed on ITN (16 08 05) that much of what had been said about the shooting of the Brazilian Jean Charles de Menezes at Stockwell tube station was nonsense. De Menezes had not been wearing a bulky jacket and had not acted suspiciously. He had simply been wrongly identified as a terrorist. Garrett got the basics of this from Lana Vandenberghe, who worked for the Independent Police Complaints Commission and was a friend of his girlfriend, Louise. All three were arrested and held for hours. Garrett's flat was turned over in his absence. When Louise later answered bail, she was put in a cell though she was pregnant. In May 2006 the case was dropped (*Guardian*, 15 05 06).

In May 2009, detectives investigating the shooting of two soldiers at an Antrim barracks used the Terrorism Act to demand notes and photographs – of an interview with the Real IRA – from Suzanne Breen, northern editor of the Dublin-based *Sunday Tribune* (*BT*, 7 05 09). Judge Tom Burgess, however, rejected the demand, saying that handing over her notes would put her life at risk (IFEX website, 24 06 09).

Earlier, freelance Shiv Malik sought a judicial review when Greater Manchester Police got a court order requiring all the material for his book *Leaving Al-Qaeda: Inside the Mind of a British Terrorist*. In June 2008 the review narrowed the order's terms but decided that the order should stand. Lord Justice Dyson said: 'Important though these rights of a journalist [to protect confidential sources] unquestionably are, they are not absolute.'

In early 2009, the Director of Public Prosecutions was talking to the media about the terms for production orders.

Immigration since the war has made British society more diverse and brought new skills. But, in a perceptive article (*FT*, 11 04 09), Christopher Caldwell, a senior editor at the *Weekly Standard*, shows that it has changed policing. The bobby of old worked in a society which shared his values. Now we have a diverse, contentious society where citizens cannot be assumed to share the culture or values of the police – who, for their part, see themselves dealing with an undeferential population which includes terrorists.

Questions

1. What efforts have you made to report on minority communities and/or tell the stories of asylum seekers?

2. What difficulties have you found and how have you overcome them?

15 Ethics: what you write could get someone killed

Accuracy derived from painstaking fact-checking, fairness – particularly when charges are made against someone – courage, honesty, oversight over public officials, lending a voice to the disadvantaged, sensitivity to differences and to deprivation and commitment to the public interest are commonly regarded as the requirements of good journalism.

Because the media are subject to human fallibility and also function under time and manpower constraints, they are obviously imperfect. Misreporting, misinterpreting facts or being plain wrong, reporting baseless charges, failing to get a response before publishing a charge, bias and cutting out one side of a story are among the common complaints against the press.

N. Ravi, editor, *The Hindu*, Chennai, speaking to the Commonwealth Journalists Association conference in Sarawak, October 2008

How reporting can affect people's lives

Denis Donaldson was traced by the *Sunday World* in a remote, ramshackle cottage in Donegal. A month later, he was shot dead (*Independent*, 5 04 06). Donaldson, a senior IRA man, had worked for the British. His killer, reported to be from the Real IRA (*BT*, 4 05 09), would probably have found him anyway. But the Donaldson story suggests that media reporting can be lethal.

It can damage innocent people. A newspaper reported that Maxine Carr, girlfriend of the Soham child-murderer, Ian Huntley, was in Coleraine, Northern Ireland. Local people turned on an English shopworker believing she was Maxine.

A Channel 4 TV programme (14 12 07) showed that she was not the only victim of Maxine hunters. A woman in Redcar on Teesside was seized by vigilantes desperate to ascertain if she was Maxine. In York, assailants attacked the home of a research student. Police protection made her neighbours the more certain she was Maxine.

Any woman the right age and height could be Maxine because she had probably changed her appearance after leaving prison. The media, Channel 4 pointed out, had turned Maxine Carr – who gave Ian Huntley a false alibi – into a national hate figure, exposing other women to this hatred.

Journalists owe a duty of fair, accurate and responsible reporting to their readers, their informants and the people they write about. This includes those who, like Maxine Carr, may have broken the law in the past. This is the principle underlying the law of libel and also underlying journalists' refusal to identify unnamed sources. We should not do people needless harm. We should report carefully, taking adequate notes.

Have a care for the unintended consequences of what you write. Columnist John Plender recalled in the *Financial Times* (29 09 08) that he once inadvertently started a run on a building society. Broadcaster Edward Stourton wrote: *If you are addressing anyone beyond your immediate social environment, there is always a possibility that your words will do things you do not expect.* (*FT*, 8 11 08).

Someone who helped you could be imprisoned or forced to emigrate, because your report angered a dictatorial government. Robert Barnett, a Tibetan expert at Columbia University, New York, wrote in the *British Journalism Review* (September 2008): 'As journalists, film makers and writers increasingly travel to the more sensitive areas of China, local people are being put at ever greater risk.'

Exposing bad situations can harm people other than the baddies. In 2008, Panorama showed Indian children doing work for Primark, which promptly fired the clothing suppliers concerned (BBC, 16 06 08). Diarist Robert Shrimsley commented drily in the *Financial Times*: *Now those poor kids are free to pursue other opportunities in quarries or child prostitution* (3 07 08).

Police and juries can be pushed into arrests, charges and convictions by media demands. After much prejudicial publicity, the disturbed and sometimes violent Michael Stone was twice found guilty of savagely murdering Lin and Megan Russell with a hammer. Yet Bob Woffinden, a specialist in miscarriages of justice, wrote in the *British Journalism Review* in June 2007 that it was hard to see on what evidence he was convicted.

After another over-hyped case, Barry George was imprisoned for seven years for the murder of TV presenter Jill Dando. In August 2008, he was cleared.

Don't inflame the anger and fearfulness of the times. Don't join in the assault on some hate figure, be it banker or paedophile or social worker or even criminal. It is unfair to report allegations about people unless there is evidence to support them. Serious allegations need to be backed by serious and thorough investigation.

A lack of trust?

In February 2009, the Media Standards Trust published a report attacking the Press Complaints Commission as inadequate to curb the press's misdeeds.

As examples of misdeeds, it quoted the Max Mosley invasion-of-privacy case (*see* p. 159), a court finding in March 2008 that the *Daily Express* and sister papers published over 100 inaccurate articles about the McCanns, and a raid by police in 2002 which showed that 305 journalists had sought confidential personal information gathered by Steve Whittamore, a Hampshire private detective. (Gerry and Kate McCann's vain search for their three-year-old daughter Madeleine, missing in Portugal, was a long-running media story.)

Other critics have added to this indictment of the press. Nick Davies alleged that *News of the World* staff had commissioned illegal interception of well-known people's phone messages (*Guardian*, 8 07 09). Kevin Marsh, editor of the BBC College of Journalim, accused the *Sun* of running a story its journalist had been told was untrue ('The Future of Journalism', BBC College, 2009). He accused the *Evening Standard* of running unfounded rumours about the Duke of Edinburgh, and the *Daily Mail* of campaigning against anti-cervical cancer vaccination in England but in favour of it in Ireland. This sort of thing, he argued, has sapped trust in journalists.

John Simpson, world affairs editor of the BBC, reviews British twentieth century reporting in *Unreliable Sources* (Macmillan, 2010). He criticizes its frequent lapses into untrustworthiness. But his conclusion is kind: 'The determination to tell people what is really going on shines out of the browning pages of the newspaper files and the transcripts of broadcasts right down to our own times'.

The Media Standards Trust report pointed out that under half the people whose opinions were polled for the *British Journalism Review* (June 2008) said that they trusted newspaper journalists to tell the truth. In a poll for the Trust itself, three-quarters of those interviewed believed that newspapers frequently published stories they knew to be inaccurate. Almost as many believed that newspaper journalists invaded people's privacy too often.

Polls asking people their opinions about journalism, when they have little knowledge of it, may not amount to much. Former broadcaster Professor Adrian Monck of City University pointed out (*BJR*, June 2008) that polls have always shown TV journalists to be more trusted than those on newspapers. Monck suggests a simple reason. People believe in what they see, particularly if it has a good-looking presenter. Anyway, an inclination to trust varies with wealth, education and geography. Wealthy, well-educated people living in cities are likely not to trust the media.

However, there is another way of looking at the argument about trust. The BBC has won trust through a reputation for being impartial.

Impartiality and independence

The BBC, from its early days, has striven for impartiality, a virtue required by law of other mainstream broadcasters. This is, above all, political impartiality. Local and regional media have mostly striven to be politically impartial, too, since the old battles between Liberal and Conservative papers ended with the death of one or the other.

But defining impartiality has its difficulties. The BBC, in 2009, defined it as ruling out the broadcasting of a disasters appeal on behalf of civilians left injured or homeless by the Israeli attack on Gaza. This much criticized decision had difficult implications. If a humanitarian appeal was partial, what was it partial against? If what it was partial against was inhumane, was partial a bad thing to be? The BBC decision raised again the question raised by Martin Bell and other journalists who covered the vicious civil war in Bosnia in the 1990s. If something was wrong, could they honourably report it impartially?

Some would argue that complete impartiality is impossible for the media. Journalists have to decide who to speak to and how to present what the speakers say. Their decisions are likely to be affected by assumptions they make and possibly by prejudices they hold. As for their informants, even academics are not necessarily impartial. Nor are other journalists. So media reports cannot be a completely impartial account of what happened or was said.

Impartiality and independence are useful aspirations; however they win people's confidence. But James Painter suggests (*Counter-Hegemonic News*, Reuters Institute, 2008) that part of the audience, especially young people, prefers opinionated news. On European election day, 4 June 2009, the *Sun's* online radio, Suntalk, broke the convention that broadcasting should be politics-free while polling stations are open. Jon Gaunt pressed listeners to explain how they voted. He aired interviews with a Conservative and Nigel Farage, leader of the United Kingdom Independence Party (Nicholas Jones's blog, 30 06 09).

Be accurate and fair despite everything

The competitive, cost-cutting environment in which newspapers operate makes accuracy harder to ensure. Journalists are expected to write more than in the past and their writing is less likely to be checked by a sub-editor. To beat competitors, they seek impact which can mean going beyond what is fair.

Broadcast journalists are not immune from the pressures. Ex-BBC man Keith Somerville argued (*BJR*, March 09) that the drive for speed and impact militates against accuracy and good practice. He gave three instances where he felt the BBC had achieved impact at a cost. One was in its coverage of Liu Xiang, hurdler and possible gold medal winner, who had to drop out of the Beijing Olympics through injury. The two others concerned men suspected of murdering Ipswich prostitutes in 2006. One report broke an understanding that an interview would not be broadcast. A second, in Somerville's view, suggested a suspect's guilt, thereby infringing contempt-of-court rules.

Reporters are not responsible for the editorial culture in their places of work. But that culture cannot be an excuse for, for example, hacking the mobile phones of all and sundry.

The important thing is to be happy in your own mind that, despite the pressures of the moment, you have done your utmost to behave well, be fair, accurate and not over-sensational and not do people undeserved harm. In many situations, the only journalist who knows whether you were fair and accurate is you. Re-read your copy. Re-write anything which might be misinterpreted. You owe it to your readers.

Magnus Linklater, Scottish editor of *The Times*, wrote (*BJR*, September 2008): *It is reporters who must decide, by listening to their own consciences, whether they are treating their subjects with decency and respect rather than cavalier disregard for everything except the next day's headline.*

An impossible standard is not required, just a thorough job done in good faith. N.Ravi, editor of *The Hindu*, Chennai, told the Commonwealth Journalists Association conference in Sarawak in October 2008: 'Journalists cannot function effectively and vigorously without making mistakes at times. A certain tolerance of honest mistakes is called for.'

Protecting sources

Journalists should not disclose the names of informants who wish to remain anonymous. However, judges can order that a wrongdoer be unmasked. What if a court thinks your anonymous source is a wrongdoer?

Lord Justice May has said: 'An order for source disclosure cannot be compatible with article 10 of the European Convention [protecting free expression] unless it is justified by an overriding requirement in the public interest' [McNae]. He was speaking during a long-running case which cost over £1 million and raised the question whether the public interest required a journalist to name the source of medical information about Moors murderer Ian Brady used in the *Daily Mirror*.

Another celebrated case concerned Bill Goodwin who, as a trainee reporter at *The Engineer* in 1989, received – from an anonymous source – information from a draft plan drawn up by a company in difficulties. The company obtained a court order requiring Goodwin to hand over notes, which would have disclosed his source. He refused and was fined £5000 for contempt of court. In 1996, the European Court of Human Rights overruled the decision, because it violated his right to free expression.

Not only judges can demand information and documents. So can the Financial Services Authority, the Serious Fraud Office and the police. Normally, the police need a judge's order to require journalists' material and journalists do not have to hand over 'excluded material'. This exclusion does not cover stolen documents.

Counsel for Derek Webb, a private detective working for national newspapers, successfully argued at Kingston Crown Court that material seized from Webb's home and car was journalistic and therefore protected by article 10 of the European Human Rights Convention (*Press Gazette*, 29 11 08). (See the Sally Murrer case, pp. 159–60.)

Anti-terrorism legislation has increased police powers to demand journalists' material if it is connected with terrorism (*see* p. 189).

Corruption

A civil servant, Humbert Wolfe, famously wrote:

> ❛ *You cannot hope to bribe or twist,*
> *thank God, the British journalist.*
> *But, seeing what the man will do,*
> *unbribed, there's no occasion to.* ❜

British journalists stoutly resist overt corruption. They resent pressure from advertisers and notables. They do not accept backhanders in brown envelopes. But they do accept many benefits: news stories, lunches, books, theatre tickets, days out, car-test opportunities, even foreign trips, which they cannot sensibly refuse because these are real opportunities for writing and reporting. They owe the providers of perks a fair report of what they have seen and heard, but they owe their readers an honest opinion if the play is boring or the car hard to drive.

Often the perk-provider's interest coincides with the journalist's interest in writing good copy. But some perks raise moral dilemmas. Is it right, for instance, to accept a free trip and write glowingly about holidays in a country with an oppressive government? Should you not tell the other side of the story, too?

You can be corrupted by your own interests and views as well as by other people's efforts to promote theirs. Don't let it happen. Don't be over-defensive of the people and organizations on which you rely for information.

Some other points:

- Checking. Be sure of your facts.

- Self-censorship. You owe readers the facts. If you withhold them, you must have a strong reason for doing so. Don't let anyone tell you what you can't publish.

- Addresses. Publishing the street where someone lives avoids confusion with other people with the same name. But don't give the house number. Don't identify a house if this puts someone in danger or attracts unwelcome attention. To avoid attracting burglars, do not give full addresses of well-known people or those away on holiday or frequently travelling abroad.

- Illustrations. Use relevant and up-to-date pictures rather than library photographs taken on some other occasion or somewhere else.

- Unwarranted assumptions. Write what you know to be true, not what you assume to be true.

- Plagiarism. Don't copy another writer's work. If you quote it acknowledge its author, check the facts and make sure your piece takes the story further.

- Politics. Don't embarrass yourself or your employer by making your political views publicly known. Be careful about what you write on Facebook, which is a public forum. 'Friending' a councillor or MP on Facebook is a way to cultivate a contact. However, this could be taken as you endorsing your friend's politics. So you also need to friend other councillors and MPs from other parties.

Free-for-all on the internet

The growth of the internet has been hailed as readers' and viewers' chance to take over from the journalists and decide what they want to write about and how they want it written. Freedom of expression for the few has become freedom of expression for the many.

But to speak, even on the internet, is not the same as to be heard. In 2009 it was still journalists who scanned the cybersphere and brought its thoughts to public attention. The BBC was using user-generated content but only after it had been checked and packaged by BBC journalists and made to fit, if possible, within the BBC's rules of impartiality. But was it, in fact, possible? Could you be impartial and, at the same time, let diversity of view have its head?

For many people, the attraction of the internet is that they can write what they choose to. They can present hearsay, rumour, belief, half-truth and invention as fact. The constraints of media ethics, if not of the law of libel, are lifted. Damian McBride, a Downing Street aide, caused a furore by seeing a new blog as a chance to 'disclose' skeletons – real or imaginary – in Tory cupboards (*Mail*, 13 04 09).

The licence of the web has an additional danger. The loudest voices will drown out others. However, web surfers who want information, not just scandal and entertainment, will want reliable suppliers. Principled writers are still in with a chance.

The PCC and the Code of Practice

Journalists' codes of conduct provide a set of benchmarks for acceptable behaviour, wrote Professor Ivor Gaber (*BJR*, March 2009). The Editors' Code of Practice is the basis on which the Press Complaints Commission (www.pcc.org.uk, 020 7831 0022) deals with complaints concerning the work of newspapers and journalists in the United Kingdom. A lay chairman, nine other laypeople and seven editors are members of the PCC. All the staff handling complaints are non-journalists.

With the PCC's kind permission the code is reproduced below apart from clauses 15 – Witness payments in criminal trials – and 16 – Payments to criminals. For these see www.pcc.org.uk/cop/practice.html. The code reads:

All members of the press have a duty to maintain the highest professional standards. The Code, which includes this preamble and the public interest exceptions below, sets the benchmark for those ethical standards, protecting both the rights of the individual and the public's right to know. It is the cornerstone of the system of self-regulation to which the industry has made a binding commitment.

It is essential that an agreed code be honoured not only in the letter but in the full spirit. It should not be interpreted so narrowly as to compromise its commitment to respect the rights of the individual, nor so broadly that it constitutes an unnecessary interference with freedom of expression or prevents publication in the public interest.

It is the responsibility of editors and publishers to apply the Code to editorial material in both printed and online versions of publications. They should take care to ensure it is observed rigorously by all editorial staff and external contributors, including non-journalists, in printed and online versions of publications.

Editors should co-operate swiftly with the PCC in the resolution of complaints. Any publication judged to have breached the Code must print the adjudication in full and with due prominence, including headline reference to the PCC.

1. Accuracy

   i)   The Press must take care not to publish inaccurate, misleading or distorted information, including pictures.

   ii)   A significant inaccuracy, misleading statement or distortion once recognized must be corrected, promptly and with due prominence, and – where appropriate – an apology published.

   iii) The Press, whilst free to be partisan, must distinguish clearly between comment, conjecture and fact.

   iv)   A publication must report fairly and accurately the outcome of an action for defamation to which it has been a party, unless an agreed settlement states otherwise or an agreed statement is published.

2. Opportunity to reply

A fair opportunity for reply to inaccuracies must be given when reasonably called for.

3. *Privacy (There may be exceptions to the clauses marked * where they can be demonstrated to be in the public interest.)

   i)   Everyone is entitled to respect for his or her private and family life, home, health and correspondence, including digital communications. Editors will be expected to justify intrusions into any individual's private life without consent.

   ii)   It is unacceptable to photograph individuals in private places without their consent.

Note – Private places are public or private property where there is a reasonable expectation of privacy.

4. *Harassment

    i)   Journalists must not engage in intimidation, harassment or persistent pursuit.

    ii)   They must not persist in questioning, telephoning, pursuing or photographing individuals once asked to desist; nor remain on their property when asked to leave; and must not follow them.

    iii)   Editors must ensure these principles are observed by those working for them and take care not to use non-compliant material from other sources.

5. Intrusion into grief or shock

    i)   In cases involving personal grief or shock, enquiries and approaches must be made with sympathy and discretion and publication handled sensitively. This should not restrict the right to report legal proceedings, such as inquests.

    *ii)   When reporting suicide, care should be taken to avoid excessive detail about the method used.

6. *Children

    i)   Young people should be free to complete their time at school without unnecessary intrusion.

    ii)   A child under 16 must not be interviewed or photographed on issues involving their own or another child's welfare unless a custodial parent or similarly responsible adult consents.

    iii)   Pupils must not be approached or photographed at school without the permission of the school authorities.

    iv)   Minors must not be paid for material involving children's welfare, nor parents or guardians for material about their children or wards, unless it is clearly in the child's interest.

    v)   Editors must not use the fame, notoriety or position of a parent or guardian as sole justification for publishing details of a child's private life.

7. *Children in sex cases

    i)   The press must not, even if legally free to do so, identify children under 16 who are victims or witnesses in cases involving sex offences.

    ii)   In any press report of a case involving a sexual offence against a child

        a)   The child must not be identified.

        b)   The adult may be identified.

        c)   The word 'incest' must not be used when a child victim might be identified.

        d)   Care must be taken that nothing in the report implies the relationship between the accused and the child.

8. *Hospitals

i)   Journalists must identify themselves and obtain permission from a responsible executive before entering non-public areas of hospitals or similar institutions to pursue inquiries.

ii) The restrictions on intruding into privacy are particularly relevant to enquiries about individuals in hospitals or similar institutions.

9. *Reporting of crime

i)   Relatives or friends of persons convicted or accused of crime should not generally be identified without their consent, unless they are genuinely relevant to the story.

ii) Particular regard should be paid to the potentially vulnerable position of children who witness, or are victims of, crime. This should not restrict the right to report legal proceedings.

10. *Clandestine devices and subterfuge

i)   The Press must not seek to obtain or publish material acquired by hidden cameras or clandestine listening devices; or by intercepting private or mobile telephone calls, messages or e-mails, or by the unauthorized removal of documents or photographs; or by accessing digitally-held private information without consent.

ii) Engaging in misrepresentation or subterfuge, including by agents and intermediaries, can generally be justified only in the public interest and then only when the material cannot be obtained by other means.

11. Victims of sexual assault

The press must not identify victims of sexual assault or publish material likely to contribute to such identification unless there is adequate justification and they are legally free to do so.

12. Discrimination

i)   The press must avoid prejudicial or pejorative reference to an individual's race, colour, religion, gender, sexual orientation or to any physical or mental illness or disability.

ii) Details of an individual's race, colour, religion, sexual orientation, physical or mental illness or disability must be avoided unless genuinely relevant to the story.

13. Financial journalism

i)   Even where the law does not prohibit it, journalists must not use for their own profit financial information they receive in advance of its general publication, nor should they pass such information to others.

ii)   They must not write about shares or securities in whose performance they know that they or their close families have a significant financial interest without disclosing the interest to the editor or financial editor.

iii) They must not buy or sell, either directly or through nominees or agents, shares or securities about which they have written recently or about which they intend to write in the near future.

14. Confidential sources

Journalists have a moral obligation to protect confidential sources of information.

The Public Interest

There may be exceptions to the clauses marked * where they can be demonstrated to be in the public interest.

1. The public interest includes, but is not confined to:

i)   Detecting or exposing crime or serious impropriety.

ii)   Protecting public health and safety.

iii) Preventing the public from being misled by an action or statement of an individual or organization.

2. There is a public interest in freedom of expression itself.

3. Whenever the public interest is invoked, the PCC will require editors to demonstrate fully how the public interest was served.

4. The PCC will consider the extent to which material is already in the public domain, or will become so.

5. In cases involving children under 16, editors must demonstrate an exceptional public interest to override the normally paramount interest of the child.

(The BBC has also issued guidance, seeing the public interest as including:

- Exposing or detecting crime, significantly anti-social behaviour, corruption or injustice.
- Disclosing significant incompetence or negligence.
- Protecting people's health and safety.
- Preventing people being misled by some statement or action of an individual; or organization.
- Disclosing information that allows people to make a significantly more informed decision about matters of public importance.
- There is also a public interest in freedom of expression itself.)

How the PCC interprets the Editors' Code

Ian Beales, secretary of the Editors' Code committee, has summarized the PCC's judgments in *The Editors' Codebook* (www.editorscode.org.uk/the_code_book.html) Beales writes that most complaints to the PCC are about accuracy – particularly important when newspapers are reporting serious allegations or dealing with emotive topics where fear or hostility may be roused, such as asylum seeking or mental health. Most detained mental patients have not appeared before a court for an offence. They are detained because health professionals have decided they need hospital care.

The PCC urges careful thought and consultation with the police and probation officers before newspapers embark on campaigns about convicted sex offenders.

The code does not require perfect accuracy but proper care – checks to establish a report is accurate plus an opportunity for likely complainants to respond. An allegation that a priest was a paedophile should not have been presented as a fact. He had not been convicted of, nor charged with, any offence. The PCC accepts, however, that, if allegations are true, it is in the public interest that they are published.

Pictures should be genuine. If a report is accompanied by a picture taken in a different place or in different circumstances, this should be made plain. Corrections of inaccurate reports should be prompt.

A quarter of complaints to the PCC are about intrusions into privacy. The PCC code of practice echoes the Human Rights Act. The code bans intrusive photography, even in a public place if someone could expect privacy there. Notre Dame cathedral in Paris and a Dorking tearoom are such public places.

People can compromise their right to privacy by writing about their private lives. However, the fact that celebrities and sports stars may present aspects of their private lives to the public does not make them fair game for intrusive reporting.

Journalists should stop pursuing or telephoning people if asked to stop, unless there are pertinent questions to be answered in the public interest. They should be sensitive in dealing with relatives of the dead and should not be the bringers of bad tidings.

Reports of suicides should not give too much detail about the method, in case other people are tempted to copy it. It is OK to say someone died from an overdose of paracetamol but not how many tablets they took.

Interviewing anyone under 16 requires consent from parent or school. If it's at school, the school must give permission. Photographing children because they are related to celebrities is out. But a picture of a child in the street – without personal details – is acceptable.

Under-16s involved in sex cases cannot be named. However, it is permissible for under-age mothers – with parents' approval – to tell their stories to newspapers.

Journalists should identify themselves and seek permission before entering non-public areas in residential homes and hospitals. However, the PCC backed the parents of a brain-damaged woman who took a photographer into hospital to picture her plight.

If journalists want to use subterfuge or hidden cameras in the public interest, they must have grounds to suspect that something illegal or damaging is going on. Normally, they should make it clear they are journalists. They should not use subterfuge to discover what they could find out by simply asking.

Journalists are morally obliged to protect confidential sources of information but should not use this obligation as a shield for inaccuracy. They should seek corroboration of what an unnamed source has said. If the source has made allegations against someone, they should give that someone a chance to comment.

The PCC has rejected claims of public interest to justify naming a boy with meningitis, a girl whose mother committed suicide, and schoolboys expelled for fighting and racial abuse. It also rejected a claim that publishing an interview with a murderer's 15-year-old girlfriend was in the public interest. But it accepted a reporter's use of subterfuge to see CCTV pictures showing a dying man was badly treated in hospital.

The PCC regards bugging of phonecalls as seriously intrusive and hard to justify.

The NUJ's Code of Conduct

The National Union of Journalists sets out these principles (reproduced by kind permission):

❝ A journalist:

1. At all times upholds and defends the principle of media freedom, the right of freedom of expression and the right of the public to be informed.
2. Strives to ensure that information disseminated is honestly conveyed, accurate and fair.
3. Does her/his utmost to correct harmful inaccuracies.
4. Differentiates between fact and opinion.
5. Obtains material by honest, straightforward and open means, with the exception of investigations that are both overwhelmingly in the public interest and involve evidence that cannot be obtained by straightforward means.
6. Does nothing to intrude into anybody's private life, grief or distress unless justified by overriding consideration of the public interest.
7. Protects the identity of sources who supply information in confidence and material gathered in the course of her/his work.

8. Resists threats or any other inducements to influence, distort or suppress information.
9. Takes no unfair personal advantage of information gained in the course of her/his duties before the information is public knowledge.
10. Produces no material likely to lead to hatred or discrimination on the grounds of a person's age, gender, race, colour, creed, legal status, disability, marital status or sexual orientation.
11. Does not by way of statement, voice or appearance endorse by advertisement any commercial product or service save for the promotion of her/his own work or of the medium by which she/he is employed.
12. Avoids plagiarism.   *,*

The NUJ believes a journalist has the right to refuse an assignment that would break the letter or spirit of the code.

For further reading see *The Ethical Journalist*, by Tony Harcup (Sage, 2007).

Questions

1. Has anyone been harmed by anything you wrote?
2. Has the accuracy of your reporting ever been challenged?
3. If so, what form did the challenge take and how did you deal with it?
4. How would you define the public interest?

Index

See also the synopsis